Born in Chatham, Kent, **Henry Stedman** studied economics at Bristol University but not even the thrill of neoclassical endogenous growth theory could keep him from his current calling as a travel writer. He has been writing guidebooks for more than six years now and is the author or co-author of half a dozen titles, including Trailblazer's *Trekking in the Dolomites*, *The Bradt Guide to Palestine*, and the *Rough Guides* to *Indonesia* and *Southeast Asia*.

When not travelling, Henry lives in England editing other people's guidebooks and putting on weight. A friend describes him as living proof that almost anyone can climb Kilimanjaro.

Kilimanjaro – a trekking guide to Africa's highest mountain
First edition: 2003; reprinted with amendments 2004

Publisher
Trailblazer Publications
The Old Manse, Tower Rd, Hindhead, Surrey, GU26 6SU, UK
Fax (+44) 01428-607571
Email: info@trailblazer-guides.com
www.trailblazer-guides.com

British Library Cataloguing in Publication Data
A catalogue record for this book is available from the British Library

ISBN 1-873756-65-8

Editor: Patricia Major
Typesetting and layout: Henry Stedman
Additional proof-reading: Anna Jacomb-Hood
Trail maps and town plans: Nick Hill
Index: Jane Thomas

Warning: mountain walking can be dangerous
Please read the notes on when to go (p16) and on mountain safety (pp160-8).
Every effort has been made by the author and publisher to ensure that the information
contained herein is as accurate and up to date as possible. However, they are unable
to accept responsibility for any inconvenience, loss or injury sustained by anyone as a
result of the advice and information given in this guide.

Printed on chlorine-free paper by
D2Print (☎ +65-6295 5598), Singapore

KILIMANJARO

A trekking guide to
Africa's highest mountain

HENRY STEDMAN

TRAILBLAZER PUBLICATIONS

For Louise. Of course.

Acknowledgements

First and foremost I should like to thank Matthew Mombo, park warden at KINAPA, for his tireless efforts in keeping me informed of the latest developments in the park, and his patience in answering my interminable (and sometimes plain stupid) questions. Thanks are also due to: Leslie Adams (US) for accompanying me to Moshi; Jon Larsen and Dave Cavanaugh (US) for information on the Lemosho Route and for the celebratory/commiserative beers on our return; to Claire Smith and Jennifer Scott (UK) for both keeping me company and keeping me smiling on the Machame Route, and Min Hazeldine and Liane Klingbeil (UK) for doing likewise on the Marangu Route; to my guides, Mohammed 'Moody' Limotko, Alex Pitari, Fredrick Munna, Humphrey, Sam, Siprian and Phillip; and to all the porters, whose names I didn't catch, or caught and have now forgotten, but who nevertheless readily shouldered this particular 'white man's burden' for little more than a few dollars a day plus the occasional boiled sweet.

Out of Africa I should like to thank Shane Winser of the Royal Geographical Society for supplying me with the information on altitude sickness on Kilimanjaro; Nick Hill in Bangkok for transforming my childlike scribbles into trail maps and town plans of beauty, and for the bird drawings; Patricia Major for turning my incoherent ramblings into something approaching English; Jane Thomas for the index; Anna Jacomb-Hood for additional checking and proofreading and Bryn, as ever, for making the whole thing possible.

A request

The author and publisher have tried to ensure that this guide is as accurate and up to date as possible. However, things change quickly in this part of the world. Agencies come and go, prices rise and ... well, rise some more, trails are re-routed, governments are toppled and glaciers shrink. If you notice any changes or omissions that should be included in the next edition of this guide, please email Henry Stedman (henry.stedman@trailblazer-guides.com) or write to Trailblazer (address on p2). You can also contact us via the Trailblazer website at ⌨www.trailblazer-guides.com). Those persons making a significant contribution will be rewarded with a free copy of the next edition, an acknowledgement in the front of that edition, and my undying gratitude.

Updated information will shortly be available on:
⌨ **www.trailblazer-guides.com**

Front cover: Kilimanjaro from the north © Torleif Svensson/Corbis

CONTENTS

CLIMBING TACKLE
(FROM *ACROSS EAST AFRICAN
GLACIERS – AN ACCOUNT OF THE
FIRST ASCENT OF KILIMANJARO*
HANS MEYER, 1891)

INTRODUCTION

Kilimanjaro is a snow covered mountain 19,710 feet high, and is said to be the highest mountain in Africa. Its western summit is called the Masai 'Ngà'je Ngài', the House of God. Close to the western summit there is the dried and frozen carcass of a leopard. No one has explained what the leopard was seeking at that altitude.
            Ernest Hemingway in the preamble to *The Snows of Kilimanjaro*

Ostensibly, climbing Kilimanjaro seems straightforward. After all, no technical skill is required to reach the summit of Africa's highest mountain beyond the ability to put one foot in front of the other; because, unless you go out of your way to find an awkward route, there is no actual *climbing* involved at all – just lots and lots of walking. Thus, anyone above the age of 10 (the minimum legal age for climbing Kilimanjaro) with the right attitude, a sensible approach to acclimatization, a half-decent pair of calf muscles and lots of warm clothing can make it to the top.

That, at any rate, is the theory, and one that a glance at the recent history of climbing Kilimanjaro would seem to bear out. With kids as young as twelve and pensioners as venerable as the Frenchman, Valtée Daniel, at 87 being the oldest man to stand on the summit, Kili conquerors come in all shapes and sizes.

The cynical could look upon the large numbers of trekkers climbing Kili as evidence that this is a relatively easy mountain to scale. For further proof, they could also point to those for whom the challenge of climbing Kilimanjaro simply wasn't, well, challenging enough, and who deliberately went out of their way to make the ascent more difficult for themselves, just for the hell of it. Men such as the Brazilian who jogged right up to the summit in just 24 hours. Or the Crane brothers from England who cycled up, surviving on Mars Bars strapped to their handlebars. And the anonymous Spaniard who, in the 1970s, drove up to the summit by motorbike. Nor must we forget Douglas Adams, the author of the *Hitchhikers' Guide to the Galaxy*, who in 1994 reached the summit for charity while wearing an eight-foot rubber rhinoceros costume; and finally there's the (possibly apocryphal) story of the man who walked *backwards* the entire way in order to get into the *Guinness Book of Records* – only to find out, on his return to the bottom, that he had been beaten by somebody who had done exactly the same thing just a few days previously.

And that's just the ascent; for coming back down again the mountain has witnessed skiing, a method first practised by Walter Furtwangler way back in 1912; snowboarding, an activity pioneered on Kili by Stephen Koch in 1997; and even hang-gliding, for which there was something of a fad a few years ago.

Cyclists to skiers, heroes to half-wits, bikers to boarders to backward walkers: it's no wonder, given the sheer number of people who have climbed Kili over the past century, and the ways in which they've done so, that so many believe that climbing Kili is something of a doddle. And you'd be forgiven for thinking the same.

You'd be forgiven – but you'd also be wrong. Whilst these stories of successful expeditions tend to receive a lot of coverage, they serve to obscure the tales of suffering and tragedy that often go with them. You don't, for example, hear much about the hang-glider who leapt off Kili a few years ago and was never seen again. Or the fact that the Brazilian who jogged up spent the next week in hospital recovering from severe high-altitude pulmonary oedema. And for all the coverage of the Millennium celebrations, when over 7000 people stood on the slopes of Kilimanjaro during New Year's week – with a 1000 on New Year's Eve alone – little mention was made of the fact that three people died on Kilimanjaro in those seven days. Or that another 33 had to be rescued. Or that well over a third of all the people who took part in those festivities failed to reach the summit, or indeed get anywhere near it.

For once, statistics give a reasonably accurate impression of just how difficult climbing Kili can be. According to the park authorities' own estimates, only 40-50% of climbers who climb up Kilimanjaro successfully reach the summit. They also admit to there being a couple of deaths per annum on Kilimanjaro; independent observers put that figure as high as ten.

The fact that the Masai call the mountain the 'House of God' seems entirely appropriate, given the number of people who meet their Maker every year on the slopes of Kili.

At one stage we were taking a minute to complete thirty-five small paces. Altitude sickness had already hit the boys and two were weeping, pleading to pack up. All the instructors with the exception of Lubego and myself were in a bad way. They were becoming violently ill. It was becoming touch and go. The descent at one stage was like a battlefield. Men, including the porters, lying prone or bent up in agony. Tom and Swato though very ill themselves rallied the troops and helped manhandle the three unconscious boys to a lower altitude.
From the logbook of **Geoffrey Salisbury**, who led a group of blind African climbers up Kilimanjaro, as recorded in *The Road to Kilimanjaro*

The high failure and mortality rates speak for themselves: despite appearances to the contrary, climbing Kilimanjaro is no simple matter.

'Mountain of greatness'
But whilst it isn't easy, it *is* achievable. As mentioned at the start, almost anyone in reasonable condition can climb this mountain.

It is this 'inclusivity' that undoubtedly goes some way to explaining Kilimanjaro's popularity, a popularity that saw 20,351 foreign tourists and 674 local trekkers visit in 2000, thereby confirming Kili's status as the most popular of the so-called 'Big Seven', the highest peaks on each of the seven continents. The sheer size of it must be another factor behind its appeal. This is the Roof of Africa, a massive massif 60km long by 80km wide with an altitude that reaches to a fraction under 6km above sea level. The renowned anthropologist,

Charles Dundas, writing in 1924 claimed that he once saw Kilimanjaro from a point over 120 miles away. It is even big enough to have its own weather systems (note the plural) and, furthermore, to influence the climates of the countries that surround it.

The aspect presented by this prodigious mountain is one of unparalleled grandeur, sublimity, majesty, and glory. It is doubtful if there be another such sight in this wide world.
Charles New, the first European to reach the snow-line on Kilimanjaro, from his book *Life, Wanderings, and Labours in Eastern Africa*

But size, as they say, isn't everything, and by themselves these bald figures fail to fully explain the allure of Kilimanjaro. So instead we must look to attributes that cannot be measured by theodolites or yardsticks if we are to understand the appeal of Kilimanjaro.

In particular, there's its beauty. When viewed from the plains of Tanzania, Kilimanjaro conforms to our childhood notions of what a mountain should look like: high, wide and handsome, a vast triangle rising out of the flat earth, its sides sloping exponentially upwards to the satisfyingly symmetrical summit of Kibo; a summit that rises imperiously above a thick beard of clouds and is adorned with a glistening bonnet of snow. Kilimanjaro is not located in the crumpled mountain terrain of the Himalayas or the Andes. Where the mightiest mountain of them all, Everest, just edges above its neighbours – and look less impressive because of it – Kilimanjaro stands proudly alone on the plains of Africa. The only thing in the neighbourhood that can even come close to looking it in the eye is Mount Meru, a fair way off to the south-west and a good 1420m smaller too. The fact that it's located smack bang in the heart of the sweltering East African plains, just a few degrees and 330km south of the equator, with lions, giraffes, and all the other celebrities of the safari world running around its base, only adds to its charisma.

And then there's the scenery on the mountain itself. So massive is Kilimanjaro, that to climb it is to pass through four seasons in four days, from the sultry rainforests of the lower reaches through to the windswept heather and moorland of the upper slopes, and on to the arctic wastes of the summit.

There may be 15 higher points on the globe; there can't be many that are more beautiful, or more tantalizing.

In sitting down to recount my experiences with the conquest of the "Ethiopian Mount Olympus" still fresh in my memory, I feel how inadequate are my powers of description to do justice to the grand and imposing aspects of Nature with which I shall have to deal.
Hans Meyer, the first man to climb Kilimanjaro, in his book *Across East African Glaciers – an Account of the First Ascent of Kilimanjaro.*

Nor is it just tourists that are entranced by Kilimanjaro; the mountain looms large in the Tanzanian psyche too. Look at their supermarket shelves. The nation's second favourite lager is called Kilimanjaro. The third favourite, Kibo Gold, is named after the higher of Kilimanjaro's two summits. Even the nation's best selling lager, Safari, has something distinctly white and pointy looming in

the background of its label. Nor can tee-totallers entirely escape Kili's presence. There's Kilimanjaro coffee (grown on the mountain's fertile southern slopes) and Kilimanjaro mineral water (bottled on its western side). On billboards lining the country's highways Tanzanian models smoke their cigarettes in its shadow, while cheerful roly-poly housewives compare the whiteness of their laundry with the mountain's glistening snows. And to pay for all of these things you can use a Tanzanian Ts5000 note – which just happens to have, on the back of it, a herd of giraffe lolloping along in front of the distinctive silhouette of Africa's highest mountain.

It is perhaps no surprise to find, therefore, that when Tanganyika won its independence from Britain in 1961, one of the first things they did was plant a torch on its summit; a torch that the first president, Julius Nyerere, hoped would '...shine beyond our borders, giving hope where there was despair, love where there was hate, and dignity where before there was only humiliation.'

To the Tanzanians, Kilimanjaro is clearly much more than just a very large mountain separating them from Kenya. It's a symbol of their freedom, and a potent emblem of their country.

And given the tribulations and hardships willingly suffered by thousands of trekkers on Kili each year – not to mention the money they spend for the privilege of doing so – the mountain obviously arouses some pretty strong emotions in non-Tanzanians as well. Whatever the emotions provoked in you by this wonderful mountain, and however you plan to climb it, we wish you well. Because even if you choose to leave the bicycle at home, forego the pleasures of wearing a latex rhino outfit and walk in the direction that nature intended you to, climbing up Kilimanjaro will still be one of the hardest things you ever do.

But it will also, without a doubt, be one of the most rewarding.

We were in an amiable frame of mind ourselves and, notwithstanding all the toil and trouble my self-appointed task had cost me, I don't think I would that night have changed places with anybody in the world. **Hans Meyer** on the evening after reaching the summit, as recorded in *Across East African Glaciers*

PART 1: PLANNING YOUR TRIP

With a group or on your own?

INDEPENDENT TREKKING NOT AN OPTION

In 1991, the park authorities made it compulsory for all trekkers to arrange their walk through a licensed agency. Furthermore, they insist that all trekkers must be accompanied throughout their walk by a guide supplied by the agency. When these laws were first introduced, it was for a while still feasible to sneak in without paying, and many were the stories that arose about trekkers who managed to climb Kilimanjaro independently, tales that were often embellished with episodes of encounters with wild animals and even wilder park rangers.

Fortunately, the authorities have tightened up security and clamped down on non-payees, so these tedious tales are now few in number. Don't try to climb Kilimanjaro without a guide, or without paying the proper fees. It's very unlikely you'll succeed, and all you're doing is freeloading – indeed, stealing isn't too strong a word – from one of the poorest countries in the world. Yes, climbing Kilimanjaro is expensive. But the costs of maintaining a mountain that big are high. Besides, whatever price you pay, trust us, it's worth it.

WITH FRIENDS . . .

It's Kili time! Time to kick back, relax and take it easy with your friends.
Printed on the labels of Kilimanjaro Beer

So you have decided to climb Kilimanjaro, and have thus taken the first step on the path that leads from the comfort and safety of your favourite armchair to the untamed glory of the Roof of Africa. The second step on this path is to consider with whom to go.

This may not be as straightforward as it sounds, because Kilimanjaro breaks friendships as easily as it breaks records. The tribulations suffered by those who dare to pit themselves against the mountain wear down the most even of temperaments, and relationships are often the first to suffer. Idiosyncrasies in your friend's behaviour that you previously thought charming now simply become irritating, while the most trivial of differences between you and your chum could lead to the termination of a friendship that, before you'd both ventured onto its slopes, you thought was as steadfast and enduring as the mountain itself. Different levels of stamina, different levels of desire to reach the top, different attitudes towards the porters and guides, even differences in the film speeds you're using or the colour of your socks: on Kilimanjaro these things, for some reason, suddenly matter.

And then there's the farting. It is a well-known fact that the regular breaking of wind is a sure sign that you are acclimatizing satisfactorily (for more about acclimatization, see pp160–6); while the onset of a crushing headache, combined with a loss of sleep and a consequent loss of humour, are all classic symptoms suffered by those struggling to adapt to the rarified atmosphere. Problems occur, of course, when two friends acclimatize at different rates: ie, the vociferous and joyful flatulence of Friend A is simply not appreciated by Friend B, who has a bad headache, insomnia and ill-temper. Put the two parties together in a remote, confined space, such as that provided by a two-man tent on the slopes of a cold and lonely mountain, and you have an explosive cocktail that can blow apart even the strongest of friendships.

It rained terrible all night, and we put most of the Wachaga porters in our tent. It was rather distressing to the olfactory nerves ... At 4am a leopard visited us but did not fancy our scent. **Peter MacQueen**, *In Wildest Africa* (an account of an expedition of 1907, published in 1910)

Of course, the above is just one possible scenario. It may be that both of you adapt equally well/badly to the new conditions and can draw pleasure/comfort from each other accordingly. (People from Northern Europe seem particularly good at making the best of the windy conditions: during the research of this book I encountered a party of four Germans holding a farting competition, and one particularly talented Dutch pair who even managed a quick game of Name that Tune. It may or may not surprise you to know that all but one of the participants in these competitions was male.)

And there are plenty of advantages in going with a friend too. There's the companionship for a start. It's cheaper, too, because you'll probably be sharing rooms, which always cuts the cost, and if you are planning on booking your climb through an agency in Tanzania your bargaining position is so much stronger if there are two of you. Having a companion also cuts the workload, enabling, for example, one to run off and find a room, while the other looks after the luggage. It also saves your being paired with someone you don't know when you book with an agency; someone who may snore and smell even more violently than your friend ever would. And if you *do* both make it to the top, it's good to know that there will be somebody to testify to your achievements upon your return.

Climbing Kili with a companion has its problems, but there's no doubting the extra pleasure that can be gained as well. As is written on the walls of Room 3 in the Kibo Huts: '*What does not break us makes us stronger*'. If you are planning on travelling with a friend, this perhaps should be your motto for the trek.

. . .OR ON YOUR OWN?

Those without friends, or at least without friends willing to climb a mountain with them, should not worry. For one thing, you'll never truly be on your own, simply because the park authorities forbid your climbing without a guide at least (see p13), and you'll need at least one other crew member to act as porter.

Furthermore, planning to go on your own means you can arrange **the trek you want**; you choose the trail to take, the time to go and for how long; the pace of the walk, the number of rest-stops, when to go to bed – these are all your decisions, and yours alone. You are the boss; you have nobody else's feelings to consider but your own.

If you want to join up with others, for companionship or simply to make the trek a little cheaper, that's not a problem: you can book your trek in your home country with a tour operator (they always insist on a minimum number of participants before the trek goes ahead); or you can book in Tanzania, and ask to be put with other trekkers (which will often happen anyway, unless you specifically say otherwise). And even if you are walking alone, you can always meet other trekkers at the campsite in the evening if you so desire.

Trekking by yourself is fun, and not the lonely experience many imagine; unless, of course, you enjoy the bliss of solitude and *want* to be alone. That's the beauty of walking solo: everything is up to you.

Budgeting

The most significant cost of your holiday – unless you opt for a few days at the Serena Inn in Zanzibar at the end of your stay (top suites $600 per night in season) is the walk itself. Set aside US$600–800 for this for a budget trek, more if you plan on ascending by an unusual route or insist on walking without other trekkers. Once on the mountain, however, you won't need to pay for anything else throughout the trek, except for the occasional chocolate bar or beer which you can buy at the ranger's huts on the way.

Away from the trek, by far the most expensive place in Tanzania is Zanzibar. Elsewhere, you'll find transport, food and accommodation, the big three day-to-day expenses of the traveller's life, are pretty cheap in Tanzania and particularly in Moshi and Arusha.

The Tanzanian shilling (Ts) is the national currency. For exchange rates and more on money see p59.

ACCOMMODATION

Basic tourist accommodation starts at around £2–3/US$3–5. You can get cheaper, non-tourist accommodation, though this is often both sleazy and unhygienic and should only be considered as a last resort. We have not reviewed these cheap hotels individually in the book, but we do give some indication of where they can be found in the introduction to the accommodation sections in the city chapters.

At the other end of the spectrum, there are hotel rooms and luxury safari camps going for anything up to US$2000 per night in the high season.

FOOD

Food can be dirt cheap if you stick to street sellers plying their wares at all hours of the day – though dirt is often what you get on the food itself too, with hygiene standards not always of the highest. Still, even in a clean and decent budget restaurant the bill should still be only £2/US$3.

TRANSPORT

Public transport is cheap in Tanzania, though it could be said you get what you pay for: dilapidated buses, potholed roads, inadequate seating and narcoleptic drivers do not a pleasant journey make, but this is the reality of public transport, Tanzanian-style. Then again, at around £0.50/US$0.75 per hour for local buses and *dalla-dallas* (the local minibuses; see p61), it seems churlish to complain. Extra safety and comfort is available on the luxury buses, and at only a slightly higher price.

When to go

The two main trekking seasons for Kilimanjaro correspond with the mountain's two dry seasons (an imprecise term, the weather being occasionally inclement during these periods too) namely January to mid-March and June to October. Of course you can walk in the rainy season, but not only is there a much higher chance of walking in the rain, but the summits of Kibo and Mawenzi are likely to be wreathed in thick cloud. Curiously, however, Christmas and New Year, when the weather is far from perfect, are actually the most popular times to go.

As to the relative merits of the two seasons, the differences are small though significant. The **January to March season** tends to be colder, and there is a much greater chance of snow on the summit at this time. The days, however, are often clearer, with only the occasional brief shower. It is an exceptionally beautiful time to climb and is usually a little quieter than the other peak season of **June to October**, which coincides with the main academic holidays in Europe and the West.

ARUSHA

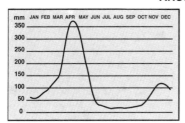

Average Rainfall (mm)

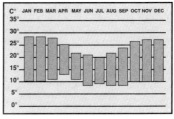

Average max/min temp (°C)

DAR ES SALAAM

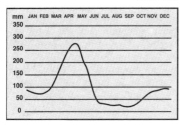

Average Rainfall (mm)

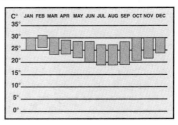

Average max/min temp (°C)

In the **June to October peak season**, following the heavy rains of March to May, the clouds tend to hang around the tree-line. Once above this altitude, however, the skies are blue and brilliant and the chance of precipitation minimal (though still present).

Although this season tends to be busier, this is not necessarily a disadvantage. For example, if you are travelling alone to Tanzania but wish, for the sake of companionship or simply to cut down on costs, to join up with other travellers for the trek, then the high visitor numbers in the June-October peak season will give you the best chance of doing this.

Star gazing

Having decided which period you wish to travel in, you may wish to refine your dates still further by timing your walk so that on the final push to the summit, which is usually conducted at night, you will be walking under the brightness of a **full moon**. Stargazers may also wish to coincide their trip with a major astronomical happening; the views of the night sky from Kili are, after all, quite exceptional.

It's good to know that it isn't just the costs of climbing Kilimanjaro that are astronomical; the rewards can be too.

And even if you do crave solitude when you walk, it can still be found on the mountain during this peak season. The trails are long, so you can always find vast gaps between trekkers to allow you to walk in peace; some of the routes – Rongai, for example, or the two trails across the Shira Plateau – almost never have more than one or two trekking groups on them at any one time, and are often completely deserted. And besides, Kilimanjaro is just so huge that its presence will dwarf your fellow trekkers, to the point where they become, if you wish them to be, quite unnoticeable.

Booking your trek

With the decision over whether or not to climb independently taken out of your hands, the next thing to decide is which agency is going to get your business.

The next few pages deal with exactly this matter. This may seem like overkill but booking with the right agency is perhaps the single most important factor in determining the success or otherwise of your trek: they are the ones who arrange everything, supply the equipment, and designate somebody to be your guide. So take your time choosing one. Because unless you are a guide, porter, guidebook writer or just plain daft, climbing Kilimanjaro will be a once-in-a-lifetime experience. It is also quite an expensive experience, so it's important to make sure that you get it right.

BOOKING WITH AN AGENCY AT HOME

Between 85 and 90% of trekkers on Kilimanjaro book their climb before they arrive in Tanzania, through an agency in their home country. Despite this overwhelming majority, there is a good case to be made for waiting until you arrive in the country before booking; see p24.

Booking from home gets rid of the hassle. It depends what kind of package you have booked, of course, but few tour companies will sell you a climb up Kilimanjaro and nothing more. Nearly all will include in their Kili package such things as airport pick-up, accommodation, sightseeing trips, transport to and from the mountain, and maybe even the odd safari or Zanzibar excursion. Pay them some more and they'll throw in the flights and insurance and sort out your visas too.

With no need to arrange these things yourself, booking from home will save you a considerable amount of time. It also ensures that you know exactly when you'll be walking, rather than having to wait around for a few days, as you may have to if you book in Tanzania.

Booking from an agency in your country also means you can plan your trek more precisely months in advance, and ask your agent any questions you may have well before you even arrive in Tanzania. Your agency at home will also either have their own guide to lead you up the mountain or, more probably, will be acting on behalf of one of the larger and better trekking operators in Moshi, providing you with peace of mind. And if the trek still turns out to be a disaster, then the big advantage of booking from home is that you have a lot more comeback, and a lot more chance of receiving compensation.

A run-down of the larger tour operators who arrange treks up Kilimanjaro follows. Before booking with anybody, have a look at the next section, Booking with an agency in Tanzania, and in particular the advice given in the sections headed Choosing an agency in Tanzania and Signing the contract. Both contain useful hints that are also relevant when dealing with agents and operators in your own country.

All prices quoted in the list below include park fees unless stated otherwise but exclude flights – again, unless stated. For details of the various routes up Kilimanjaro mentioned in the following list, please see p36.

Agencies in the UK
● **Abercrombie & Kent** (☎ 0845-0700 610; 🖳 www.abercrombiekent.co.uk) Sloane Square House, Holbein Place, Sloane Square, London SW1W 8NS. Upmarket holiday company with treks on the Machame trail from £2000 upwards including flights.

● **Acacia Adventure Holidays** (☎ 020-7706 4700; 🖳 www.acacia-africa.com), Lower Ground Floor, 23A Craven Terrace, London W2 3QH. Africa specialist with a budget Marangu trek, using Nairobi as a base, for £395 excluding park fees. An extra day's acclimatization (essential) is another £60 plus park fees.

● **Africa Reps** (☎ 020-8750 5655; 🖳 www.africareps.co.uk) Sovereign Court, Simpson Road, Heathrow UB7 DJE. Agents for Moshi's Shah Tours (see p153).

● **Alpine Mountaineering** (☎ 0114-258 8508; 🖳 www.ottexpeditions.co.uk) South West Centre, Suite 5b, Troutbeck Rd, Sheffield S7 2QA, is a mountaineering and adventure trekking company, and thus one of the few to offer an assault on the summit via the Umbwe/Western Breach Route. Accommodation in Moshi is at the lovely Key's Hotel.

● **Dragoman** (☎ 01728-861133; 🖳 www.dragoman.com) Camp Green, Debenham, Stowmarket, Suffolk, IP14 6LA. Runs a rather hurried seven-night tour beginning and ending in Nairobi and taking in the Marangu Route to the top of Kili, with one guide for every two climbers. They use Zara International (p154), so accommodation in Moshi is in the Springlands Hotel.

● **Exodus Expeditions** (☎ 020-8675 5550; 🖳 www.exodustravels.co.uk) 9 Weir Rd, London SW12 OLT. Offers a 17-day Kilimanjaro, Serengeti and Zanzibar trip using the little-used Rongai Route (6 days) for upwards of £1732 (excluding park fees). Also offer Kilimanjaro-only treks using the Shira/Rongai routes for £1099/965 respectively, and a Roof of Africa tour for the hardy combining Kili and Mount Kenya from £1471 (excluding park fees).

● **Explore Worldwide** (☎ 01252-760 000; 🖳 www.exploreworldwide.com) 1 Frederick St, Aldershot, Hants GU11 1LQ. Twenty-year old company offering small-group treks (12–16 people) on the Machame and Marangu routes, either on their own or combined with a safari or trip to Zanzibar. Also do an interesting Tanzanian Volcano Trek, taking in the Ngorongoro Crater, Mount Meru and the Machame Route starting at £1085 excluding park fees (another US$720).

● **Footprint Adventures** (☎ 01522-804 929; 🖳 www.footventure.co.uk) 5 Malham Drive, Lincoln LN6 0XD. Offers several guided treks on Kilimanjaro (beginning at £555) on all the established trails as well as a nip up Mount Meru (£450), staying at either the Springlands or Leopard Hotel. They also run an equipment hire service, eg four-season sleeping bags £25.

● **Gane & Marshall International** (☎ 020-8441 9592; 🖳 www.kilimanjarosa faris.com), 98 Crescent Road, New Barnet, Herts EN4 9RJ. A small company that, using the Lemosho Route, claims to have a 95% success rate of trekkers reaching the summit. Also do the Machame, Umbwe and, reluctantly, Marangu routes and have recently developed their own tough 'Julius Route' (named after the guide who helped them 'discover' it) which crosses Kibo from north to south. They are also one of the few to do a circuit around Kibo before ascending via the Western Breach. A company for Kili connoisseurs methinks.

● **Guerba Expeditions** (☎ 01373-858 956; 🖳 www.guerba.co.uk), Wessex House, 40 Station Rd, Westbury, Wilts BA13 3JN. Offers an eight-day trek on the Rongai Route, seven days on Marangu and eight on Machame, beginning at less than £1000 including park fees – a pretty good deal.

● **Hoopoe/Tropical Trekking** (☎ 020-8428 8221; 🖳 www.tropicaltre kking.com) Suite F1, Hartsbourne House, Carpenders Park, Watford, Herts, WD1 5EF. Tropical Trekking is the sister company of Hoopoe Safaris that deals specifically with walks and climbs in Tanzania. It's an excellent organization with high ideals, very eco-friendly and involved on many community projects; it runs treks on all the popular routes (though the Marangu Route only reluctantly), including a climb via the difficult Western Breach and a set departure every month on the Machame trail. They have also established a semi-luxury eco-camp on the western side of Kilimanjaro, near Ol Molog overlooking Amboseli National Park, which is good for game viewing, and which they use as a base for their Lemosho trek. They also offer a Mount Meru walk, and a three-day Kili trek up Machame to the Lava Tower and down across the Shira Plateau to Londorossi Gate. They have an office in Arusha (see p142).

● **KE Adventure Travel** (☎ 01768-773 966; 🖳 www.keadventure.com) 32 Lake Rd, Keswick, Cumbria CA12 5DQ. Trekking specialists running a popular seventeen-day Mount Kenya and Machame Route combination from £1500 excluding park fees, as well as separate treks on the Rongai and Shira trails. Accommodation after the trek is in Arusha at the Impala.

● **Mountain Travel & Sobek** (☎ 01494-448 901; 🖳 www.mtsobek.com) 67 Verney Ave, High Wycombe, Bucks, HP12 3ND (see Trekking Agencies in the USA, p22).

● **Sherpa Expeditions** (☎ 020-8577 2717; 🖳 www.sherpa-walking-holida ys.co.uk) 131a Heston Rd, Hounslow, Middx TW5 0RF. Machame Route trek or Mount Meru-Machame combination for a very reasonable £665 plus park fees.

● **Terra Firma** (☎ 01691-870 321; 🖳 www.terrafirmatravel.com) 'eunant', Lake Vyrnwy, Wales, SY10 0NF. Offer a seven-day Shira trek, which is one of the few led by a Western climbing leader, for just over £1000 plus park fees; not cheap, but recommended by a number of trekkers.

● **Tribes Travel** (☎ 01728-685 971; 🖥 www.tribes.co.uk) 7 The Business Centre, Earl Soham, Woodbridge, Suffolk IP13 7SA. Eco-friendly company offering all the routes including, wonderfully, the chance to spend the night on Kibo and visit the Reusch Crater and Ash Pit (£1666). Other treks are fairly standard. Prices include park fees.

● **World Expeditions** (☎ 0800-0744 135, 020-8870 2600; 🖥 www.worldexpe ditions.com), 3 Northfields Prospect, Putney Bridge Rd, London SW18 1PE. (See p23, Trekking Agencies in Australia.)

Trekking agencies in Continental Europe

● **Austria** Charisma (☎ 1-585 3680; 🖥 abyss@tauchreisen.at) Hofmuhgasse 20, A-1060 Wien; **Oekista** (☎ 1-401 487 001; 🖥 www.oekista.at), Turkenstrasse 6, 1090 Wien; **Supertramp Reisen** (☎ 01-533 07 48; 🖥 www.su pertramps.co.at), Helferstorferstrafle 4, A-1010 Wien.

● **Belgium** Boundless Adventures (☎ 02-426 4030; 🖥 boundlessadven tures@joker.be), Verdilaan 23/25, 1083 Brussels-Ganshoren; **Joker Tourisme** (☎ 02-502 19 17; 🖥 www.joker.be) Lemonnierlaan 37, 100 Brussels; **Divantoura** (☎ 09-223 00 69; 🖥 www.divantoura.com), Bagattenstraat 176, B-9000, Ghent, and (☎ 03-233 19 16) St Jacobsmarkt 5, 2000 Antwerpen; **Road-runner** (☎ 052-21 15 11), Grote Markt 22, 9200 Dendermonde.

● **Denmark** Inter-Travel (☎ 33-15 00 77; 🖥 www.inter-travel.dk), Frederiks-holms Kanal 2, DK-1220 Kobenhavn K; **Marco Polo Tours** (☎ 33-28 18 75 40; 🖥 www.marcopolo-tours.dk), Borgergade 16, 1300 Kobenhavn K; **Topas** (☎ 33 -11 69 62; 🖥 info@topas.dk), Frederiksborggade 50, 1360 Kobenhavn.

● **France** Club Aventure (☎ 08-25 30 60 32; 🖥 www.clubaventure.fr), 18 rue Séguier, 75006 Paris; **CTS Voyages** (☎ 01-43 25 00 76; 🖥 www.ctsworld.com), 20 rue de Carmes, Paris 75005.

● **Germany** Hauser Exkursionen (☎ 089-23 50 06; 🖥 www.hauser-exkursi onen.de/main.asp) Marienstraße 17, D-80331 München. One of Germany's main trekking operators; runs different tours to Kili, mostly via Kenya using the little-walked Loitokitok Route. **DAV Summit Club** (☎ 089-64 24 20; 🖥 www .dav-summit-club.de), Am Perlacher Forst 186, 81545 München; **Explorer Fernreisen** (☎ 0211-99 49 02; 🖥 marketing@explorerfernreisen.com) Huttenstrasse 17, 40215 Dusseldorf; **Kilroy Travels** (☎ 30 31 00 040; 🖥 www .kilroytravels.com), Hardenbergstrasse 9, 10623 Berlin. **Skantur** (☎ 0391-60 31 35; 🖥 www.skantur.de), Skandinavisches Reisezentrum, Halberstädter Str 188, 39122, Magdeburg.

● **Netherlands** SNP Travel (☎ 024-327 7000, 024-327 7099; 🖥 www.snp.nl), PO Box 1270, 6501 BG Nijmegen. Run two treks up Kili, combined with a safari and trip to Zanzibar. **Adventure World** (☎ 023-5382 954, 🖥 atc@eu ronet.nl), Muiderslotweg 112, Haarlem 2026 AS; **Snow Leopard Adventure**

Reizen (☎ 070-388 28 67; 🖳 www.snowleopard.nl), Treubstraat 15 F, 2288 EG Rijswijk; **Himalaya Trekking** (☎ 0521-55 13 01; 🖳 www.htwande lreizen.nl), Ten Have 13, 7983 KD Wapse; **Nederlandse Klim en Bergsport Vereniging** (☎ 030-233 40 80) Oudkerkhof 13, 3512 GH Utrecht.

● **Norway** Worldwide Adventures (☎ 22-40 48 90; 🖳 post@worldwide.no), AS Nedre Slottsgate 12, Oslo 0157.

● **Spain** Banoa (☎ 944-23 20 39), Ledesma (Musico), 10-bis, 2°, 48011 Bilbao and (☎ 93-318 96 00), Ronda de Sant Pere, 11, 8906 Barcelona. **CTS Viages** (☎ 91 559 31 81; 🖳 www.cts.world.com), Edificio Espana, Plaza de Espana, 28013 Madrid and (☎ 933 18 25 93), El Palau Nou de la Rambla, Las Ramblas 88-94, Ir C 08002 Barcelona.

● **Sweden** Himalayaresor (☎ 08-605 57 60; 🖳 www.himalaya.se) Bjorkallen 45, 14266 Trangsund, Stockholm.

● **Switzerland** Acapa Tours (☎ 062-843 01 16; 🖳 exodus_ch@gmx.ch).

Trekking agencies in the USA
North American trekking agencies tend to quote land cost only.
● **Adventure Center** (☎ 510-654 1879, ☎ 800-228 8747; 🖳 www.adventurece nter.com) 1311 63rd St, Suite 200, Emeryville, CA 94608. Agents for Explore and Guerba (see Trekking Agencies in the UK, p20).
● **G.A.P. Adventures** (☎ 416-260 0999, ☎ 800-692 5495; 🖳 adv enture@gap.ca) 760 North Bedford Rd, Suite 246, Bedford Hills, New York, 10507. Agents for Exodus (UK). Run standard Marangu Route in seven days, to and from Nairobi.
● **Geeta Tours & Travels** (☎ 312-262 4959) 1245 West Jarvis Ave, Chicago.
● **Geographic Expeditions** (☎ 415-922 0448, ☎ 800-777 8183) 2627 Lombard St, San Francisco, CA 94123.
● **Himalayan Travel** (☎ 800-225 2380) 2nd Floor, 112 Prospect St, Stamford CT 06901. Agents for Sherpa Expeditions (UK).
● **Holbrook Travel** (☎ 800-451-7111; 🖳 www.holbrook.com) 3540 NW 13th Street, Gainesville, FL 32609. Run a standard six-day trek on the Marangu Route for US$1255 (excluding fees).
● **Journeys International** (☎ 313-665 4407, ☎ 800-255 8735; 🖳 www.journe ys-intl.com) 107 Aprill Drive, Suite 3, Ann Arbor, MI 48103-1903. Does Rongai, Marangu and Lemosho-Shira routes. Also includes some treks specifi- cally for families.
● **Journey to Africa** (☎ 877-558 6288; 🖳 www.journeytoafrica.com), 11191 Westheimer 410, Houston, TX 77042. Organizes treks on the two most popular routes up Kilimanjaro.
● **Mountain Madness** (☎ 206-937 8389; 🖳 www.mountainmadness.com), 4218 SW Alaska Suite 206, Seattle, WA 98116. Sister company of top agency African Environments (p141); offer Machame/Shira Plateau routes. Expensively reliable.
● **Mountain Travel & Sobek Expeditions** (☎ 510-527 8100, ☎ 888-687 6235; 🖳 www.mtsobek.com) 6420 Fairmount Ave, El Cerrito, CA 94530-3606.

Upmarket treks including Machame and Rongai routes. They can also tailor-make itineraries.

● **Wilderness Travel** (☎ 510-558 2488, ☎ 800-368 2794; 🖳 www.wilder nesstravel.com) 1102 9th St, Berkeley, CA 94710. Offers nine-day upmarket trek on the Shira Plateau Route.

● **World Expeditions** (🖳 www.weadventures.com) 580 Market St, 6th floor, San Francisco, CA 94104. Australian company now based in California, offers a challenging 16-day trekking trip encompassing both Mount Kenya and Kilimanjaro (Rongai Route), or a more sedate Machame trek.

Trekking agencies in Canada

● **Canadian Himalayan Expeditions** (☎ 416-360 4300, 800-563 8735; 🖳 ww w.himalayanexpeditions.com) 2 Toronto St, Suite 302, Toronto, Ontario M5C 2B6. This is one of the few Canadian outfits that run their own treks, rather than acting as agents for foreign companies. Run a couple of standard treks on the Machame and Marangu routes. Land costs are around $1500CA.

● **G.A.P. Adventures** (☎ 416-260 0999, ☎ 800-465 5600; 🖳 www.gapadventu res.com) 19 Duncan St, Suite 401, Toronto, Ontario M5H 3H1. Agents for Exodus UK. Run standard (but rather rushed) Marangu Route treks in seven days to and from Nairobi.

● **Travel Cuts** have offices in **Edmonton** (☎ 780-488 8487) 10127a 124 St, Edmonton, Alberta, T5N 1P5, **Toronto** (☎ 416-979 2406) 187 College St, Toronto, Ontario M5T 1P7 and **Vancouver** (☎ 604-659 2887) 120 West Broadway, Vancouver BC, V5Y 1P3.

● **Trek Holidays**, agents for Explore (UK), have offices in **Calgary** (☎ 403-283 6115), 336 14th St NW, Calgary, Alberta T2N 1Z7, **Edmonton** (☎ 403-439 9118), 8412 109th St, Edmonton, Alberta T6G 1E2, **Toronto** (☎ 416-922 7584) 25 Bellair St, Toronto, Ontario M4Y 2P2 and **Vancouver** (☎ 604-734 1066), 1965 West 4th Ave, Vancouver BC V6J 1M8. They are currently running a clean-up Machame campaign – a worthy endeavour, though I have to say there are plenty of other places in Africa more deserving of a clean-up than Kili.

● **Worldwide Adventures Inc** (☎ 416-633-5666; 🖳 travel@worldwid equest.com) 45-1170 Sheppard Avenue, West Toronto, Ontario, Canada M3K 2A3. Agents for World Expeditions (Australia).

Trekking agencies in Australia

● **Adventure World** (🖳 www.adventureworld.com) has branches in **Perth** (☎ 08-9226 4524), 4th floor, 197 St Georges Terrace, Perth, WA 6000 and **Sydney** (☎ 02-8913 0755), 3rd floor, 73 Walker St, North Sydney, NSW 2060.

● **Outdoor Travel** (☎ 03-9670 7252) 382 Lt Bourke St, Melbourne, Vic 3000. Agents for Sherpa Expeditions (UK).

● **Peregrine Adventures** has branches in **Melbourne** (☎ 03-9663 8611), 2nd floor, 258 Lonsdale St, Melbourne, Vic 3000, and **Sydney** (☎ 02-9290 2770), 5th floor, 38 York St, Sydney, NSW 2000. Large agency and agents for Exodus UK.

● **Peregrine Travel** (08-223 5905) 192 Rundle St, Adelaide, SA 5000.

● **Summit Travel** (☎ 09-321 1259) 1st floor, 862 Hay St, Perth WA 6000.

● **World Expeditions** (☎ 02-9279 0188; 🖥 www.worldexpeditions.com.au) Level 5, 71 York St, **Sydney** NSW 2000. Branches also in **Melbourne** (☎ 03-9670 8400) 1st Floor, 393 Little Bourke St, Melbourne Victoria 3000 and **Brisbane** (☎ 07-3216 0823), Shop 2, 36 Agnes St, Fortitude Valley, Queensland 4006. The main competition for Peregrine Travel. Offers a challenging 16-day trekking trip encompassing both Mount Kenya and Kilimanjaro (Rongai Route), or a Machame trek.

Trekking agencies in New Zealand
● **Adventure World** (☎ 09-524 5118) 101 Great South Rd, Remuera, PO Box 74008, Auckland. Agents for Explore (UK).
● **Venture Treks** (☎ 09-379 9855) PO Box 37610, 164 Parnell Rd, Auckland. Agents for Sherpa Expeditions (UK).
● **World Expeditions** (☎ 09-368 4167) Level 1, 11 Cheshire St, Parnell, Auckland.

Trekking agencies in South Africa
● **Destination Africa Tours** (☎ 12-333 7110; 🖥 www.climbingkiliman jaro.com) 671 31st Avenue, Villeria, Pretoria 0186. Agency that covers all routes, and claims to have a 96% success rate for leading trekkers to the top. Also offers gear rental, and their comprehensive website includes full-moon dates, Swahili terms, a fitness programme and a menu.

For a review of **trekking agencies in Tanzania and Kenya**, see p111 (Dar es Salaam), p122 (Nairobi), pp140–2 (Arusha) and pp151–4 (Moshi); and read the following section.

BOOKING WITH AN AGENCY IN TANZANIA

The main advantage of booking in Tanzania is one of economy: you're cutting out the middleman. Many foreign tour operators don't actually use their own staff to take the treks; instead, they use the services of a Tanzanian tour operator. By booking in Tanzania, therefore, you are dealing directly with the people who are going to take you up the mountain, and not the Western agent.

So it can be quite a bit cheaper booking your trek in Tanzania after you've arrived, particularly if you are willing to shop around, and especially if you are willing to bargain. There are other advantages too. If you ask, there should be no reason why you cannot meet the guides and porters before you agree to sign up – and even your fellow trekkers, all of whom have a huge role to play in making the trek an enjoyable one. You can also personally check the tents and camping equipment before booking. Furthermore, the fact that you can book a trek up to 24 hours beforehand (though see note on p172) gives you greater flexibility, allowing you to alter your plans so that you can pick a day that suits you – when booking with an agency at home you often have to book months in advance, the tour is usually organized to a pretty tight schedule, and altering this schedule at a later date is often impossible. Another point: while the money you spend on a trek may not be going to the most destitute and deserving of Tanzania's population, at least you know that *all* of it is going to Tanzanians, with none going into the pockets of a Western tour company. And finally, with the rise of the Internet, you don't even need to wait until you arrive in Tanzania before booking: the bigger agencies in Moshi and Arusha (see p151 and p140) now have Internet booking services, and while it may seem a little scary sending a deposit to people in East Africa you've never met, the bigger companies at least are used to receiving bookings this way and can be relied upon.

And if you're planning to go with an agency recommended in this book or by friends, then there's no reason why it should be any more risky than if you were booking at home; indeed, there's a slim chance that you might even end up joining a group who *did* book their tour abroad, and paid more as a consequence.

Choosing an agency in Tanzania

The best place to look for an agency is either **Arusha**, which has the greatest number of tour and trekking operators, or **Moshi**. A third option, Marangu, is smaller and has fewer agencies, though it is also covered in this book on p156. Agencies in Dar es Salaam and other Tanzanian towns are usually nothing more than middlemen for the operators in Moshi and Arusha: book a tour with an agency in Dar, for example, and the chances are you'll still end up on a trek organized by an agency in Moshi or Arusha, only you would have paid more for it. Furthermore, if you book outside of Arusha or Moshi, you have less chance of inspecting the equipment or testing your guide before you set off.

Of the two, Moshi is probably preferable. The town is home of some of the most established trekking agencies – including many of those used by tour operators in Europe and the West. It's usually a little cheaper too. Besides, most of the Arusha agencies are, first and foremost, safari organizers; Kili isn't really their thing, and once again many are just acting as middlemen for one of the agencies in Moshi. Nevertheless, it is still worth looking around Arusha for a suitable agent, particularly if you plan to go on safari as well. Booking a safari and a Kili trek with the same agency *should* give you a better deal for both.

The golden rule when shopping around is: **stick to those agencies that have a licence**, and check that licence thoroughly to ensure it covers trekking. If they don't have a licence, or the one that they show you looks a bit suspect, is out of date, or looks like a fake, take your business elsewhere. Don't take a chance on this matter.

Other useful advice includes:

● Decide what sort of trek you want, what route you wish to take, how long you wish to go for, and with how many people.
● Ask other travellers for their recommendations of a good agency.
● Shop around: don't sign up with the first agent you talk to – at least not without consulting some other agencies first to compare.
● Read the section on signing contracts on p26, and learn it off by heart, so you know what to ask the agency.
● Ask about the number of other people on your trek, and the number of porters you'll be taking.

● Ask if you can see their comment book. This is a book where previous clients have written their thoughts on the agency. Nearly every agency will have one, and if they are any good they will show it to you with little or no prompting. Indeed, if they don't have one, or are reluctant to show you, be very suspicious.
● If you have any dietary requirements or other special needs, ask them if these will be a problem, if it will cost any more, and how exactly they propose to comply with your requirements (for example, if you are a vegetarian, ask the agent what kind of meals you can expect to receive on the trek).
● Ask to see a print-out of the day-to-day itinerary (though some, admittedly, will not have this, all agencies should be able to describe all the trekking routes and their itineraries without any problem); if you're negotiating with an agency at the upper end of the market, you may even be able to get a preview of the daily menus.
● If you think you've found a good company, ask to see the equipment you will be using, and make sure the tent is complete, untorn, and that all the zips work.
● Check the sleeping arrangements, particularly if you're not trekking with friends but have joined a group: are you going to have a tent to yourself, or are you going to be sharing with somebody you've never met before.
● If you are alone and on a budget, ask if it is possible to be put with a group, which should make things cheaper. (This is normally done automatically anyway; indeed, if you are travelling alone and were quoted a very low price, you can expect to be put with another group.)

Following on from the last point, many of the operators at the budget end often band together to lump all their customers into one large trekking group, thereby making it cheaper for them (because there are fewer guides required). So don't be surprised if, having signed up with one company, you end up being joined by trekkers who booked with another company. Once again, make sure you know in advance about any arrangements like this *before* you sign anything or hand over any money. And if you want to be on your own, tell them.

For a list of trekking agencies in Tanzania, see the relevant sections in the Arusha and Moshi chapters on pp140–2 and pp151–4.

SIGNING THE CONTRACT

You've found a suitable agency offering the trek you want for the required duration at an acceptable price. Before you sign on the dotted line, however, there are a number of questions to be asked, matters to consider and points to discuss with the agency. (And if there is no dotted line to sign on – ie no contract – then don't even think about handing over any money or going with them.) What is vitally important is that you **sort out *exactly* what is and isn't included in the price of the trek**. Don't just ask what is included in the price: ask what isn't included – ie what you yourself will need to pay for.

The following is a brief checklist of items that should be included:
● All park fees, rescue fees, hut/camping fees for both yourself and the porters and guides.

● Hire of porters, assistant guides and guides, their wages and food.

● Food and water for the entire trek. Try to get a breakdown of exactly how many meals per day you will be getting: normally trekkers are served three meals per day plus a snack – typically a hot drink with popcorn and biscuits – upon arrival at camp at the end of the day's walking; see p171 for more details about food on the trek.

● Transport to and from the park at the beginning and end of the trek.

● Hire of camping and cooking gear. If you have brought your own gear, you should be able to persuade the agency to reduce the cost of your trek, though it will be only by a small amount.

● Hire of any equipment – torches, ski poles, spare water-bottles etc – that you have forgotten to bring with you.

● Any special dietary requirements or other needs, all of which should be stipulated in the contract.

● Any free night's accommodation at the beginning or end of your trek that the trekking company has agreed to pay for.

Please note that items that are rarely, if ever, included in the package include cigarettes, soft drinks and the tips you dish out to staff at the end.

Having sorted that out, you then need to make sure that *everything* that the agency has said they will provide, including everything listed above, is **specified in the contract**. This is important because, as you probably already know, a verbal contract is simply not worth the paper it isn't written on. The trekking companies all have standard contracts already drawn up which should include most of the above, but will not include specific things such as the hire of any equipment that you need or any free nights' accommodation that you have managed to negotiate into the package. However, these will need to be written in as well. It is also useful to have a breakdown of the **day-by-day itinerary** written somewhere into the contract. Though it's rare now, in previous years some trekkers failed to reach the summit simply because they started out too late on the final, night-time push to the top.

THE COST: WHY IS IT ALL SO EXPENSIVE?

With little change from US$500 for even the cheapest trek, it cannot be denied that climbing Kili is a relatively expensive walk, particularly when compared to other famous treks (the Annapurna Circuit in Nepal, for example, costs around US$30 for the entrance fee, while the Inca Trail is around US$50 for the permit); with no refund available to those who fail either, at first sight this trek can seem very bad value too – though to those who successfully reach the summit, of course, the sense of achievement and the enjoyment of the trek makes any amount seem worth it.

To give you some idea of where your US$500-plus is going the following is a breakdown of fees, wages and other costs incurred on the trek. The box on p29 is an example of the breakdown of costs for an average trek. Don't forget that, in addition to the official costs outlined below, there is also the matter of tips: see below for further details.

Park fees

Rescue fee	US$20 per trip
Park entry fee	US$30 per day
Camping fee	US$40 per night
Hut fee (Marangu Route only)	US$50 per night
Porter/guide entrance fees	US$1 per person per trip

Take a quick look at these figures and already you can see just why the cost of climbing Kilimanjaro is so high. Even if you took the quickest (and thus not recommended) five-day yomp up the Marangu Route, your fees alone still come to $370. See opposite for how much a typical trek could cost.

Other costs

Wages (per trip) Wages vary from company to company of course, though no agency pays their porters or staff that well – which is why they rely so heavily on the tips you give out. The most generous employers are reputed to be African Environments (p141), who are rumoured to pay their porters up to Ts45,000, around 50% more than the average. But then they do expect 50% more work too: this is the company, so rumour has it, that willingly carried up a proper porcelain Armitage Shanks toilet bowl for one pampered customer. As one of my guides put it, if a banana became lost or broken en route, they'd radio the office to bring up a replacement.

Porters	Ts20–25,000 per porter (US$21–26)
Assistant guides	Ts45–50,000 per assistant guide (US$48–53)
Guide	Ts65–70,000 per guide (US$69–74)

Transport The only significant cost that can be divided between trekkers, a gallon of premium petrol is Ts650 per litre, with diesel a little less. The total cost for your trek will depend, of course, on which route you are taking, and how long the journeys to and from the trek are.

Food Difficult to calculate precisely, the best guess we can come up with for the food bill is around Ts10,000 per person; remember, though, that your total bill has to cover not only your food, but the food of the porters and guides too.

TIPPING

In addition to the cost of booking your trek, you will also need to shell out tips to your crew at the end of it all. The gratuity system on Kilimanjaro follows the American-style: that is to say, a tip is not so much a bonus to reward particularly attentive service or honest toil, as a mandatory payment to subsidize the poor wages the porter and guides receive. In other words, tipping is obligatory.

To anybody born outside the Americas this compulsory payment of gratuities seems to go against the very spirit of tipping. Nevertheless, it is very hard to

❏ **AN EXAMPLE: THE MACHAME TREK**

For a six-day Machame trek, taking one guide, one assistant guide and two porters, the basic cost would be as follows:

Park fees

Rescue fee		US$20
Park entry fee	$30 x 6 days	US$180
Camping fee	$40 x 5 nights	US$200
Porter/guide entrance fees		US$4

Wages

Porters (two)	US$45
Assistant guide	US$50
Guide	US$70

Food

Five people at Ts10,000	US$51

Transport

Estimate per person		US$20
	TOTAL	**US$640**

Obviously if there are more of you then some costs, such as the food for the porters and the transport costs, can be divided between the group, thus making it cheaper. Nevertheless, the above example gives you an idea of just how quickly the costs add up. Any excess over these costs goes straight to the agency. But they have significant costs of their own, including an annual licence fee of US$200, and a Ts200,000 (US$206) municipality fee (in Moshi) that they must pay before they can even open their door to begin trading. Remember, too, when working out your budget, to add on tips for your crew.

begrudge the guides and porters a decent return for their labours – and depriving your entourage of their much-needed gratuities is not the way to voice your protest against this system.

As to the **size of the remuneration**, there are no set figures or formulas, though I do urge you to let your conscience instruct you on this matter as much as your wallet. One method that's currently very popular is for everybody to contribute 10% of the total cost of their trek towards tips. So if you paid US$750 for your trek, you should pay US$75 into the tip kitty. (If there are only one or two of you, it would be better to pay slightly more than 10%.) Another approach I've heard about is where each member of the trekking staff receives a set amount, from $20 to each of the porters to $40–50 to the assistant guides, and US$60–70 to the guides. These are mere guidelines, and you may wish to alter them if you feel, for example, a certain porter is deserving of more than his normal share, or if your trek was particularly long or difficult.

Having collected all the money, the usual form is either to hand out the individual shares to each porter and guide in turn; or, more usually, to give the whole lot to the guide and let him deal it out. This alternative is perhaps better, for your crew may have already decided how to divide up the tips amongst themselves, and it's not unknown for fights to break out at the bar by Marangu Gate if they think you've given somebody more than they deserve. By letting the guide distribute the money you could save yourself from being embroiled in any controversy – though if you do give all the money to the guide, make sure that he realizes that it is not all for him! See opposite for more information about giving tips to porters.

The crew

PORTERS

My guide was as polite as Lord Chesterfield and kindly as the finest gentleman of the world could be. So I owe much to the bare-footed natives of this country, who patiently for eight cents a day bear the white man's burden. **Peter MacQueen** *In Wildest Africa* (1910)

The wages may have gone up – a porter today will earn on average Ts20,000–25,000 for a six-day trip – and all now have footwear of some description, but the opinion expressed way back at the beginning of the twentieth century by the intrepid MacQueen is pretty much the same as that voiced by thousands of trekkers today.

These men (and the ones hired by trekkers are always male) never fail to draw both gratitude and, with the amount they carry and the minimum of fuss they make it about it, admiration from the trekkers who hire them. Ranging in age from about 18 (the minimum legal age, though some look a good deal younger) to 40 (and occasionally presumably beyond this), porters are amongst the hardest workers on Kilimanjaro. To see them traipsing up the mountain, water in one hand, cooker in another, rucksack on the back and picnic table on the head, is staggering to behold. And though they are supposed to carry no more than 15kg, many, desperate for work in what is an over-supplied market, carry much, much more.

And if that isn't enough, while at the end of the day the average trekker spends his or her time at camp moaning about the hardships they are suffering – in between cramming down mouthfuls of popcorn while clasping a steaming hot cup of tea – these hardy individuals are putting up the tents, helping with the preparation of the food, fetching more water and generally making sure every trekker's whim is, within reason, catered for.

Yet in spite of appearances, porters are not indestructible. Though they don't actually climb to the summit themselves, a few still expire each year on the slopes of Kilimanjaro. The most common cause of death, perhaps unsurprisingly given the ragged clothes many wear, is exposure. For this reason, if you see a porter dozing on the wayside and it's getting a bit late, put aside your concerns about depriving him of some much needed shut-eye and wake him up: many are the tales of porters who have perished on Kilimanjaro because they took forty winks, and then couldn't find their way back to camp in the dark.

How many . . .

The first question regarding porters is: how many do you actually need? This particular issue won't actually concern many people, for agencies typically work this out for you. Those looking to save every last shilling, however, often ask the agency to cut down on the number of porters. But this is neither particularly easy nor – given that the cost of a porter's wages is usually less than the food bill – a particularly brilliant idea. Remember that even if you do carry your own rucksack, there is still all the food, cooking equipment, camping gear and so forth to lug up the mountainside. Then there is the guide's rucksack too, for which he will expect you to hire a porter.

As a general rule, the larger the number of trekkers, the less porters per person required, and if you take the Marangu Route (where no tent is required) you can probably get away with about two per trekker, and often less if the group is large. On other routes, where tents are necessary, two to three porters per person is the norm. (Just for the record, and just in case taking porters up a mountain makes you feel a little less virile, you may like to know that the great Count Teleki – see p87 – took no less than 65 of them up the mountain with him!)

. . . and how much?

The porters' wages are paid by the agency you sign up with. All you need to worry about is how much to give them as a **tip** at the end of the trek. Given the privations they suffer over the course of an average trek, their efforts to extract as much money as possible from the over-privileged *mzungu* (Swahili for white person) is entirely forgivable. One elaborate yet surprisingly common method is to pretend that there are more of them than there actually are; which, given the vast numbers of porters running around each campsite, and the fact you don't actually walk with them on the trail, is a lot easier to achieve than you may think. It's a technique hinted at by John Reader in his excellent book *Kilimanjaro*:

I hired four porters for part of my excursion on Kilimanjaro. The fourth man's name was Stephen, or so the other three told me. I never met Stephen himself. Our gear seemed to arrive at each campsite without his assistance and I am not aware that he ever spent a night with us. I was assured that he was engaged elsewhere on tasks essential to the success of my journey, but I occasionally wondered whether Stephen actually existed. I was particularly aggrieved when he failed to collect his pay in person at the end of the trip. The other guides collected it for him. They also collected his tip.

This sort of thing shouldn't happen if you're with a reputable company, but it's a good idea anyway to make sure you meet your team at the start of the trail before you set off. This will help to prevent this sort of scam, and it's good manners too.

Please note that however much you lavish on them at the end, the porter's reaction will always be the same. Simply put, porters are not above play-acting, in the same way that the sea is not above the clouds. On being given their gratuity all porters will grimace, sigh, tut, shake their head, roll their eyes in disgust and stare at the money in their hand with all the enthusiasm and gratitude of one who has just been handed a warm jar of the contents of the Barranco Camp toilets. A few of the more talented ones may even manage a few tears. Nevertheless, providing you have paid a reasonable tip (and for guidance over what exactly is the correct amount, see p29), don't fall for the melodramatics, but simply thank them warmly for all their endeavours over the course of the trek. Once they realize your conscience remains unpricked it will all be handshakes and smiles, and having trousered the money they'll soon trot off happily enough.

GUIDES

Mzee Yohana Lauwo, the porter guide who accompanied the first Europeans up the Kilimanjaro Mountain a century ago, was the centre of attention in a commemorative ceremony in Moshi on Friday.

Mzee Lauwo, now over 118 years, was presented with a prize in cash. The Deputy Minister for Lands, Natural Resources and Tourism, Ndugu Chabanga Hassan Dyamwalle, suggested that Mwee Lauwo also be given a house to be built in his own village.

The ambassador to the Federal Republic of Germany (FRG) to Tanzania, Christel Steffler, presented Mzee Lauwo with a letter which expressed gratitude for his service in cementing German-Tanzanian relations. She said it was high time porters and guides were given the recognition they deserved for their work.

At the same ceremony, the deputy minister presented cash prizes and certificates to the winners of the Bonite tree planting competition.

Press cutting from the *In Brief* section of a local newspaper, found stuck on the wall of the *Kibo Hotel*, Marangu.

If portering is the first step on the career ladder of Kilimanjaro, then it is the guides who stand proudly on the top rung. Ornithologist, zoologist, botanist, geologist, tracker, astronomer, chef, butler, manager, doctor, linguist and teacher, a good guide will be all of these professions rolled into one. With luck over the course of the trek they'll also become your friend.

The metamorphosis from porter to guide is a lengthy one. Having served one's apprenticeship by lugging luggage as a porter, a few lucky and ambitious ones are eventually promoted to the position of **assistant guide**. These gentlemen are probably the hardest working people on the mountain. While they still essentially remain a porter, in that they have to carry their fair share of equipment, they are also expected to perform many of the duties of a fully fledged guide – including, most painfully of all, the escorting of trekkers on that final, excruciating push to the summit.

Their reward for all this effort is a slightly higher wage than a porter (Ts50,000 per six-day trip is about the average), a commensurately greater proportion of the tips – and, perhaps most importantly, the knowledge that they have taken that first crucial step towards becoming a guide, when they can leave all this hard graft behind and wallow in the privileges that seniority brings.

Standing between them and a guiding licence is a period of intensive training conducted by the park authorities. This mainly involves a two- to three-week tour of the mountain, during which time they cover every designated route up and down Kilimanjaro. On this course they are also taught the essentials of being a guide, including a bit about the fauna and flora of Kili, how to take care of the mountain environment, how to spot the symptoms of altitude sickness in trekkers and, just as importantly, what to do about it.

Choosing a guide

At the moment, all guides carry the same licence regardless of their ability. As a result, tourists have no idea whether they are hiring a knowledgeable guide who can instruct them in the geology, flora, fauna and so on of the mountain, or whether they are getting a guide whose knowledge extends little beyond knowing where the path is, and how to cook popcorn. For this reason, KINAPA are planning to introduce a system whereby the guides will be categorized according to their ability: so, for example, the top guides (who for the moment have been given the title of Chief Interpreters by KINAPA) will be issued with one licence, while those of lesser ability (dubbed, temporarily at least, Route Guides by KINAPA) hold another. Naturally, those who hold the Chief Interpreter licences will command a higher wage and will tend to be employed by the more expensive agencies. But the Route Guides should still be able to find employment among the cheaper agencies catering to those trekkers who want to climb the mountain, but aren't overly interested in its features; in other words, those who are hiring a guide simply because the rules say they have to.

This initiative, if it works, can only be good news for trekkers: your guide is one of the most important factors in determining whether your trek is an enjoyable one, and a good guide can truly enhance any walk on Kilimanjaro.

Unless and until that initiative is introduced, it is very important that you meet your guide before you go, in order to test his abilities and, even more importantly, to make sure that you can trust him: remember, you are putting your life into his hands for the next five or six days, and his decisions could determine whether you come down with a gold certificate or on a stretcher. It's not just his talent on the mountain that needs to be tested either. You need to make sure you can get along with him; his ability with the English language could be crucial too. You may even, if you're feeling particularly vindictive, test him on his knowledge of Kilimanjaro by asking him about a few facts that you've gleaned from this book (though bear in mind, knowledge of the mountain is only one area in which he should be proficient). Remember, it's you who is paying for this trek, and it's a lot too; for that reason alone you should be entitled to check that you are getting your *shilingis*' worth.

That complete, they receive their licences and are free to tout themselves around the agencies looking for work. While a few of the better guides are snapped up by the top agencies and work exclusively for them, the majority are freelance and have to actively seek work in what is already an over-supplied market. For this reason, guides' wages are not that much more than those of their assistants, being about Ts65,000–70,000 for a six-day trip.

Getting to Kilimanjaro

One of the gladdest moments in life, methinks is the departure upon a distant journey into unknown lands. Shaking off with one mighty effort the fetters of habit, the leaden weight of routine, the cloak of many cares and the slavery of home, man feels once more happy... The blood flows with the fast circulation of childhood ... afresh dawns the morn of life.
Diary entry of **Richard Burton** (the explorer, not the actor), December 2 1856.

BY AIR

Tanzania has three major international airports: Dar es Salaam, Zanzibar and Kilimanjaro. The latter, as you may expect, is the most convenient for Kilimanjaro, standing only 48km away from the mountain town of Moshi, and a similar distance from Arusha, where most people arrange their trek and begin their adventure. An approximate timetable of international flights to and from Kilimanjaro can be found in Appendix C, p232. Unfortunately, the lack of airlines flying into KIA (the acronym for Kilimanjaro International Airport, though the three-letter international airport code more commonly used is JRO) – KLM, Ethiopian, Air Tanzania and Precision Air being the major ones – results in airfares from Europe and elsewhere being rather inflated; this, combined with the fact that many trekkers will want a few days on a beach at the start or end of their holiday, means that most visitors to Tanzania fly to one of the other two airports. Of the two, Zanzibar is often, surprisingly, the cheaper destination. It is, however, rather inconveniently located for Kilimanjaro, being around 40km off the Tanzanian coast, and as such those flying out for the specific purpose of climbing the mountain should really discard this option and look instead at flights to Dar es Salaam.

In addition to the Tanzanian destinations, you may also wish to consider Mombasa and Nairobi in Kenya, both of which are conveniently situated for Kilimanjaro and which are usually rather cheaper to fly to. This also gives you the chance of taking in one of Kenya's world-renowned game reserves (which are cheaper, when compared to Tanzanian park fees). Note, however, that by choosing this option you may need a multiple-entry visa for Kenya, which for Brits and others can be as much as £70 – thereby reducing or eliminating any saving you may have made in airfares. (For details of whether you will require a multiple-entry visa, or can get away with a single-entry visa for Kenya, see p58.) Furthermore, the Kenyan capital in particular has a reputation for violence and robbery that is entirely deserved.

You will find brief guides in this book to Nairobi (p117), as well as Dar es Salaam (p108) and Kilimanjaro International Airport (p128); while a timetable for flights to Kilimanjaro International can be found in Appendix C, p232.

From the UK

A cheap flight to Kilimanjaro from London with KLM via Amsterdam will set you back a minimum of £500, while for Dar the determined may be able to find one for around £420. You have to add on to these places departure taxes from both the UK (£20, or £40 for first and business passengers) and Tanzania (around US$20, and not usually included as part of the ticket price)

In addition to the travel agencies listed below, net-heads may also like to check out ▣ www.cheapflights.co.uk, which gives a summary of the flight offers to your destination from a number of different agents. There are also online **flight auctions**; you log on to the website (such as ▣ www.skya uction.com), fill in the details of when you want to go, and say how much you're prepared to pay. You can offer any amount (though remember that the bid must be high enough to persuade the airlines to sell it to you), and it is possible to pick up real bargains this way.

But be warned: the auction houses want your credit card details before you make a bid for a flight, because if your bid is accepted, the seat is considered sold and *you cannot back out*. Furthermore, these tickets are non-changeable and non-refundable so it is absolutely essential that you fill out the details of when you can travel extremely carefully, or you could end up with a ticket that you cannot use. For this reason, most travellers forego these online flight auctions, preferring to buy from a regular travel agent instead.

Of these 'regular' agencies, famous names include: STA Travel (⌨ www.st atravel.com; London ☎ 020-7937 9962, Bristol ☎ 0117-929 4399, Manchester ☎ 0161-839 0668, Cambridge ☎ 01223-366 966, Oxford ☎ 08701-636 373, and many other places around the country too) and Trailfinders (⌨ www.trailfin ders.com; London ☎ 020-7938 3939, Manchester ☎ 0161-839 6969, Glasgow ☎ 0141-353 2224, Bristol ☎ 0117-929 9000, Dublin ☎ 01-677 7888 and others).

From the USA
In the US, check out Air Brokers International of San Francisco (⌨ www.airbr okers.com; ☎ 1-800-883 3273), Sky Link of New York (☎ 212-599 0430) and STA Travel (⌨ www.statravel.com; toll free helpline ☎ 1-800-836 4115, with 24 offices nationwide).

From Australia and New Zealand
In Australia and New Zealand try Flight Centre (Melbourne ☎ 03-9650 2899, Auckland ☎ 09-209-6171), Thomas Cook (Sydney ☎ 02-9248 6100) and Trailfinders (Sydney ☎ 02-9247 7666, Brisbane ☎ 07-3229 0887).

OVERLAND

A big country lying at the heart of East Africa, Tanzania has borders with many countries, including Burundi, Kenya, Malawi, Mozambique, Rwanda, Uganda and Zambia. The **Burundi** border has been shut since 1995 due to the civil war going on in that country. The peace deal signed in November 2001 was rejected by the Hutu rebels committed to overthrowing president Buyoya, and fighting continues to this day. A number of travellers were, at least in the early years of the war, crossing over the Kobero Bridge, though with so few people visiting Burundi these days, we have no update on whether that bridge is still open.

The Burundi upheaval is affecting other border crossings, all of which should be open. The border between **Rwanda** and Tanzania, for example, while open, can be negotiated only with an armed guard because of huge numbers of Burundi rebels in the area. For this you shouldn't have to pay, though you probably will.

The border with **Uganda** (most commonly crossed at Mutukula, north-west of Bukoba), **Zambia** (main crossing Tunduma), **Mozambique** (Kilambo), **Malawi** (Songwe River Bridge) and **Kenya** (see the Nairobi chapter for details) are all relatively straightforward and served by public buses. Tanzania and Zambia are also linked by express train, running twice weekly between Dar es Salaam and Mbeya.

Route options

GETTING TO THE MOUNTAIN

This book aims to take you from your armchair to the summit of Africa's highest mountain. If you have booked a package from home, of course, your transport to and from the mountain will already have been sorted out and you needn't worry. If you haven't then this book will tell you about the city you are flying to, and the towns of Arusha, Moshi and Marangu that lie nearest to the mountain. It also goes into some detail about which trekking company to book with and where you can find them; and once you have booked your trek with a company in Tanzania, it will invariably include transport to and from the Kilimanjaro National Park gates.

GETTING UP THE MOUNTAIN   [SEE COLOUR MAP, p242]

Kilimanjaro has two main summits. The higher one is Kibo, the glacier-clad circular summit that stars on all the pictures of Kilimanjaro. While spiky Mawenzi, to its east, is impossible to conquer without knowledge of advanced climbing techniques and no small amount of courage, it is possible to walk up to the top of Kibo at a height of 5892–5896m (for a discussion of the exact height of the mountain, see p70).

Look down at Kilimanjaro from above and you should be able to count eight paths trailing like ribbons up the sides of the mountain. Five of these are ascent-only paths (ie you can only walk up the mountain on them and are not allowed to come down on these trails), two are descent-only paths, and only one – the Marangu Route – is both an ascent and descent trail. At around 4000m these trails meet up with a path that loops right around Kibo. From here, three further paths lead up the slopes to the summit itself. For a brief description of the trails, and a look at their relative merits, read on. For further details about the trails, check out the full descriptions of each, beginning on p169. Note that some trekking agencies vary the routes slightly, particularly on the Shira Plateau. Any agency worth its salt will provide you with a detailed itinerary, enabling you to check exactly which path you will be taking each day.

Ascending Kilimanjaro: the options

There are six main ascent trails leading up to the foot of Kibo peak. These are (running anti-clockwise, beginning with the westernmost trail): the Shira Route, Lemosho Route, Machame Route, Umbwe Route, Marangu Route and, running from the north, the Loitokitok (Rongai) Route. Each of these six routes eventually meet with a path circling the foot of the Kibo cone, a path known as either the **Northern Circuit** or the **Southern Circuit** depending on which side of the mountain you are. (It is possible and very worthwhile to walk right around Kibo on this path, though this needs to be arranged beforehand with your agency, takes a long time, and permission from KINAPA will need to be sought before embarking on such an expedition.) Three trails then lead up from this circular path to Kibo's crater rim: the **Arrow Glacier Route** and **Barafu Route** (both named after the campsites from which the trails start) and the most popular but nameless third path which runs up from Kibo Huts to Gillman's Point, and which we shall call the **Kibo Hut Route**. Which of these you will take to the summit depends largely upon which of the six paths you took to get this far: the Shira, Lemosho, Machame and Umbwe routes can use either the difficult Arrow Glacier Route or the easier (but longer) Barafu Route, while the Marangu and Rongai trails use the Kibo Hut Route. You can deviate from this rule and design your own combination of trails to take you to the summit, but it will require special permission from KINAPA, and the agencies will charge a lot more to organize such a trek.

A brief description of each of the six main trails follows:

The Marangu Route (5–6 days) is the oldest and most popular trail, and the one that comes closest (though not very) to the trail Hans Meyer took in making the first successful assault on the summit. It is the only trail where camping is not necessary, with trekkers sleeping in dormitory huts along the way. From the Kibo Huts, trekkers climb up to the summit via Gillman's Point. The average trekker will take five days and four nights to complete the trail though an extra night is often taken after the second day to allow trekkers to acclimatize.

The Machame Route (6–7 days) is the next most popular trail, and the one many guides consider the most enjoyable. Though widely regarded as more difficult than the Marangu trail, the success rate on this trail is higher, possibly because it is a day longer at six days and five nights (assuming you take the Barafu Route to the summit) which gives trekkers more time to acclimatize. An extra acclimatization day can also be taken in the Karanga Valley. You can also take the Arrow Glacier Route but this shortens the trek by a day.

The Rongai Route (5–6 days) is the only trail to approach Kibo from the north. Indeed, the original trail began right against the Kenyan border, though recently the trail shifted eastwards and now starts at the Tanzanian town of Loitokitok, after which the new trail has been named (though everybody still refers to it as the Rongai Route). For the final push to the summit trekkers on this trail take the Kibo Hut Route, joining it at the 5000m mark just below Hans Meyer Cave. Again the trek can be completed in five days and four nights, though trekkers usually take a detour to the campsite beneath Mawenzi peak, adding an extra day.

The Umbwe Route (5–6 days) is the hardest trail, a tough vertical slog through the jungle, in places using the tree roots as makeshift rungs on a ladder. Having reached the Southern Circular Route, trekkers then traditionally continue north to tackle Kibo from the west and the difficult Arrow Glacier Route, though you can also follow the Southern Circular Route east round to Barafu and approach the summit from there. The entire walk up and down takes about six days (with a day's acclimatizing at Karanga Valley) if going via the Barafu Campsite, or five if going via the Western Breach.

The Shira Plateau and Lemosho routes (5–8 days each) Both run from west to east across the centre of the Shira Plateau, and are perhaps the least popular trails on the mountain, mainly because of the difficulty involved in getting to the start of them. The **Shira Plateau Route** is the original plateau trail, though it is seldom used these days, for walkers embarking on this trail actually begin their walk above the forest in the moorland zone. After traversing the plateau the trekker has a choice of climbing Kibo via the Arrow Glacier Route,

---

The topography of Kilimanjaro

And surely never monarch wore his royal robes more royally than this monarch of African mountains, Kilimanjaro. His foot rests on a carpet of velvety turf, and through the dark green forest the steps of his throne reach downward to the earth, where man stands awestruck before the glory of his majesty. Art may have colours rich enough to fix one moment of this dazzling splendour, but neither brush nor pen can portray the unceasing play of colour – the wondrous purples of the summit deepening as in the Alpine afterglow; the dull greens of the forest and the sepia shadows in the ravines and hollows, growing ever darker as evening steals on apace; and last, the gradual fading away of all, as the sun sets, and over everything spreads the grey cloud-curtain of the night. It is not a picture but a pageant – a king goes to his rest.

Hans Meyer *Across East African Glaciers*

Kilimanjaro is not only the highest mountain in Africa, it's also one of the biggest volcanoes on Earth, covering an area of approximately 388,500 hectares. In this area are three main peaks that betray its origins as the offspring of three huge volcanic eruptions.

The oldest and smallest peak is known as **Shira**, and lies on the western edge of the mountain. This is the least impressive peak, being nothing more than a heavily eroded ridge, 3962m tall at its highest, **Johnsell Point**. This ridge is, in fact, merely the western and southern rims of the original Shira crater, the northern and eastern sides being covered by later material from Kibo (see below).

The Shira Ridge separates the western slopes from the **Shira Plateau**. This large, rocky plateau, 6200ha in size, is one of Kilimanjaro's most intriguing features. It is believed to be the caldera of the first volcano (a caldera is a collapsed crater) that has been filled in by lava from later eruptions which then solidified and turned to rock. The plateau rises gently from west to east until it reaches the youngest and main summit on Kilimanjaro, **Kibo**. This is the best preserved crater on Kilimanjaro; its southern lip is slightly higher than the rest of the rim, and the highest point on this southern lip is Uhuru Peak – the highest point in Africa and the goal of just about every Kilimanjaro trekker.

Kibo is also the only one of the three summits which is permanently covered in snow, thanks to the large **glaciers** that cover much of its surface. Kibo is also the one peak that really does look like a volcanic crater; indeed, there are not one but three concentric craters on Kibo. Within the inner **Reusch Crater** (1.3km in diameter) one can still see signs of volcanic activity, including fumaroles, the smell of sulphur and a third crater, the **Ash Pit**, 130m deep by 140m wide. *(Continued opposite.)*

or the longer and easier Barafu Route. If opting for the former, expect the trek to last a total of five nights and six days. By the latter trail the walk could last as many as eight days if extra overnight stops on the plateau and in the Karanga Valley are taken – if not, six days is more likely. The **Lemosho Route** is a new trail that improves on the Shira Plateau Route by starting below the Shira Ridge, thus providing trekkers with both a walk in the forest at the start of the trek and more time to acclimatize. As with the Shira Plateau Route, you can ascend Kibo either by the Arrow Glacier Route or by the Barafu Route; allow four to five nights for the former, up to seven nights for the latter if stops at Shira 1, Shira Huts and in the Karanga Valley are taken.

The topography of Kilimanjaro *(Continued from opposite page)* The outer, **Kibo Crater** (1.9 by 2.7km), is not a perfect, unbroken ring. There are gaps in the summit where the walls have been breached by lava flows; the most dramatic of these is the **Western Breach**, through which many climbers gain access to the summit each year. The crater has also subsided a little over time, leading to a landslide 100,000 years ago that created the **Barranco** on Kibo's southern side (see p68). On the whole, though, Kibo's slopes are of a gentle gradient, allowing trekkers as well as mountaineers to reach the summit. (For more details on the Kibo summit, see p224.)

Separating Kibo from the second peak, Mawenzi, is the **Saddle**, at 3600ha the largest area of high altitude tundra in tropical Africa. This really is a beautiful, eerie place — a dusty desert almost 5000m high, featureless except for the occasional parasitic cone dotted here and there, including the **Triplets**, **Middle Red** and **West Lava Hill**, all running south-east from the south-eastern side of Kibo. These are just some of the 250 parasitic cones that are said to stand on Kilimanjaro

Nothing could be more marked than the contrast between the external appearance of these two volcanoes – Kibo, with the unbroken, gradual slopes of the typical volcanic cone – Mawenzi with its bewildering display of many-coloured lavas and its fantastically carved outlines, the result of long ages of exposure, combined with the tendency of its component rocks to split vertically rather than horizontally. The hand of time has left its impress upon Kibo too, but the havoc it has wrought is not to be detected at a distance. **Hans Meyer** *Across East African Glaciers*

Seen from Kibo, **Mawenzi** looks less like a crater than a single lump of jagged, craggy rock emerging from the Saddle. This is merely because its western side also happens to be its highest, and hides everything behind it. Walk around Mawenzi, however, and you'll realize that this peak is actually a horseshoe shape, with only the northern side of the crater having been eroded away. Its sides too steep to hold glaciers, there is no *permanent* snow on Mawenzi, and the gradients are enough to dissuade all but the bravest and most technically accomplished climbers. Mawenzi's highest point is Hans Meyer Peak at 5149m, but so shattered is this summit, and so riven with gullies and fractures, that there are a number of other distinctive peaks including Purtscheller Peak (5120m) and South Peak (4958m). There are also two deep gorges, the Great Barranco and the Lesser Barranco, scarring its north-eastern face.

Few people know this, but Kilimanjaro does actually have a crater lake. **Lake Chala** (aka Jala) lies some 30km to the south-east, and is said to be up to 2.5miles deep.

For details on how exactly Kilimanjaro came to be this shape, see the geology section on p67; for flora and fauna that can be found growing on the mountain, see p94.

> **Day trips**
> If for some reason you cannot climb all the way to the top but nevertheless wish to experience the pleasure of walking on Africa's most beautiful mountain, it is possible to enter the Kilimanjaro National Park for one day only. There are some advantages to doing this. It's safer for one thing, for few will get beyond 3000m at most in one day. With no camping or rescue fees, porters' wages or food to pay, it will work out much cheaper too: just US$30 per day entry fee plus a wage for the compulsory guide. And as well as being wonderfully pleasant, if you're fit and start out early enough, there's no reason why you can't climb above the tree-line to the heathland, thereby covering two vegetation zones, and giving yourself a good chance of a reasonably close-up view of Kibo and Mawenzi. There are even designated picnic spots on the way.
>
> Marangu Gate has a **three-hour nature loop** through the cloud forest which is lovely, and from which you can descend either via the trekkers' trail or the less scenic but faster porters' route. There are also a number of seldom visited waterfalls in the area. The ambitious can attempt to reach the Mandara Huts (p176) and descend again in one day. Furthermore, just 15 minutes beyond the Mandara huts, through a small patch of forest alive with monkeys, is the Maundi Crater (p176), with excellent views of Kibo and Mawenzi to the north-west, and the flat African plains stretching away to the east.
>
> The other place where day trips are allowed is on the Shira Plateau, where your chances of spotting big game are much greater, though the time taken in entering the park from the west deters most day-trippers.

Descending Kilimanjaro – the designated descents

In an attempt to control the number of people walking on each trail, and thus limit the amount of soil erosion on some of the more popular routes, KINAPA have introduced new regulations regarding the descent routes, and which ones you are allowed to take. In general, the main rule is as follows: those ascending Kilimanjaro from the south or west (ie by taking the Machame, Umbwe, Lemosho or Shira routes) must take as their descent route the **Mweka** or **Alternative Mweka** trails (which of these two you take will be decided by KINAPA); whereas if you have climbed the mountain from the east or north (ie on the Marangu or Rongai/Loitokitok trails) you must descend by the **Marangu Route**. The only exception to this rule is that, for the time being at least, you can take the Marangu Route up and the Mweka Route down. But remember that if you do this, you are going to need to pay for an extra porter to carry a tent, even though you actually use this tent only on the last night; the rest of the time you will be on the Marangu Route, and therefore sleeping in huts.

Those trekkers who wish to **deviate from these rules** should first seek permission from KINAPA. Before doing so, bear in mind that the choice of different ascent/descent combinations is somewhat restricted by the limits of your porters. For example, one attractive and seemingly possible combination would be to climb to the summit from the west, starting off from the Arrow Glacier Camp and ascending via the Western Breach, and then descend via the Marangu Route from Gillman's Point to the Kibo Huts – thereby allowing you to walk along all of the southern half of the summit (assuming, of course, you make it to the top in the first place). Unfortunately, while it will take you just one night and a bit of the next morning to complete this walk and reach the Kibo Huts, for the porters, who do not climb to the summit but circumambulate Kibo instead, it would take a couple of days. That doesn't mean to say that such a route is impossible, for there are always porters who will willingly undertake such a walk and make it in time to meet you at the Kibo Huts, just as there are trekking agencies willing to organize such an endeavour – but be prepared to pay a considerable premium to realize such a plan.

What to take

CLOTHES

The best head-gear for all weathers is an English sun-helmet, such as are supplied by Messrs. Silver & Co., London; while a soft fez or smoking cap should be kept for wearing in the shade – one with flaps for drawing down over the ears on a cold night to be preferred.
Hans Meyer *Across East African Glaciers*

According to his book *Life, Wanderings, and Labours in Eastern Africa*, when Charles New attempted to climb Kili in 1861 he took with him a party of thirteen porters, all of whom were completely naked. New and his crew became the first to reach the mountain's snow-line, which is a rather creditable effort considering their lack of suitable apparel. Assuming your goal is to reach more than just snow, however, you will need to make sure you (and indeed your porters) are appropriately attired for the extreme conditions.

The fact that you will be paying porters to carry your rucksack does, to some degree, make packing simpler – allowing you to concentrate on warmth rather than weight. However, packing for warmth does not mean packing exclusively warm clothes. The secret to staying warm is to **wear lots of layers**. Not only does this actually make you warmer than if you just had one single, thick layer – the air trapped between the layers heats up and acts as insulation – but it also means you can peel off the layers one by one when you get too warm, and put them on again one by one when the temperatures drop.

A suitable mountain wardrobe would include:

● **Walking boots** Mountain boots are unnecessary unless you're taking an unusual route that demands them. If you're not, a decent pair of trekking boots will be fine. The important thing about boots is comfort, with enough toe room, remembering that on the ascent up Kibo you might be wearing an extra pair or two of socks, and that on the descent the toes will be shoved into the front of the boots with every step. Remember these points when trying on trekking boots in the shop. Make sure they are also sturdy, waterproof, durable, and high enough to provide support for your ankles. Finally, ensure you break them in *before* you come to Tanzania, so that if they do give you blisters, you can recover before you set foot on any mountains.

● **Socks** Ahhh, the joy of socks ... a couple of thick thermal pairs and some regular ones should be fine; you may stink but you'll be comfortable too, which is far more important. Some people walk in one thick and one thin pair of socks changing the thin pair regularly, rinsing them out in the evening and tying them to their pack to dry during the day.

● **Down jacket** Not necessary if you have enough fleeces, but nevertheless wonderfully warm, light and compact – and very expensive. Make sure it is large enough to go over all your clothes.

● **Fleece** Fleeces are light, pack down small, dry quickly and can be very, very warm. Take at least two: one thick 'polar' one and one of medium thickness and warmth. Make sure that you can wear the thinner one over all of the T-shirts and shirts you'll be taking, and that you can wear your thick one over all of these – you'll need to on the night-walk up Kibo.

● **Thermals** The value of thermal underwear lies in the way it draws moisture (ie sweat) away from your body. A thermal vest and long johns are sufficient.

● **Trousers** Don't take jeans, which are heavy and difficult to dry. Instead, take a couple of pairs of trekking trousers, such as those made by Rohan, preferably one light and one heavy.

● **Sun-hat** Essential: it can be hot and dazzling on the mountain ...

● **Woolly/fleecy hat** ... but it can also be very cold. Brightly-coloured bobble hats can be bought very cheaply in Moshi; or, better still, invest in one of those knitted balaclavas on sale in Moshi, which look a bit like a furnace with the door open, but which will protect your face from the biting summit wind.

● **Gloves** Preferably fleecy; many people wear a thin thermal under-glove too.

● **Rainwear** While you are more likely to be rained on during the walk in the forest, where it's still warm, once you've got your clothes wet there will be little opportunity to dry them on the trek – and you will not want to attempt to climb freezing Kibo in wet clothes. A waterproof jacket – preferably made from gore-tex or similar breathable material, hopefully with a warm or fleecy lining too, and big enough to go over all your clothes so you can wear it for the night-walk on Kibo – is ideal; waterproof trousers are perhaps a luxury rather than a necessity, but if you have a pair bring them with you.

● **Summer clothes** T-shirts and shorts are the most comfortable things to wear under the humid forest canopy. You are strongly recommended to take a shirt with a collar too, to stop the sun from burning the back of your neck.

OTHER EQUIPMENT

Any trekking agency worth its licence will provide a **tent**, as well as **cooking equipment, cutlery and crockery**. You will still need to pack a few other items, however, if you don't want to return from your trek as a sun-burnt, snow-blinded, dehydrated wretch with hepatitis and hypothermia. Most of these items can be bought or rented in Moshi, Arusha, or Nairobi. Your agency can arrange equipment rental, which is the most convenient way, though you may well find it cheaper to avoid going through them as they will, of course, take their cut. Note that the following lists concern the trek only. It does not include items necessary for other activities you may have planned on your holiday, such as binoculars for your safari, or a bucket and spade for Zanzibar.

Essentials

● **Sleeping bag** The warmest you've got. A three-season bag is probably the most practical, offering a compromise between warmth and cost. A two-season plus thermal fleecy liner, available in camping shops back at home for about £20–30, is another solution.

● **Sleeping mat** Essential in camping, but unnecessary if you're following the standard Marangu Route, when you'll be sleeping in huts.

● **Water bottles/Platypus Hoser system** You'll need to carry two litres of water up Kibo *at the very least*. Make sure they are thermally protected, otherwise they will freeze on the summit. The Platypus Hoser system (a kind of soft, plastic bladder with a long tube from which you can drink as you walk along) has a number of advantages over a regular bottle: it saves you fiddling about with bottle tops and you can keep your hands in your pockets while you drink – great on the freezing night-time walk to the summit; it means you don't have to stop to drink but can carry on walking; and it encourages you to drink more, which could help keep AMS at bay.

● **Water purifiers/filter** Also essential, unless you intend to hire an extra porter or two to transport your drinking water up from the start. While you can get your cooking crew to boil you some water at the end of every mealtime, you'll still find purifiers and/or a filter essential if you're going to drink the recommended four–five litres every day, for which you'll have to collect water from the mountain streams. Of the two, purifying tablets, such as iodine, are more effective, as they kill everything in the water, though they taste awful. A cordial will help to mask this taste. Filters are less effective and more expensive, though the water they produce tastes much better.

● **Torch** A head-torch, if you have one and don't find it uncomfortable, is far, far more practical than a handheld one, allowing you to keep both hands free; on the last night this advantage is pretty much essential, enabling you to keep your hands in your pockets for warmth.

● **Sunscreen** High factor essential.

● **Ice axe/ski stick** Only useful if you plan to take the Arrow Glacier Route to the summit. Otherwise leave it, your snow boots, rope, karabiners and all that other mountaineering gear at home.

● **Towel** The controversy here is over which sort of towel to bring. Many just bring one enormous beach towel, because they plan to visit Zanzibar after the trek and don't see the point of packing two towels. At the other extreme there are the tiny so-called 'travel towels', a sort of chamois-cloth affair sold in camping shops and airport lounges the world over. Some people swear by these things, but others usually end up swearing at them, finding that they have all the absorbency of your average block of obsidian stone. Nevertheless, I grudgingly admit that they do have their uses on Kilimanjaro, where opportunities to wash anything other than face and hands are minimal. You can dry your towel by attaching it to the outside of your rucksack with clothes-pegs (see p45).

Medical kit

According to Meyer, the Chagga treated their cuts and scars with the liberal application of cow dung. We advise you don't; instead take a medical kit with you onto the mountain – as few agencies, at least at the budget end, will have one. In theory many of the mountain huts have first-aid kits, but take one anyway just to be on the safe side, for you never know what they'll have, how old it will be or how far you'll be from the nearest station when you need help.

A medical kit should include the following:

- **Antiseptic cream** For small cuts and grazes.
- **Plasters** Ditto.
- **Bandages** Useful for twists and sprains as well as for larger flesh wounds.
- **Compeed** For blisters.
- **Elastic knee supports** For steeper gradients, particularly if you have knee problems.
- **Anti-malarials** Though you're highly unlikely to catch malaria on the mountain (you'll be above the anopheles mosquito's maximum altitude for nearly all the trek), if you're on a course of anti-malarials you should continue taking them.
- **Ibuprofen/Aspirin/Paracetamol** Or other painkillers, though do read the discussion on AMS (pp160–6) and the medical indications in the packet before scoffing these.
- **Imodium** Stops you going when you don't want to go, which could come in useful.
- **Insect repellent** Useful on the first and last day, though above the tree-line the climate is too cold for most insects to survive.
- **Rehydrating powders** Such as Diarolyte. Usually prescribed to people suffering from diarrhoea but useful after a hot day's trekking as well.
- **Lip salve or chapstick/vaseline** See under highly desirables opposite.
- **Throat pastilles** Useful, as the dry, dusty air causes many a sore throat.
- **Any current medication you are on** Bring with you all your needles, pills, lotions, potions and pungent unguents.
- **Diamox** Diamox is the brand name for Acetazolamide, the drug that fights AMS and which many people use prophylactically on Kilimanjaro. See the box on p165 to help you decide whether you want to bring some of these with you.
- **Sterile needles** If you are having an injection in Tanzania, insist that the doctor uses your new needles.

Carry everything in a waterproof bag or case, and keep at least the emergency stuff in your daypack – where hopefully it will lie undisturbed for the trek's duration.

- **Sunglasses** Very, very necessary for the morning after you've reached the summit, when the early morning light on Kibo can be really painful and damaging. If you're climbing via the glacier route or are going to spend some time on the summit, they could be essential for preventing snow-blindness.
- **Money for tipping** For a rough guide as to how much you should take, see p28, then add a few dollars, just in case.
- **Toothbrush and toothpaste** Ensure your dental checks are up-to-date; if there is one thing more painful than climbing to the summit of Kili, it's climbing to the summit of Kili with toothache.
- **Toilet paper**
- **Tampons/sanitary towels**
- **Contraceptives**

Highly desirables
- **Ski poles** If you've done some trekking before you'll know if you need ski-poles or not; if you haven't, assume you will. While people often use them the whole way, poles really come into their own on the descent, to minimize the strain on your knees as you trudge downhill. Telescopic poles can be brought from trekking/camping outfitters in the West, or you can invest in a more primitive version, a stick freshly chopped from the nearby forest, at Machame or Marangu Gate – and anywhere else where enterprising local children gather.
- **Boiled sweets/chocolate** For winning friends and influencing people. Good for energy levels too. And morale.
- **Chapstick/ lip salve or vaseline** The wind on the summit will rip your sunburnt lips to shreds. Save yourself the agony by investing in a chapstick, available in strawberry and mint flavour from pharmacists in Moshi and Arusha.
- **Money** For sundry items on sale at huts en route.
- **Camera and equipment** See box on p46.

Usefuls
- **Earplugs** Some porters have stereos and even mobile phones, and they love advertising this fact by playing the former and speaking into the latter extremely loudly at campsites. A set of earplugs will reduce this disturbance.
- **Gaiters** Useful on the dusty Saddle.
- **Soap** Though you won't get through much of it on the mountain.
- **Sandals/flip-flops** Useful in the evenings at camp, but make sure they are big enough to fit round a thick pair of socks.
- **Candles** But don't use them in the tent, and keep them away from everybody else's tent too.
- **Bootlaces/string**
- **Clothes pegs** Very useful for attaching wet clothes to the back of your rucksack to allow them to dry in the sun while you walk.
- **Penknife** Always useful, if only for opening beer bottles at the post-trek party.
- **Matches** As with the penknife, always useful, as any boy scout will tell you.
- **Sewing kit** For repairs on the trail.
- **Trowel** If you envisage needing to defecate along the trail at places other than the designated toilet huts, this will help to bury the evidence and keep the mountain looking pristine; see pp159–60.
- **Insulating tape** Also for repairs – of shoes, rucksacks, tents etc, and as a last resort for mending holes in clothes if you have forgotten your sewing kit, or are incapable of using it.
- **Watch** Preferably cheap and luminous for night-time walking.
- **Compass** Not essential, but useful when combined with ...
- **Map** See p47 for a list of our preferred maps; again not essential, but will, in combination with a compass, help you to determine where you are on the mountain, and where you're going.
- **Whistle** It's difficult to get lost on Kilimanjaro but if you're taking an unusual route – on the northern side of the mountain, for example, or around Mawenzi – a whistle may be useful to help people locate which ravine you've fallen into.

Luxuries

● **Mobile phone** Some people manage to get reception at Horombo Huts, a great place to phone friends stuck behind their desks at work on a rainy day in Europe.

● **CD players** Really unnecessary, as you won't want to listen to music during the day, and you'll probably be too tired to listen in the evening. Nevertheless, while most find the idea abhorrent, people do still bring Walkmans on the trek with them, including many porters. There is nothing wrong with a little mountainside music of course. But do remember that while you may think that the perfect soundtrack to climbing up Kili is something by Mussorgsky (*A Night on the Bare Mountain*, perhaps?) or Atomic Kitten, others on the mountain may disagree: bring headphones, so as not to disturb.

● **Diary/reading material** Though you'll probably be too tired to read or write much. A list of appropriate reading matter can be found in Appendix A on p227.

● **Champagne** For celebrating, of course, though don't try to take it up and open it at the summit – the combination of champagne and altitude sickness could lead to tragedy, and besides, the glass could well crack with the cold.

WHAT TO PACK IT IN

You'll need two bags, a **rucksack** and a smaller, lighter **daypack**. While sensible trekkers spend a long time finding the rucksack that's most comfortable for

---

Cameras and camera equipment

Film is readily available in the larger towns of Tanzania, though the choice is limited, and the films are sometimes either past their sell-by date or have been stored in the baking hot sun and have perished. Therefore, you are strongly advised to **bring all your film from home**. (The same applies if you have a digital camera: bring plenty of memory cards, for you'll be lucky to find any out here.)

Regarding regular film, there is plenty of light on Kilimanjaro, so 100 or 200ASA film should be fine. A **polarizing filter** is also a good investment to bring out the rich colours of the sky, rocks and glaciers. A **tripod** is useful for those serious about their photography, in order to keep the camera steady and allow for maximum depth of field – though remember, you're the one who's going to have to carry it if you want to use it during the day. You should also bring a couple of sets of **spare batteries** with you; the cold on Kibo can play havoc with batteries, and you may be extremely glad of them, particularly as both digital cameras and the later, flashier automatic SLRs seize up altogether without power.

One other useful investment is a **camera-cleaning kit**. Your camera goes through a lot of hardship on Kili, not least because of the different vegetation zones you pass through, from the humidity of the forest to the dusty desert of the Saddle. Either buy a ready-made kit from a camera shop, or make one yourself by investing in a soft cloth, cotton buds, a blow brush and tweezers.

Finally, many people with expensive SLR cameras also bring along a cheap point-and-shoot **compact**; this is not a bad idea, as it doubles your chances of getting some photographic record of your journey. As an alternative, why not invest in a disposable panoramic camera – you can pick them up for about a tenner in the UK – which both acts as a back-up to your main camera *and* offers an alternative picture of the mountain.

them, few bother to spend as long when choosing a daypack; however, on Kili it is the porters who traditionally carry your rucksack for you (usually on their heads), while you will carry your daypack yourself. So make sure your **choose your daypack with care**, and that it is both comfortable and durable. It also needs to be big enough to hold everything you may need with you when walking, as it is unlikely that you will see your rucksack from the moment you break camp in the morning to the time you arrive at camp in the evening. See p170 for a possible list of these things. Don't leave anything valuable in your rucksack; though porters are very trustworthy, it's only fair that you do not put temptation in their path.

Finally, put everything in **plastic bags** inside your backpack and daypack to keep the contents dry.

MAPS

Maps of Kilimanjaro are available in Arusha, Moshi and your own country, though we've yet to find one that is entirely satisfactory. The most common map is the cartoon-ish *New Map of the Kilimanjaro National Park*, published by the safari-cum-trekking agency Hoopoe Adventure (see p20 and p142). It's not a bad map – bright and colourful, and drawn in 1998, which makes it one of the newest – though some of the trails have disappeared and some that do exist are missing. Its cartoon-style means it's of little practical use, but it's packed full of information and not bad.

The *Tourist Map of Kilimanjaro* (1:100,000) by the Ordnance Survey is the biggest and most beautiful, though once again of little practical use: the routes themselves have been drawn, seemingly without thought of precision, over the top of what looks an accurate topographical map. Over a decade old, it's a little out of date too.

A third map, *Kilimanjaro* (1:50,000), by Mark Savage, is harder to track down – though the shop at Marangu Gate stocks some. The descriptions of the trails are not brilliant, and the map itself is a little ugly, though it is up to date and the black-and-white drawings of wild flowers are good – though would be far more useful in colour. Finally, the Canada-based ITM (International Travel Maps) series has recently produced a full colour map of Kilimanjaro; it is the most up-to-date map available.

RECOMMENDED READING

For a list of recommended books, see the Appendix on p227. Please note that many of these are rare, and a number are extremely difficult to find except at the British Library or a similar institution. Among those that are readily available are Hemingway's *The Snows of Kilimanjaro* and John Reader's excellent (though rather bulky) *Kilimanjaro*, which you may have more luck tracking down in Tanzania than in your home country. If you're visiting Zanzibar before Kilimanjaro, you may want to wait and buy your reading material for the mountain there: some of the bookshops in Stonetown have fine selections.

Internet sites

You could spend a happy decade or two simply by typing the word Kilimanjaro into your search engine and sifting through the results. In fact, a quick check just now with the search engine Lycos has found 377,771 relevant sites; you can add a few hundred thousand more by typing in Marangu or Machame.

Most of these sites fall into two categories, being either websites promoting trekking companies or personal accounts of people's experiences on Kilimanjaro. Some of the former are rather good and packed full of useful info; these sites have not been listed below, though details of the best of them can be found in the sections on trekking agencies on p18, p140 and p151. As for the personal accounts, these tend to be short on practical information and long on both pretty pictures and phrases such as 'spiritual awakening', 'inner drive', and other guff. One or two of the better ones have been listed below, along with details of other useful and relevant websites.

● www.tanzania.go.tz/ Official website of the government of Tanzania.

● www.mos.org/kili/index.html Site of the Museum of Science in Boston which includes a trailer for their IMAX film *Kilimanjaro – to the Roof of Africa*.

● www.geo.umass.edu/climate/kibo.html University of Massachusetts' geoscience website covering their study of the climate on Kibo using a weather station they have installed on the summit, and the rate of disappearance of the glaciers.

● www.distantsuns.com Very useful astronomy site with details of the sky over Kili.

● www.kilimanjarotrust.org Website of the Kilimanjaro Environmental Conservation Management Trust Fund, an African body working towards the preservation of Kilimanjaro's natural resources and the prevention of degradation of the mountain through man's activities such as fires, forestry and farming.

● www.lonelyplanet.com Website of well-known guidebook publisher. Their Thorn Tree message board, in which travellers answer other travellers' questions, has been hijacked of late by some Tanzanian trekking agencies who, posing as regular travellers, use the site to give themselves some free publicity. Still, there's some useful stuff on it.

● www.wesleyrd.freeserve.co.uk This personal account of two people's trek lacks the pretentious self-indulgence of other Kili sites, and, just as uniquely, is not trying to sell you something either. It's useful too; nice one!

● www.high-altitude-medicine.com/ Website covering everything you need to know about altitude sickness.

● www.tanzania-web.com/home2.htm Official site of the Tanzanian Tourist Board.

● www.sas.upenn.edu/African_Studies/NEH/tz.html Website of all things African, with a large section devoted to Tanzania.

● www.expedia.co.uk/daily/resources/currency/ One of the few currency converters to feature the Tanzanian shilling in its list.

● http://gorp.com/gorp/location/africa/tanzania/home_kil.htm Detailed guide to Kili including all routes courtesy of this guide to outdoor recreation.

● www.tanzaniawebsiteaddresses.com List of Tanzanian firms' web addresses.

● www.leica-geosystems.com/innovative/application/kilimanjaro.pdf Interesting couple of pages devoted to the latest attempts to measure the height of Kilimanjaro.

● www.digitalbrain.com/Kilimanjaro/web/Kilimanjaro Star-gazers guide to Kili.

● www.intotanzania.com/safari-guide/TZ-N-2-1-1.doc Concise and comprehensive printable factfile on Kilimanjaro by UK-based company Africa Travel Resource.

● www.calle.com/~carl/kili.html Personal account filled with 142 photos, and one of the few Internet accounts that deal with the ascent of Kibo via the Western Breach.

Health precautions, inoculations and insurance

FITNESS

I ascribe the almost perfect health I have always enjoyed in Africa to the fact that I have made every step of my journey on foot, the constant exercise keeping my bodily organs in good order. **Hans Meyer** *Across East African Glaciers*

There's no need to go overboard with fitness preparations for climbing Kili. The main reason why people fail to reach the summit is due to altitude sickness rather than lack of necessary strength or stamina. That said, the trek will obviously be more enjoyable for you the fitter you are, so anything you can do in the way of training can only help. A weekend of walking would be a good thing to do; it won't improve your fitness to a great degree, but it will at least confirm that you can walk for more than a few hours, and for more one day. Wear the clothes you plan to bring to Kilimanjaro with you – particularly your boots and socks – and carry the daypack that you hope to be carrying all the way to the top of Kibo too.

One more thing: if you're planning on relying on it on the mountain, try a Diamox (see p165) before you go to make sure it has no severe adverse reaction on you.

INOCULATIONS

The only vaccination that you must have to enter Tanzania is **yellow fever**, which you must have if you've been to an infected area in the last seven days. As yellow fever is prevalent in Tanzania anyway, it's only wise to have an inoculation against it, which in the UK costs about £25. Remember to collect a health card or some other written evidence from your doctor to prove you've had the jab.

Sort out your vaccinations a few months before you're due to fly. Recommended inoculations include:

● **Typhoid** This disease is caught from contaminated food and water. There are a number of alternative inoculations; the most common lasts for ten years though is said to offer only 50% protection.

● **Polio** The polio vaccine is usually administered by sugar-lump, making it one of the more pleasant inoculations.

● **Hepatitis A** This debilitating disease of the liver is spread by contaminated water, or even by using cutlery that has been washed in this water. The latest inoculations involve two injections adminstered one month apart and cover you for ten years.

● **Tetanus** Tetanus vaccinations last for ten years and are absolutely vital for visitors to Tanzania. The vaccination is usually given in combination with one for **diphtheria**.

● **Meningococcal meningitis** This disease of the brain is often fatal, though the vaccination, while not free, is safe and effective and should be obtained.

● **Rabies** If you're spending some time with animals or in the wilderness, it's also worth considering having a course of **rabies** injections.

Malaria

Malaria is a problem in Tanzania, which is considered one of the highest risk countries in the world. While you are highly unlikely to contract malaria on Kilimanjaro, which is too high and cold for the anopheles mosquito (the species that carries malaria), it is rife in coastal areas and on Zanzibar. When beginning a course of **anti-malarials**, it is very important to begin taking them before you go; that way the drug is established in your system by the time you set foot on Tanzanian soil, and it will give you a chance to see if the drug is going to cause a reaction or allergy. Once started, complete the full course, which usually runs for several weeks after you return home.

  Which anti-malarial you will need depends on which parts of Africa you are visiting and your previous medical history. Your doctor will be able to advise you on what drug is best for you. With Tanzania in the highest risk category, the chances are you will be recommended either Lariam (the brand name for mefloquine), Doxycycline or the new drug Malarone. Stories of Lariam causing hallucinations, nightmares, blindness and even death have been doing the rounds in travellers' circles for years now; but if you feel no adverse reaction to taking them – and millions don't – carry on and don't worry.

  Of course the best way to combat malaria is not to get bitten at all. A **repellent** with 30% Diethyltoluamide (DEET) in the evenings when the malarial anopheles mosquito is active should be effective in preventing bites. Some use it during the day too, when mosquitoes that carry yellow and dengue fevers are active. Alternatively, you could just keep covered up with long sleeve shirts and long trousers, sleep under a **mosquito net** and burn **mosquito coils**; these are available within Tanzania.

Travellers' medical clinics

For all your jabs, malaria advice and anything else you need to know regarding health abroad, visit one of the following clinics:

● **Trailfinders Travel Clinic** (☎ 020-7938 3999; 🖥 www.trailfinders.com) 194 Kensington High Street, London.

● **Nomad Travellers Store and Medical Centre** (☎ 020-7833 4114; 🖥 www.nomadtravel.co.uk) 40 Bernard Street, Russell Square, London.

● **British Airways** (☎ 020-7439 9584; 🖥 www.britishairways.com/health) 156 Regent St, London.

Also worth looking at is the informative website of the **US Center for Disease Control** (🖥 www.cdc.gov), packed full of advice and the latest news.

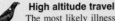

High altitude travel

The most likely illness you are going to suffer from is altitude sickness; indeed, it's a rare trekker on Kilimanjaro who doesn't in some degree. Altitude sickness is caused by the body's inability to adapt quickly enough to the thinner mountain air present at high altitudes. It can be fatal if ignored or left untreated but is also entirely preventable. For an extensive run-down on the causes, symptoms and treatments of altitude sickness, read carefully the section on pp160–6.

Before you go, if you suffer from heart or lung problems, high blood pressure or are pregnant, you must visit your doctor to get advice on the wisdom of climbing up Africa's highest mountain; many of the deaths on the mountain are due to heart failure.

INSURANCE

When buying insurance you must make clear to the insurer that you will be trekking on a very big mountain. If you are going to be climbing and using ropes then you need to tell them that too. This will probably increase your premium (it usually doubles it), and may even exclude you from being covered altogether. But if you don't make this clear from the start and pay the lower premium you may find, should you have to make a claim, that you weren't actually covered at all.

Remember to read the small print of any insurance policy before buying, and shop around too, for each insurance policy varies slightly from company to company. Details to consider include:

● How much is the deductible if you have to make a claim?
● Can the insurers pay for your hospital bills etc immediately, while you are still in Tanzania, or do you have to wait until you get home?
● How long do you have before making a claim and what evidence do you require (hospital bills, police reports etc)?
● Does the policy include mountain rescue services, helicopter call-out and so forth? (If it doesn't, don't buy it!)

Remember you must expect the premium for the entire trip to double when you mention that you are climbing Kilimanjaro, even though you will actually be on the mountain for only a few days. However, you will need to be covered for your entire trip: there are just as many nasty things that can happen to you – indeed more – when off the mountain than on it, and theft becomes a much bigger issue too.

PART 2: TANZANIA

Although this book concentrates specifically on Kilimanjaro, some background knowledge of the country in which it stands, Tanzania, is necessary. For the chances are that climbing Kilimanjaro forms only one part of your trip to Tanzania, and as such you are going to need to know what this beautiful country is like, and how you are going to negotiate travelling around it. With this in mind, the following chapter tackles these considerations and is split into two halves. The first provides a background of the country by looking at the history, economy, culture etc. This should both increase your enjoyment of visiting it and serve to put Kilimanjaro in its national context. The second half of this chapter deals with the more practical side of things, offering advice and tips to help the visitor in Tanzania.

Facts about the country

GEOGRAPHY

Tanzania occupies an area of 945,090 sq km – a little over twice the size of California – made up of 886,040 sq km of land (including the offshore islands of Pemba, Mafia and Zanzibar) and 59,050 sq km of water. This makes it the largest country in the geo-political region of East Africa. It is bounded to the north by Uganda and Kenya, to the west by Zaire, Burundi and Rwanda, to the south by Mozambique, Malawi and Zambia, and to the east by the Indian Ocean. The terrain in that 886,040 sq km of land includes a wide, lush coastal plain, and a large and dusty central plateau flanked by the eastern and western branches of the **Great Rift Valley** (see p68). There are highlands in both the north and south of the country, and in the centre of the plateau are some volcanic peaks, which again owe their existence to the Rift Valley. Interestingly, over a quarter of the country is given over to national parks or nature reserves.

Tanzania is also a land of extremes, housing Africa's largest game reserve, the **Selous** (covering approximately 55,000 sq km, and with an approximately equal number of elephants), and the Serengeti, the park with the greatest concentration of migratory game in the world. Its borders also encompass a share in the continent's largest lake, **Lake Victoria**, and a share in **Lake Tanganyika**, the longest and, after Lake Baikal in Siberia, deepest freshwater lake in the world. The third largest lake in Africa, **Lake Malawi**, also forms one of the Tanzanian borders. These lakes were formed when the Great Rift Valley, which runs through the heart of the country, opened up about 30 million years ago. As a direct result of the formation of this valley, Tanzania contains Africa's lowest point, the floor of Lake Tanganyika, some 350m below sea level. It is also, of course, the proud owner of Africa's highest...

Beautiful as this country undoubtedly is, it is also beset by enormous environmental problems, from deforestation to desertification and soil degradation and erosion to reef bombing. Significant damage has already occurred, and is still occurring, with added pressures on the land, the result of the meteoric rise in tourism over the past couple of decades. For details of how you can minimize your impact on the environment of Kilimanjaro, see pp159–60.

CLIMATE

Tanzania's climate varies greatly, and you'll be encountering just about all of the variations in the four or five days it takes you to walk to the top of Kilimanjaro. For more about this, see the Kilimanjaro climate section on p71. Away from the mountain, the narrow coastal strip tends to be the most hot, humid and tropical part of the country, with the inland plateau being of sufficient elevation to offer some cooler temperatures and respite from the heat. On the coast the average temperature during the day is a sticky 27°C; luckily the sea breezes temper this heat and make it bearable. On the inland plateau you're looking at an average temperature of around 20–26.5°C during the cooler months of June to August, up to a roasting 30°C between December and March. The **rainy seasons** extend from November to early January (the short rains), and from March to May (the long rains). On the coast the average annual rainfall is around 1400mm; inland it is a much drier 250mm, though in mountainous areas it can be a magnificent 2000mm; unsurprisingly, flooding can be a problem at this time.

HISTORY

We, the people of Tanganyika, would like to light a candle and put it on the top of Mount Kilimanjaro, which would shine beyond our borders, giving hope where there was despair, love where there was hate, and dignity where before there was only humiliation.
Julius Nyerere in a speech to the Tanganyika Legislative Assembly, 1959. In December 1961, following independence, his wish was granted and a torch was placed on Kili's summit.

The discovery of the 1,750,000-year-old remains of an early hominid, **Australopithecus Zinjanthropus Boisei**, at Olduvai Gorge in the Ngorongoro Crater, (near footprints that could be as much as three and a half million years old), suggest that Tanzania has one of the longest histories in the world. We are now going to cram these three and a half million years into the next three and a half pages – a task made considerably simpler by the fact that this history has been, until the last 200 years or so, unrecorded. (For a detailed history of Kilimanjaro, see p72.)

We know that **Khoisan speakers** moved into the area of modern Tanzania around 10,000 years ago, to be joined between 3000BC and 1000BC by Cushitic-speakers from the Horn of Africa (Ethiopia and Eritrea), who brought with them more advanced agricultural techniques. Over the next few hundred years **Bantu**

speakers from West Africa's Niger Delta and Nilotic peoples from the north and Sudan also migrated to the area we now know as Tanzania.

By 400BC merchants from Classical Greece knew about and traded with the coast of East Africa, which they called **Azania**. Some of them eventually settled here to take advantage of the trading opportunities, to be joined later by **traders from Persia** and, by the end of the first millennium AD as trade routes stretched into China, merchants from **India**. The majority of immigrants, however, proved to be the seafaring **traders from Arabia**, and soon the Swahili language and culture, an amalgamation of the cultures of Arabia and the Bantu speakers who had also settled on the coast, began to emerge there.

Life on the coastal strip of modern-day Tanzania continued, as far as we know, pleasantly enough for a number of centuries, a fairly idyllic existence that was rudely shattered by the arrival of the **Portuguese** following Vasco da Gama's legendary expedition at the end of the fifteenth century. As greedy as they were intrepid, they built the coastal village of Kilwa Kisiwani into a major trading port which, in typical Portuguese style, they later sacked. Understandably unpopular, the Portuguese nevertheless held on grimly and gamely to their East African possessions for almost 200 years until the end of the seventeenth century; that they managed to survive for so long is largely due to a lack of a united opposition, which didn't arrive until 1698 in the form of **Omani Arabs**, summoned to help by the long-suffering traders of Kilwa.

Portuguese, Arabs, Germans and British

Unlike the Portuguese, the Omani Arabs were keen to forge trading links with the interior. They pushed new routes across the plains to Lake Tanganyika, thereby facilitating the extraction of gold, **slaves** and ivory from the interior. With their capital on Zanzibar Island, the Arabs grew inordinately wealthy from the fat of Africa's land, to the extent that the Omani sultan eventually decided to pull up his tent pegs from the desert sands of Arabia and relocate, establishing his new capital at Stonetown on Zanzibar.

While this was going on, the Europeans returned to Africa. Initially it was just a trickle of **missionaries** and **explorers**, hell-bent (if that's the right term) on making converts and mapping continents respectively. Indeed, one man who famously combined both vocations, Dr David Livingstone, spent a while in Tanzania as part of his efforts to find the source of the Nile, and it was at the village of Ujiji, on the Tanzanian shore of Lake Tanganyika, that HM Stanley is believed to have finally caught up with him and uttered those immortal words 'Dr Livingstone, I presume'.

With intrepid, independent Europeans now roaming all over the continent, it could only be a matter of time before one European country or another would come up with the idea of full-scale colonization. By the late **1880s** Britain had already secured a dominant role on Zanzibar. But over on the mainland it was Germany who was making the most progress.

Or rather, a German, for it was one **Carl Peters** who, acting independently of his government, established German influence on the mainland at this time, negotiating treaties with local chiefs in order to secure a charter for his

Deutsch-Ostafrikanische Gesellschaft (DOAG) or German East Africa Company. A few years later, and with his homeland's government now supporting his work, Peters' DOAG was formally given the task of administering the mainland. This left the British on Zanzibar fuming – and not a little scared – at the German's impertinence, and war was averted between the two superpowers only with the signing of an accord in 1890, in which Britain was allowed to formally establish a protectorate over her Zanzibar territories. One year and further negotiations later and the land we now know as Tanzania (Zanzibar excluded) officially came under direct German control as **German East Africa**.

The Germans brought a Western education, a rail network, and a higher level of healthcare with them to Africa. They also brought harsh taxes, suppression, humiliation, and no small amount of unrest. They were eventually replaced as colonial overlords after World War One by the **British** following a League of Nations mandate. The territory was renamed Tanganyika at this time. After World War Two Britain clung on to administrative control, though officially Tanganyika was now a 'trust territory' of the fledgling United Nations.

Independence

Life under the British was marginally better than under the Germans, with greater political freedom and an improved economy thanks to the cultivation of export crops; but it was only marginal, and soon political groups were springing up all over the country with each campaigning for the same thing: independence. The most important of these was the Dar es Salaam-based Tanganyika Africa Association, which in 1953 elected teacher **Julius Nyerere** as its president. Pressure from Nyerere and his party (now known as TANU, or the Tanganyika African National Union) forced Britain to agree to the formation of an internal self-government. Indeed, so impressed was Britain with Nyerere that the only condition they placed on the establishment of this new regime of self-government was that he should be its first chief minister.

Now a mere formality, **independence** for Tanganyika was eventually declared on the 9 December 1961; exactly one year later it was formally established as a **republic**, with Nyerere, as Britain had hoped, as the first president.

On **Zanzibar**, meanwhile, things were going less smoothly. Whilst the Zanzibaris won their independence just a year later (December 1963), the two parties that formed the first government did not enjoy popular support, but instead had been thrust into power by the departing British because of their pro-British leanings. With a tenure that was decidedly shaky, it came as no surprise when they were toppled in a revolution just a month later. In their place came the popular, radical Afro Shirazi Party (ASP). Less than a year after independence, on 26 April 1964 the ASP leader, Abeid Karume, was signing an act of union with his mainland neighbours, and the **United Republic of Tanganyika** was formed.

In October of the same year the name was changed to the **United Republic of Tanzania**, the name being a neat combination of the two former territories. The two maintained separate governments, however, even after 1977 when ASP and TANU were combined by Nyerere to form **Chama Cha Mapinduzi**, or **CCM**, the party which maintains political control of Tanzania to this day.

Modern history

From 1967 to the late 1980s Nyerere and his party followed a socialist course; the economy was nationalized, the tax regime was deliberately aimed at redistributing wealth, and entire villages were established in order to modernize the agricultural sector and give the rural poor greater access to social services. Unfortunately, the twenty-year experiment was eventually deemed a flop, with the economy in seemingly perpetual decline. By 1992 things had got so desperate that the CCM took the unprecedented step of legalizing opposition parties, after pressure from Western donors for more democracy in the country.

Curiously, this move seems to have done little to achieve this. Three years after the legalization of political opponents to CCM, the first democratic elections were held, with the CCM, now under the leadership of **Benjamin Mkapa** following Nyerere's resignation in 1985, emerging once again as the major force in Tanzanian politics. The elections of late 2000 confirmed their dominance, with over 95% of parliamentary seats won by CCM candidates. While they remain the most creditable political party in Tanzania, the scale of the victory suggests that proper political debate will be stifled for years to come.

On semi-autonomous **Zanzibar** things, as usual, have been a little more explosive. In 1995 the incumbent CCM president, Salmin Amour, was returned to office after an election that many believe was rigged. Fresh elections in 2000 resulted in yet more controversy, with widespread reports of ballot rigging and intimidation of opposition leaders. Zanzibar is still in political disarray and anger is fomenting between the two sides. On 27 January 2001 27 protesters were shot dead in Pemba as they marched through the streets protesting against these voting irregularities. In response, President Mkaba announced the formation of a body to investigate the shootings. The situation continues to smoulder to this day.

The future

Tanzania is often portrayed as a model African nation, garnering international acclaim for its fight against corruption and its efforts to reform itself peacefully – as exemplified by the move towards democracy in the 1990s. It is, however, still a nation beset by problems. The usual African ailments – poverty, AIDS, a lack of clean water, basic healthcare and decent education – are as prevalent in Tanzania as they are over much of the continent. In addition, Tanzania has other local problems to contend with, from a lack of credible opposition to the main autocratic CCM party to the secessionist grumblings of many on Zanzibar who were never happy with the union with the mainland – a dissatisfaction that three subsequent decades of turmoil have done little to dispel. It remains to be seen whether the moderate line that Tanzania has taken throughout its independence will continue into the future; and whether this thoughtful, conservative (with a small 'c') attitude will be enough to help it to overcome these difficulties.

ECONOMY

Tanzania is one of the poorest countries in the world. Its per capita GDP stands at a modest US$264. Just over 50% live below the poverty line. Infant mortality stands at a level of 85 per 1000 births, 31% of children under five are malnourished, and life expectancy is just 49 years. One of the biggest contributors to the economy is foreign aid: in 1997 it received US$973 million in donations.

Tanzania is still largely an **agricultural** country. The style of agriculture is mainly traditional, the large collective farms introduced under Nyerere's socialist experiment having been rejected on the whole in favour of the age-old system whereby each farmer cultivates a small plot of land called a *shamba*. The most popular home-grown crops are cotton, rice, sorghum, sugar and coconuts; sisal, coffee and tea are produced principally for the export market, while cloves and other spices are still grown on Zanzibar and the coast. Agriculture accounts for half of Tanzania's GDP, contributes an enormous 85% of its exports, and employs 80% of the workforce.

As well as agriculture, Tanzania has a solid **mining** base with oil, tin, iron, salt, coal, gypsum, phosphate, natural gas, nickel and diamonds all extracted in the country. Tourism is now a major contributor to the GDP of the country and is a vital source of much-needed foreign currency, particularly in the north.

THE PEOPLE

With 36,232,074 people (CIA world factbook estimate 1999) split into more than a hundred different ethnic groups, numerous local languages and dialects, and three main religions, Tanzania is something of an **ethnic and cultural hotchpotch**, and it is a credit to the country that they exist largely in harmony, without succumbing to the sort of ethnic hatred that has riven many other countries around these parts. Native Africans make up 99% of the population; of these, the vast majority (estimate 95%) are of Bantu origin, though even here there are over 130 tribes. The other 1% are of European, Arabian or Indian origin. Around Kilimanjaro it is the Chagga people, one of the more wealthy and powerful groups in Tanzania, who dominate; for details about the Chagga, see p100.

The **religious** division is a lot more equal. The slight majority (45%) are Christian, with 35% professing the Islamic faith, and traditional indigenous beliefs accounting for the other 20%. (Presumably adherents of the Hindu faith are too small in number to register in the statistics, though they are undoubtedly a highly visible presence in Tanzania with some large, ostentatious Hindu temples in Dar, Arusha and Moshi.) The Chagga people around Kilimanjaro are largely Christian; again, you can read more about them, their culture and beliefs on p100.

Language

The first and most common language in Tanzania is **Swahili**, the language originally used by traders on the coast and thus based on Arabic and various Bantu dialects. Zanzibar is still known as the home of Swahili, where the purest form of the language is spoken.

A few words of Swahili will go a long way in Tanzania and, although the prefixes and suffixes used in the language can be a little tricky to grasp, any efforts to speak a few words will endear you to the local people. Appendix B on p230 provides an introduction to Swahili.

Around Kilimanjaro, however, it is not Swahili but the language of the Chagga people, a tongue sometimes known as Wichagga, that predominates. See the box on p105 for an introduction.

Practical information for the visitor

DOCUMENTS AND VISAS

Visas for Tanzania are required by most visitors **except** citizens of the following countries:

Antigua & Barbuda, Barbados, Belize, Bermuda, Botswana, Brunei, Cyprus, Dominica, Grenada, Guyana, Jamaica, Kenya, Kiribati, Lesotho, Malaysia, Malawi, Malta, Maldives, Mauritius, Namibia, Nauru, Sao Tome & Principe Island, Saint Lucia, Saint Vincent, Saint Christopher and Nevis, Seychelles, Singapore, Solomon Island, Swaziland, Tuvalu, Tonga, Uganda, Vanuatu, Zambia, Zimbabwe.

Note that while Commonwealth countries are included in that list, citizens of Canada, India, Nigeria and the UK **do require visas**.

A single entry visa costs £38 for UK citizens, US$50 for US citizens, €30 for those with a German passport, Netherlands €40, France €30, Australia US$30, New Zealand US$30, Israel US$20, South Africa US$25. A visa is typically valid for three months from the **date of issue**. Please note that it is rumoured that these fees are due to rise again very shortly to £46 for British passport holders, US$50 Australian, US$40 Israeli, US$40 German, US$45 France, US$70 Canada, US$50 New Zealand, US$70 South Africa. Multiple entry visas cost around the US$100 mark, or £45 for British citizens (again, this is a price that is expected to rise) and are also valid for three months. Unless coming from a country without Tanzanian representation, you should buy your visa at the consulate/embassy beforehand. A list of the addresses of some of the more popular Tanzanian embassies and consulates is given in Appendix D on p233. With all applications you will need to present a passport that's valid for at least six months and two passport photos. If applying in person, some consulates/high commissions (including the ones in London and Washington) insist that you pay in cash.

If you don't have a Tanzanian representative in your country you can pick up a visa only at one of the **four border controls**: Dar-es-Salaam International Airport, Kilimanjaro International Airport, Zanzibar International Airport, and the Namanga border crossing between Tanzania and Kenya.

Remember that, if flying in and out of Kenya you will need a **Kenyan visa** too (typically £35 for UK citizens). If you plan to fly to Kenya and cross into Tanzania from there, you can return to Kenya using the same single-entry visa you arrived with *providing* your visit to Tanzania lasted for less than two weeks, and that your Kenyan visa has not expired. Otherwise, you will need to buy a multiple-entry visa, which typically costs double the single-entry (ie UK£70). See Appendix E (p234) for a list of addresses of Kenyan embassies abroad.

Yellow-fever vaccination certificate
In addition to a visa, a **yellow-fever vaccination certificate** is required to prove that you have been immunized against the disease. This can be picked up from your doctor after you have received the jab, and is usually free – though the jab itself is not.

AIRPORT TAX

Airport tax is currently US$20 for international flights. Internal flights are subject to airport taxes too, though these vary from airport to airport.

MONEY

Currency
The Tanzanian shilling (Ts) is the national currency. It's fairly stable. Local currency cannot be imported except by residents of Tanzania, Kenya and Uganda, and cannot be exported.

Foreign currency
Foreign currency can be imported and exported without limit. **Dollars** and, to a lesser extent, **sterling** are the best currencies to bring. One assumes that, in time, given the number of

> ❏ **Exchange rates**
> To get the latest rates visit www.expedia.com. At the time of writing they were:
> UK£1 = Ts1559
> €1 = Ts1000
> US$1 = Ts990
> Can$ = Ts634
> A$ = Ts558
> NZ$ = Ts498

tourists from Europe, the **Euro** will also be widely accepted but at the present moment it is definitely the 'third' currency.

Tanzanian banks usually offer a better rate for cash than for travellers' cheques, but with robbery not unheard of in East Africa, it's better to bring most of your money in the form of **travellers' cheques**, which have the advantage over cash of being replaceable should anything unfortunate happen. Furthermore, park fees can be paid for in US dollar travellers' cheques directly to the offices at the start of the Machame and Marangu routes, and at Londorossi. That said, **cash dollars** are useful for those occasions when the Tanzanian shilling is not accepted, such as for hotel rooms, park fees and air tickets, all of which, officially at least, must be paid for in hard currency. Usually the hotels and some of the airline companies will waive this rule. Nevertheless, it's worth bringing plenty of US dollars just in case. My advice: bring a few hundred dollars in cash, and the rest of your money in travellers' cheques. As back-up, bring along a credit card too (see p60).

Banks and moneychangers
Banking hours are typically 8.30am–4pm Monday to Friday, and 8.30am–1pm on Saturday. As a general rule, only banks and the larger exchange bureaux can

change travellers' cheques, but since currency controls were relaxed a few years ago and the black market for foreign currency has largely disappeared, this is not the major drawback it once was. You get a significantly better rate for large denomination bills (US$50 and $100 bills) than small ones. Keep your **exchange receipts** so that when you leave the country you can change your spare shillings back into hard currency. They rarely check, but you never know.

There are few **ATM**s ('cashpoints') in either Tanzania or Kenya; bring enough cash or travellers' cheques with you. That said, Standard Chartered have **Visa** ATMs, and Barclays (who currently have just one office in Tanzania, in Dar es Salaam) have similar, with a **MasterCard** option too.

Credit cards

Credit cards are of little use except in major tourist hotels, restaurants and gift shops. Visa is probably the more useful card, in that you can withdraw money from the few ATMs in the country. MasterCard is all but useless; you can still get money out from the occasional ATM, but only after paying huge commission – sometimes 10% or more of the transaction!

TOURIST OFFICES

Dar es Salaam and Arusha have tourist offices (see p109 and p133), but they're the only ones who do. Outside Tanzania, there's a tourist office in New York (☎ 212-972 9160), 8th Floor, 205 East 42nd Street, New York 10017. Consulates and embassies around the world also have the odd brochure and information, or you can look at the online information services on the net (see p48).

GETTING AROUND

Transport in Tanzania is unreliable, uncomfortable, slow, and not recommended for those with either long legs or haemorrhoids. It is also dangerous. A little-known but highly pertinent fact about Tanzania's transport system is that 8% of deaths in Tanzanian hospitals are road-accident victims. According to one source, Tanzania suffers an average of 9780 road accidents annually, resulting in the loss of 1189 lives; and these are just the ones the authorities know about.

That said, Tanzanian transport is also cheap, convenient and, it must be said, cheerful: conversation usually flows pretty easily on a train, bus or dalla-dalla (providing you can make yourself heard above the noise of the stereo). And while the average road is little more than a necklace of potholes strung together with tyre tracks, the main roads between towns are splendid, well-maintained tarmac strips – with speed ramps to deter the bus drivers from going too fast.

The most luxurious form of ground transport is provided by the **express bus** companies; a few of them, such as Scandinavia and Fresh Ya Shamba, deserve their reputation for safety and comfort; you may want to ask your hotel or a local which bus company is currently the most reliable. These express buses run to a fixed timetable, and will leave without you if you're late. The cheaper alternative is the **ordinary buses**, which leave when full. These are cheap, but you definitely pay for what you get! As with all forms of local transport, ask your fellow passengers what the correct fare is before handing any money over to the 'conductor'; rip-offs are the rule rather than the exception on many journeys.

In addition to the buses there are the indigenous **dalla-dallas**: minibuses plying routes around and between neighbouring towns. They're usually a tight squeeze as the drivers pile in the customers to maximize their takings. If you're being pushed into one that looks full-to-bursting, simply refuse to enter; there'll be another along in a minute. In Kenya these minibuses are known as **matatus**.

It is possible to **hire a car** in Tanzania; we give details of some of the more reliable companies in Dar es Salaam; you can also hire cars from many of the bigger tour and trekking agencies in Moshi and Arusha. Make sure you choose a vehicle that is suitable for your requirements. Don't, for example, be tempted to conduct your own off-road safari in a two-wheel drive.

You can of course **hitch** around the country, though payment will often be expected from a Western tourist; it is, of course, wiser not to hitch alone.

Tanzania does still have a skeleton **train** service; services to Arusha and Moshi have long since stopped, though the stations and tracks are still there in both towns and are interesting places to look around if you're very bored.

Flying is a great way to cover the vast distances of Tanzania, and there are a number of small chartered and scheduled airlines serving visitors, including ZanAir, Precision Air, Air Excel and the national airline Air Tanzania. For details of airlines flying to Kilimanjaro see p232.

ACCOMMODATION

Tanzania's guesthouses and hotels can be split into three sorts: those that welcome tourists, those that accept them, and those that refuse them altogether. The latter are usually the cheapest, double as brothels, have minimum security, minimal advertizing, and can safely be ignored. Room rates for the other two start at about Ts3000 per night; dorms are a rarity. Always take your time when choosing a hotel, particularly in the towns featured here where there are lots of options. Standards vary widely, but you'll probably be surprised at how pleasant some of them can be, with mosquito nets and attached bathrooms. In Nairobi safety is a concern in some of the hotels, though the ones we have chosen to recommend in this book were fine. Accommodation on Zanzibar, incidentally, is generally much more expensive. Note, too, that in Swahili *hotel* or *hoteli* means restaurant rather than accommodation.

For details of **accommodation on the mountain**, see p171.

❏ **Abbreviations**
Throughout this book we have used the following abbreviations when writing about accommodation: **s/c** is short for self-contained, a local term meaning that the room comes with a bathroom (ie the room is en suite or attached); **sgl/dbl/tpl** means single/double/triple rooms. For example, where we have written 's/c sgl/dbl/tpl US$35/40/45', we mean that a self-contained single room costs US$35 per night, a self-contained double costs US$40, and a self-contained triple costs US$45.

ELECTRICITY

Tanzania is powered by a 250V, 50 cycles, AC network. Those bringing electrical items from home may wish to invest in a power breaker: Tanzania's electricity supply can be erratic on occasions, and power surges could seriously impair the efficacy of your electrical instruments, if not melt them altogether. Plugs and sockets vary in style, though by far the most common are the British three-square-pin or European two-round-pin style.

TIME

Tanzania is **three hours ahead of GMT**, and thus two hours ahead of Western Europe, eight ahead of New York, eleven ahead of San Francisco, one ahead of Johannesburg, seven hours behind Sydney and nine behind Wellington.

A point of endless confusion for travellers, and with the potential to cause major problems for the uninitiated, is the concept known as **Swahili time**, used mainly on the coast and other regions where Swahili is the *lingua franca*. Swahili time begins at dawn, or more precisely at 6am: ie 6am is their hour zero (and thus equivalent to our midnight), 7am is actually hour one and so on.

To add further confusion, this system for telling the time is not prevalent throughout the whole of Tanzania, with most offices, timetables etc using the standard style for telling the time. Whenever you're quoted a time it should be blatantly obvious which clock they are using, but always double check.

POST AND TELECOMMUNICATIONS

Telephone and fax

The phone system in Tanzania is archaic and expensive, at about US$4 per minute for an international call. If you're planning to go to Kenya you may want to save your phone calls for there; the official phone system is a little cheaper, while an unofficial phone office (see p120 for an example) could save you a small fortune.

Cardphones have been installed in the larger Tanzanian towns, but they are seldom used, frequently vandalized, and often the only place where you can buy the cards themselves is from a Telecom building anyway. In Dar, you have a choice between the Red Smile Simu Poa phones and the yellow TTCL cardphones; outside Dar, currently only the TTCL phones are available. The TTCL Telcards come in denominations of 10, 20, 40, 100, 150 and 500 units, and cost Ts50 a unit. Even if you do manage to secure the correct phonecard, and find a phone that will accept it and hasn't been vandalized beyond use, there is still no guarantee that you'll be able to call home. If you are having trouble ringing home, try to tack an extra '0' on to the front of the international dialling code: for example, if you wish to ring the UK but the phone continues to bar your call, dial ☎ 00044 (or ☎ 000144) rather than just ☎ 0044 (or ☎ 00144).

❏ The telephone country access code for Tanzania is ☎ 255.

Given this hassle, you may consider it worthwhile spending a little more and using the service at the **Telecom building**, of which there is one in every major town (including Moshi and Arusha). Most Telecom offices open from 8am until 10pm on weekdays. The procedure is simple: pick up a scrap of paper from the counter; if the office is posh you will have a form to fill out, but if it's not then you'll just have to write the name and number of the person you wish to call and how long you wish the call to last. Hand it over and the operator will dial the number and direct you to a booth where you can take the call. If you did not speak for your allotted time, the operators are usually scrupulously fair in giving back the correct change; if you do speak for the full number of minutes, the operator will come online to tell you when your time is up.

Email

In contrast to the phones, Tanzania's Internet cafés are havens of efficiency and value, at about Ts1000 for thirty minutes (a rate that is continually tumbling as competition grows). Most cafés are open from about 9am until late (typically 9pm). Some of the equipment is a little dated, as you'd probably expect, and the speed of the connection, particularly in the afternoon, can be a little slow. Nevertheless, if you've already tried to make a phone call or post a letter here, you'll come to regard the Internet cafés with something approaching affection: they're your best chance of keeping in regular touch while you're in East Africa. In the city guides beginning on p108 we have picked out some of the better cafés.

Post

Thanks to the presence of the English missionaries, matters have already advanced so far in Jagga that the Europeans stationed there get their letters and newspapers not more than a month old. **Hans Meyer** *Across East African Glaciers*

The postal system in Tanzania has improved since Meyer's day, but not massively. Reasonably reliable and reliably sluggish, things do occasionally get 'lost in the post' but most gets through ... eventually. You should allow about two weeks for letters to reach their destinations from Dar, a day or two longer from regional post offices. There is a poste restante system operating in Tanzania too; letters sent to post offices in Tanzania for collecting are generally held indefinitely, usually in a shoebox in a dusty corner somewhere.

Media

You'll find that **BBC World** and **CNN** are both popular in Tanzania and often fill air-time on the national channels during the day (ITV, for example, switches to BBC at 8am every morning). **Channel O** is Africa's MTV equivalent, and a favourite with waitresses who often have it blaring out in the restaurant while you're trying to eat. **Radio Tanzania** is the most popular radio station, with some broadcasts in English. The *Guardian* is the pick of the English-language newspapers for world events, while the *Daily News* is more Tanzania-centric.

Office hours

These are typically 8am–noon and 2–4.30pm Monday to Friday, and 8am–12.30pm for some private businesses on Saturdays.

❑ HOLIDAYS AND FESTIVALS

The following are public holidays in Tanzania; note that some, (eg Zanzibar's Revolutionary day) are not held nationwide but are celebrated locally only.

1 Jan	New Year	**7 July**	Industrial Day
12 Jan	Zanzibar Revolutionary Day	**8 Aug**	Farmers' Day
April	Good Friday/Easter	**9 Dec**	Independence/Republic Days
26 April	Union Day (National Day)	**25 Dec**	Christmas Day
1 May	International Labour Day	**26 Dec**	Boxing Day

Islamic holy days

The dates of the following holidays are determined according to the Islamic lunar calendar, and as such do not fall on the same date each year. Their **approximate** dates for the next few years are given. The extent to which these days are celebrated and whether these celebrations will impact on your holiday depend to a great extent on where you are in Tanzania; remember that around Kilimanjaro the people are largely Christian, and so the impact tends to be minimal, though there will be some shops and businesses closed.

Idul Fitri (End of Ramadan – a two-day celebration)
approx dates: November 25, 2003; November 14, 2004; November 4, 2005.
Eid El-Hajj (also known as Eid El-Adha or Eid Al-Kebir)
approx dates: February 12, 2003, February 2, 2004, January 21, 2005.
Maulidi Day (Prophet Mohammad's birthday)
approx dates: May 14, 2003; May 2, 2004; April 21, 2005.

FOOD

The native foods do not offer much variety, though they do differ widely in different districts; but if the traveller is not too dainty and is prepared to make the best of what is to be had, it is wonderful what can be done. **Hans Meyer** *Across East African Glaciers*

Tanzanian food is, on the whole, unsubtle but tasty and filling. If there's one dish that could be described as quintessentially East African, it would be **nyama choma** – nothing more than plain and simple grilled meat. If the restaurant is any good they will add some sauces – often curry, and usually fiery – to accompany your meat, and the whole lot will usually come with either rice, chips, plantains or the ubiquitous **ugali**. This is a stodgy cornmeal or cassava mush. Usually served in a single cricket-ball sized lump that you can pick up with your fork in one go, ugali has the consistency of plasticine and gives the impression of being not so much cooked as congealed. A bit bland, it nevertheless performs a vital role as a plate-filler, and can act as a soothing balm when eating some of the country's more thermogenic curries.

With the indigenous cuisine catering for carnivores, the country's significant Indian minority has cornered the market for vegetarian fare. Indian restaurants

---

Opposite: Lobelia and everlastings (see p96) flourish in the Barranco Valley.

abound in Dar, Moshi, Arusha and Nairobi, catering mainly for the budget end of the market though the cuisine at a top-notch Indian restaurant in Tanzania is amongst the best served outside Britain or India. For details about food on the trail, see p171.

DRINKS

The usual world-brand **soft drinks** are on sale in Tanzania. Juices are widely available and pretty cheap, though be warned: a lot of upset stomachs are caused by insanitary juice stalls. Far safer, coconuts are ubiquitous on the coast and Zanzibar. **Alcoholic** drinks include a range of beers: Kibo, Safari and Kilimanjaro from Tanzania, Tusker from Kenya, and the potent Chagga home-brew *mbege*, or banana beer.

THINGS TO BUY

kíRìmíyà – A Chagga term meaning a treat brought home by mother to kids upon completion of a successful day at market From **University of Oregon**'s *Word of the Week* website

Tanzania has the usual supply of weavings and woodcarvings, T-shirts, textiles and trinkets. Amongst the T-shirts, at least in Moshi, are a number of variations on the 'I climbed Kili' motif. Witchcraft items, battle shields, Masai beads and necklaces and bows and arrows are all up for grabs in the high streets of Moshi and Arusha. Kilimanjaro coffee makes for a good and inexpensive present for the person who's been feeding your cat while you've been away; buy it in a wooden box or velvet bag in a souvenir store, or pick a simple bag of it up for a third of the price in a supermarket. Another popular souvenir is the *kanga*, the typical Tanzanian woman's dress that usually has a message or motto running through the print, or the similar but smarter and message-less *kitenge*.

In the afternoon I bought some small capes made of hyrax skins, of a style formerly much in vogue, and two long spears of the most modern narrow-bladed pattern, which were quite works of art. **Hans Meyer** *Across East African Glaciers*

It depends on your taste, of course, but Zanzibar is widely reckoned to have a better selection and higher quality of souvenirs. Some of them, particularly the carved door jambs and furniture, are lovely, though difficult to get home; furthermore, these people are extremely tough negotiators, know the true price of everything, and bargains are few.

SECURITY

Tanzania is a pretty safe country, at least by the standards of its neighbours. That said, the standards of its neighbours are very, very low indeed – as anybody who has already been to Kenya's capital, known to many travellers as 'Nairobberi',

---

Opposite Top: The long and lonely path across the Saddle to Kibo.
Bottom: Tough terrain on the way to the Barafu Huts.

will testify – so do take care. (See the warning on p118.) Violent crime is relatively rare, but not unknown, especially in Dar es Salaam, while pickpockets are common throughout the country and reach epidemic proportions in busy areas such as markets and transport terminals. The best (if somewhat contradictory) advice is to:

● Keep a close eye on your things. ● Don't flaunt your wealth.

● Wear a moneybelt. ● Be on your guard against scams and con merchants ... but at the same time don't let a sense of paranoia ruin your holiday, and remember that the vast majority of travellers in East Africa spend their time here suffering no great loss beyond the occasional and inevitable overcharging. If you are unfortunate enough to become the victim of a mugging, remember that it's your money that they're after, so hand it over – you should be insured against such eventualities anyway. Report the crime as soon as possible to the police, who are generally quite helpful, particularly when the victim is a tourist. This will help to back up your claim from the insurers, and may help to prevent further crimes against tourists in the future.

HEALTH

Diarrhoea is often symptomatic of nothing more than a change of diet rather than any malignant bacteria, so if you get a vicious dose of the runs and your sphincter feels like a cat flap in the Aswan Dam, don't panic and assume you've got food poisoning. That said, there are problems with hygiene in Tanzania, so it's wise to take certain precautions. Take heed of that old adage about patronizing only places that are popular – so food doesn't have a chance to sit around for long – as well as that other one about only tucking in to food that has been cooked, boiled or peeled. Stick to **bottled**, **purified** or **filtered water** and avoid ice unless certain it has been made from treated water. Washing fruit, vegetables, and your hands (with purified water, of course) and ensuring food is thoroughly cooked can all help to prevent food poisoning. Shellfish, ice cream from street vendors and under-cooked meat should all be avoided like the plague, or you could end up feeling like you've got it. Slathering yourself in an **insect repellent** to prevent you from being eaten alive by the smaller members of Tanzania's animal kingdom is a good idea too.

We could go into a detailed examination here of all the possible diseases you could catch in Tanzania. But the truth is for most of the worst ones you should have already had an inoculation or be taking some sort of prophylactic. Besides, it's unlikely that you'll suffer anything more in Tanzania than a dose of **the runs**, some **altitude sickness** or, if you're careless, a touch of **sunstroke**. If you've got the former, just rest up and take plenty of fluids until you recover; to protect against the latter wear a high-factor suntan lotion and a hat, and drink a lot of fluids – maintaining a reasonable salt intake will also help to prevent dehydration. As for altitude sickness, which the majority of trekkers on Kili suffer from to some extent, as well as other ailments that you may contract on the trail, read the detailed discussion on p160.

PART 3: KILIMANJARO

Geology

Our geological work was especially delightful.... Every rock seemed to differ from another, not only in form but in substance. In half-an-hour it was no uncommon thing for us to pick up specimens of as many as two-and-twenty different kinds.
Hans Meyer *Across East African Glaciers*

Rising 4800m above the East African plains, 270km from the shores of the Indian Ocean, and measuring up to 40km across, Kilimanjaro is a bizarre geological oddity, the tallest freestanding mountain in the world and one formed, shaped, eroded and scarred by the twin forces of fire and ice. It is actually a volcano, or rather three volcanoes, with the two main peaks, **Kibo** and **Mawenzi**, the summits of two of those volcanoes. The story of its creation goes like this:

About three-quarters of a million years ago (making Kilimanjaro a veritable youngster in geological terms) molten lava burst through the fractured surface of the **Great Rift Valley**, a giant fault in the earth's crust that runs through East Africa (see p68). The huge pressures behind this eruption pushed part of the earth's crust skywards, and as the pressure continued, three huge conical shapes were thrust ever further into the air – forming the three volcanoes of Kilimanjaro.

These three volcanoes continued to grow over the course of the next hundred thousand years or so until all three passed the 5000m mark. Of the three, the **Shira Cone** was the first to expire, collapsing as it did so to form a huge caldera (the deep cauldron-like cavity on the summit of a volcano) many times the size of its original crater. **Mawenzi** followed suit, dying soon after though keeping its shape. But continual subterranean pressure forced Kibo to erupt several times more, forcing the summit ever higher until reaching a maximum height of about 5900m some 450,000 years ago.

A further huge eruption from Kibo 100,000 years later led to the creation of Kilimanjaro's characteristic black stone – which in reality is just solidified black lava, or **rhomb porphyry**. This spilled over from Kibo's crater into the Shira caldera and around to the base of the Mawenzi peak, forming the so-called Saddle. Later eruptions created a series of distinctive mini-cones, or **parasitic craters**, that run in a chain south-east and north-west across the mountain, as well as the smaller **Reusch Crater** inside the main Kibo summit. The last volcanic activity of note, just over 200 years ago, left a symmetrical cone of ash in the Reusch Crater, known as the **Ash Pit**, that can still be seen today.

Today, **Uhuru Peak**, the highest part of Kibo's crater rim and the goal of all trekkers, stands at around 5895m. The fact that the summit is ten metres shorter today than it was 450,000 years ago can be ascribed in part to some improved technology which has enabled scientists to measure the mountain more accurately; and in part to the simple progress of time and the insidious glacial erosion down the millennia. These glaciers, advancing and retreating across the summit, created a series of concentric rings like **terraces**, near the top of this volcanic massif on the western side. The Kibo peak has also subsided slightly over time, and about one hundred thousand years ago a landslide took away part of the external crater, creating **Kibo Barranco** (see p191). The glaciers were also behind the formation of the valleys and canyons, eroding and smoothing the earth into gentle undulations all around the mountain, though less so on the northern side where the glaciers on the whole failed to reach, leaving the valleys sharper and more defined.

While eruptions are unheard of in recent times, Kibo is classified as being dormant rather than extinct, as anybody who visits the inner **Reusch Crater** can testify. A strong sulphur smell still rises from the crater, the earth is hot to touch, and certainly too hot for any ice to form, while occasionally fumaroles escape from the Ash Pit that lies at its heart.

THE GLACIERS

It is now time to consider the discovery on which Mr Rebmann particularly prides himself, namely, that of perpetual snow. **W D Cooley** *Inner Africa Laid Open* (see box p79)

At first sight, Kilimanjaro's glaciers look like nothing more than big smooth piles of slightly monotonous ice. On second sight they pretty much look like this too. Yet there's much more to Kili's glaciers than meets the eye: for these cathedrals of gleaming blue-white ice are not only dynamic repositories of climatic history; they could also be providing us with a portent for impending natural disaster.

You would think that with the intensely strong equatorial sun, glaciers wouldn't exist at all on Kilimanjaro. In fact, it is the brilliant white colour of the

---

The Great Rift Valley

According to the theory of plate tectonics, the Earth's exterior is made up of six enormous plates that 'float' across the surface. Occasionally they collide, causing much buckling and crumpling and the creation of huge mountain ranges such as the Himalayas. At other times, these plates deteriorate and break up because of the massive forces bubbling away in the earth's interior. When this happens, valleys are formed where the Earth fractures.

The Great Rift Valley, whose origins are in Mozambique but which extends right across East Africa to Jordan, is a classic example of a fracture in the Earth's surface caused by the movement of these plates. The same monstrous internal forces that two million years ago caused the disintegration of the tectonic plate and the Rift Valley to form are also responsible for the appearance of volcanoes along the valley, as these forces explode through the surface, pushing the Earth's crust skywards and forming – in the case of Kilimanjaro – one huge, 5895m-high geological pimple.

Of Africa's sixteen active volcanoes, all but three belong to the Rift Valley. Kili was just one of a number of volcanic eruptions to hit the valley; others included Ol Molog (to the north-west of Kilimanjaro) and Kilema (to the south-east).

ice that allows it to survive as it reflects most of the heat from the sun. The dull black lava rock on which the glacier rests, on the other hand, does absorb the heat; so while the glacier's surface is unaffected by the sun's rays, the heat generated by the sun-kissed rocks underneath leads to glacial melting.

As a result, the glaciers on Kilimanjaro are inherently unstable: the ice at the bottom of the glacier touching the rocks melts, the glaciers lose their 'grip' on the mountain, and 'overhangs' occur where the ice at the base has melted away, leaving just the ice at the top to survive. As the process continues the ice fractures and breaks away, exposing more of the rock to the sun ... and so the process begins again. The sun's effect on the glaciers is also responsible for the spectacular structures – the columns and pillars, the towers and cathedrals – that are the most fascinating part of the upper slopes of Kibo.

One would have thought that, after 11,700 years of this melting process, (according to recent research, the current glaciers began to form in 9700BC) very little ice would remain on Kilimanjaro. The fact that there are still glaciers is due to the prolonged 'cold snaps', or ice ages, that have occurred down the centuries, allowing the glaciers to regroup and reappear on the mountain. According to estimates, there have been at least eight of these ice ages, the last a rather minor one in the fifteenth and sixteenth centuries, a time when the Thames frequently froze over and winters were severe. At these times the ice on Kilimanjaro would in places have reached right down to the tree line, and both Mawenzi and Kibo would have been covered. At the other extreme, in between these ice ages there have been periods when Kilimanjaro was completely free of ice, perhaps for up to twenty thousand years.

The slush of Kilimanjaro – where have all the glaciers gone?

Of the 19 square kilometres of glaciers to be found on Africa, only 2.2 square kilometres can be found on Kilimanjaro. Unfortunately, both figures used to be much higher: Kili's famous white mantle has shrunk by a whopping 82% since the first survey of the summit in 1912. Even since 1989, when there were 3.3 sq km, there has been a decline of 33 per cent. At that rate, say the experts, Kili will be completely ice-free within the next two decades.

'We found that the summit of the ice fields has lowered by at least 17 metres since 1962,' said Professor Lonnie Thompson of Ohio State University. 'That's an average loss of about a half-metre (a foot and a half) in height each year.' You don't need to be a scientist to see that the glaciers on Kili are shrinking. Take a look at old photos of Kibo, even those taken as late as the 1960s, and compare them with the ice on the summit today and the difference is obvious.

The big question, therefore, is not whether they are shrinking, but why – and should we be concerned? Certainly glacial retreats are nothing new: Hans Meyer, the first man to conquer Kilimanjaro, returned in 1898, nine years after his ascent, and was horrified by the extent to which the glaciers had shrunk. The ice on Kibo's slopes had retreated by 100m on all sides, while one of the notches he had used to gain access to the crater in 1889 – and now called the Hans Meyer Notch – was twice as wide, with the ice only half as thick. Nor are warnings of the complete disappearance of the glaciers anything new: in 1899 Meyer himself predicted that they would be gone within three decades, and the top of Kili would be decorated with nothing but bare rock.

What concerns today's scientists, however, is that this current reduction in size of Kili's ice-cap does seem to be more rapid and more extensive than previous shrinkages. But is it really something to worry about, or merely the latest in a series of glacial retreats experienced by Kili over the last few hundred years?

So how high is it then?

Ever since Hans Meyer ambled down from the summit of Kibo and told anybody who'd listen that he'd reached 19,833ft above sea level (6010m), an argument has been raging over just how high Africa's highest mountain really is. For though Meyer's estimate is now unanimously agreed to be a wild over-estimate (an inaccuracy that can be ascribed to a combination of the imprecise nineteenth-century instruments that he had at his disposal, and perhaps a touch of hubris) finding a figure for the height of Kili that meets with a similar consensus of opinion has proved altogether more difficult.

For years the accepted height of Kilimanjaro was 5892m, that being the figure set by the colonial German authorities some five years after Meyer's ascent. You'll see this figure crop up time and again in many a twentieth-century travelogue as well as on pre-World War Two maps of the Kilimanjaro region. Not many people at the time bothered to question this estimate; the few dissenting voices almost invariably belonged to climbers whose own estimates (which were, perhaps unsurprisingly, nearly always over-estimates, ranging from 5930m to 5965m) are today regarded as even more inaccurate than the German's figure.

Under British rule the figure was revised to 5895m following the work of the cartographers of the Ordnance Survey, who mapped Kilimanjaro in 1952; and it is this figure that those trekkers who reach the summit will find written on the sign at the top, as well as on the certificates they receive from KINAPA, and on the souvenir T-shirts on sale back in Moshi.

The trouble was, of course, that whereas the Ordnance Survey's techniques and equipment may have been state of the art in the 1950s, so were the Ford Edsel and vinyl records. Technology has moved on a couple of light years since then. The Ordnance Survey's readings for Kilimanjaro had been taken from a distance of over 55km away from the mountain; as such, the probability that the OS's figure was not entirely accurate was rather high.

So in 1999 a team of specialists at the University College of Land and Architectural Studies in Arusha together with experts from Karlsruhe University in Germany set out to measure the precise altitude using a technique involving GPS (Global Positioning Satellites) that had previously been used on Everest, and which resulted in that mountain shrinking by a couple of metres to 8846.10m.

The result of their findings in Africa? Kilimanjaro was now a full 2.5 metres shorter than the traditionally accepted figure, at **5892.55m**.

So is Kilimanjaro shrinking? Or was the old estimate of 5895m just plain inaccurate. Unfortunately, the scientists have yet to tell us that. And while they have every confidence in the accuracy of their latest readings, the old figure of 5895m is still the official figure, and the one you'll hear bandied about by tour operators, guides, porters and anybody else you care to speak to; and until we are told otherwise, 5895m is the one we're going to use in this book too.

Professor Thompson and his team are attempting to find answers to all these questions. In January and February 2000 they drilled six ice cores through three of Kibo's glaciers in order to research the history of the mountain's climate over the centuries. A weather station was also placed on the Northern Icefield to see how the current climate affects the build-up or destruction of glaciers.

Although results are still coming in from Professor Thompson's work, early indications are not good. In a speech made at the annual meeting of the American Association for the Advancement of Science in February 2001, the professor declared that, while he cannot be sure why the ice is melting away so quickly, what is certain is that if the glaciers continue to shrink at current rates, the summit could be completely ice-free by 2015.

This doesn't surprise locals who live in the shadow of Kilimanjaro, some of whom believe they know why the ice is disappearing. According to an AllAfrica.com news report, a 50-year-old native of Old Moshi, Mama Judith Iyatuu, reckons that it's the evil eyes of the white tourists which are melting the ice, while 65-year old Mzee Ruaici Thomas from Meela village believes that the ice is disappearing because God is unhappy with mankind.

Whatever the reasons, if Kilimanjaro is to lose its snowy top, the repercussions would be extremely serious: Kilimanjaro's glaciers are essential to the survival of the local villages, supplying their drinking water, the water to irrigate their crops and, through hydroelectric production, their power; never mind the blow the loss of the snow-cap would deal to tourism.

And these are just the local consequences. If the scientists are to be believed, what is happening on Kilimanjaro is a microcosm of what could face the entire world in future. Even more worryingly, more and more scientists are now starting to think that this future is probably already upon us.

Climate

Kilimanjaro is big enough to have its own weather pattern. The theory behind this pattern is essentially very simple. Strong winds travel across the oceans, drawing moisture up as they go. Eventually they collide with a large object – such as a mountain like Kilimanjaro. The winds are pushed upwards as they hit the mountain slopes, and the fall in temperature and atmospheric pressure leads to precipitation or, as it's more commonly called, snow and rain.

In one year there are two rain-bearing seasonal winds buffeting Kilimanjaro. The south-east trade wind bringing rain from the Indian Ocean arrives between March and May. Because the mountain is the first main obstacle to the wind's progress, and by far the largest, a lot of rain falls on Kili at this time, and for this reason the March-to-May season is known as the **long rains**. This is the main wet season on Kilimanjaro. As the south-east trade winds run into the southern side of Kili, so the southern slopes tend to be damper and as a consequence more fertile, with the forest zone much broader, than on the northern slopes.

Then there are the dry **'anti-trade' winds** from the north-east which carry no rain and hit the mountain between May and October. These anti-trade winds, which blow, usually very strongly, across the Saddle (the broad valley between Kilimanjaro's two peaks), also serve to keep the south-east trade winds off the upper reaches of Kilimanjaro, ensuring that the rain from the long monsoon season stays largely on the southern side below 3000m, with little falling above this. This is why, at this time of year, the first day's walk for trekkers following the Marangu, Umbwe or Machame routes is usually conducted under a canopy of cloud, while from the second day onwards they traditionally enjoy unadulterated sunshine.

A second seasonal rain-bearing wind, the north-east monsoon, having already lost much of its moisture after travelling overland for a longer period, brings a **short rainy season** between November and February. While the northern side receives most of the rain to fall in this season, it is far less than the rain brought by the south-east trade winds, and as a result the northern side of the mountain is far drier and more barren in appearance. Once again, the rain falls mainly below 3000m.

This theory seems fine in principle but it does pose a tricky question: if the precipitation falls below 3000m, how did the snows on the summit of Kibo get there in the first place? The answer, my friend, is blowing in the (anti-trade) wind: though these winds normally blow very strongly as those who walk north across the Saddle will testify, they occasionally drop in force, allowing the south-east trade winds that run beneath them to climb up the southern slopes to the Saddle and on to the summit. Huge banks of clouds then develop and snow falls.

This, at least, is the theory of Kilimanjaro's climate. In practice, of course, the mountain is rarely so predictable. What is certain is that, with rain more abundant the further one travels down the mountain, life, too, is more abundant further down the slopes as the Flora and Fauna section on p94 illustrates.

The history of Kilimanjaro

EARLY HISTORY

Thanks to several primitive **stone bowls** found on the lower slopes of Kilimanjaro, we know that man has lived on or around the mountain since at least 1000BC. We also know that, over the last 500 years, the mountain has at various times acted as a navigational aid for traders travelling between the interior and the coast, a magnet for Victorian explorers, a political pawn to be traded between European superpowers who carved up East Africa, a battlefield for these same superpowers, and a potent symbol of independence for those who wished to rid themselves of these colonial interlopers. Unfortunately, little is known about the history of the mountain during the intervening two thousand five hundred years.

It's a fair bet that Kilimanjaro's first inhabitants, when they weren't fashioning stone bowls out of the local terrain, would have spent much of their time hunting and gathering the local flora and fauna, Kilimanjaro being a fecund source of both. Add to this its reputation as a reliable region both for fresh drinking water and materials – wood, stones, mud, vines etc – for building, and it seems reasonable to suppose that Kilimanjaro would have been a highly desirable location for primitive man, and would have played a central role in the lives of those who chose to take up residence on its slopes.

Unfortunately, those looking to piece together a comprehensive history of the first inhabitants of Kilimanjaro rather have their work cut out. There are no documents recording the life and times of the people who once lived on the mountain; not much in the way of any oral history that has been passed down through the generations; and, stone bowls apart, little in the way of archaeological evidence from which to draw any inferences. So while we can *assume* many things about the lives of Kilimanjaro's first inhabitants, we can be certain about nothing, and if Kilimanjaro did have a part to play in the pre-colonial history of the region, that history, and the mountain's significance within it, has, alas, now been lost to us.

And so it is to the notes of Western travellers that we must turn in order to find the earliest accounts of Kilimanjaro. These descriptions are usually rather brief, often inaccurate, and more often than not based on little more than hearsay and rumour rather than actual firsthand evidence. One of the first ever descriptions of East Africa is provided by the ***Periplus of the Erythraean Sea***, written anonymously in AD45. The *Periplus* – a contender for the title of the world's first ever travel guide – is a handbook for seafarers to the ports of Africa, Arabia and India and includes details of the sea routes to China. In it the author tells of a land called Azania, in which one could find a prosperous market town, Rhapta, where 'hatchets and daggers and awls ... a great quantity of ivory and rhinoceros horn and tortoise shell' were all traded. Yet interestingly, there is no mention of any snow-capped mountain lying nearby; indeed, reading the *Periplus* one gets the impression that the author considered Rhapta to be just about the end of the world:

Beyond Opone [modern day Ras Harun on the Somalian coast] *there are the small and great bluffs of Azania ... twenty-three days sail beyond there lies the very last market town of the continent of Azania, Rhapta ...*

Less than a hundred years later, however, **Ptolemy of Alexandria**, astronomer and the founder of scientific cartography, wrote of lands lying to the south of Rhapta where barbaric cannibals lived near a wide shallow bay and where, inland, one could find a '**great snow mountain**'. Mountains that wear a mantle of snow are pretty thin on the ground in Africa; indeed, there is only one candidate that is permanently adorned in snow, and that, of course, is Kilimanjaro.

How exactly Ptolemy came by his information is unknown, for he almost certainly never saw Kilimanjaro for himself. Nevertheless, based on hearsay though it may have been, this is the earliest surviving written account of Africa's greatest mountain. It therefore seems logical to conclude that the out-

Kilimanjaro – the name

The meaning of the name Kilíma Njáro, if it have any meaning, is unknown to the Swáhili... To be analysed, it must first be corrupted. This has been done by Mr Rebmann, who converts Kilíma Njáro into Kilíma dja-aro, which he tells us signifies, "Mountain of Greatness." This etymology... is wholly inadmissible for the following reasons: 1st. It is mere nonsense....

So said W D Cooley (see p79), leading British geographer during the mid-nineteenth century, in his book *Inner Africa Laid Open*. Nonsense Rebmann's suggestion may have been, but in the absence of better alternatives, the translation is as valid as any other. For the fact of the matter is that despite extensive studies into the etymology of the name Kilimanjaro, nobody is really sure where it comes from, or what exactly it means.

When looking for the origin of 'Kilimanjaro', it seems only sensible to begin such a search in one of the local Tanzanian dialects, and more specifically, in the language spoken by those who live in its shadow, namely the Chagga people. True, the name Kilimanjaro bears no resemblance to any word in the Chagga vocabulary; but if we divide it into two parts then a few possibilities present themselves. One is that Kilima is derived from the Chagga term *kilelema*, meaning 'difficult or impossible', while *jaro* could come from the Chagga terms *njaare* ('bird') or *jyaro* ('caravan'). In other words, the name Kilimanjaro means something like 'That which is impossible for the bird', or 'That which defeats the caravan' – names which, if this interpretation is correct, are clear references to the sheer enormity of the mountain.

Whilst this is perhaps the most likely translation, it is not, in itself, particularly convincing, especially when one considers that while the Chagga language would seem the most logical source for the name, the Chagga people themselves do not actually have one single name for the mountain! Instead, they don't see Kilimanjaro as a single entity, but as two distinct, separate peaks, namely Mawenzi and Kibo. (These two names, incidentally, are definitely Chagga in origin, coming from the Chagga terms *kimawenzi* – 'having a broken top or summit' – and *kipoo* – 'snow' – respectively.)

side world first became aware of Africa's tallest mountain in the years between the publication of the Periplus in AD45, and that of Ptolemy's work, sometime during the latter half of the second century AD.

THE OUTSIDERS ARRIVE

Arabs, An Anonymous Chinaman and some Portuguese

Following Ptolemy's description, almost nothing more is written about Kilimanjaro for over a thousand years. The Arabs, arriving on the East African coast in the sixth century, must have heard something about it from the local people with whom they traded. Indeed, the mountain would have proved essential to the natives as they travelled from the interior to the markets on the East African shore: as one of the few unmissable landmarks in a largely featureless expanse of savannah and scrub, and with its abundant streams and springs, the mountain would have been both an invaluable navigational tool and a reliable source of drinking water for the trading caravans. But whether the merchants from the Middle East actually ventured beyond their trading posts on the coast

❏ **Kilimanjaro – the name (cont'd)**

Assuming Kilimanjaro isn't Chagga in origin, therefore, the most likely source for the name Kilimanjaro would seem to be Swahili, the majority language of the Tanzanians. Rebmann's good friend and fellow missionary, Johann Ludwig Krapf, wrote that Kilimanjaro could either be a Swahili word meaning 'Mountain of Greatness' – though he is noticeably silent when it comes to explaining how he arrived at such a translation – or a composite Swahili/Chagga name meaning 'Mountain of Caravans'; *jaro*, as we have previously explained, being the Chagga term for 'caravans'. Thus the name could be a reference to the many trading caravans that would stop at the mountain for water. The major flaw with both these theories, however, is that the Swahili term for mountain is not *kilima* but *mlima* – *kilima* is actually the Swahili word for 'hill'!

The third and least likely dialect from which Kilimanjaro could have been derived is Masai, the major tribe across the border in Kenya. But while the Masai word for spring or water is *njore*, which could conceivably have been corrupted down the centuries to *njaro*, there is no relevant Masai word similar to *kilima*. Furthermore, the Masai call the mountain *Oldoinyo Oibor*, which means 'White Mountain', with Kibo known as the 'House of God', as Hemingway has already told us at the beginning of this book. Few experts, therefore, believe the name is Masai in origin.

Other theories include the possibility that *njaro* means 'whiteness', referring to the snow cap that Kilimanjaro permanently wears, or that Njaro is the name of the evil spirit who lives on the mountain, causing discomfort and even death to all those who climb it. Certainly the folklore of the Chagga people is rich in tales of evil spirits who dwell on the higher reaches of the mountain, and Rebmann himself refers to 'Njaro, the guardian spirit of the mountain'; however, it must also be noted that the Chagga's legends make no mention of any spirit going by that name.

And so we are none the wiser. But in one sense at least, it's not important: what the mountain means to the 20,000 who walk up it every year is far more meaningful than the name we ascribe to it.

to see the mountain for themselves seems doubtful, and from their records of this time only one possible reference to Kilimanjaro has been uncovered, written by a thirteenth-century geographer, **Abu'l Fida**, who speaks of a mountain in the interior that was 'white in colour'.

The Chinese, who traded on the East African coast during the same period, also seemed either ignorant or uninterested in the land that lay beyond the coastline, and in all their records from this time once again just one scant reference to Kili has been found, this time by an anonymous chronicler who states that the country to the west of Zanzibar 'reaches to a great mountain'.

After 1500, and the exploration and subsequent conquest of the African east coast by Vasco da Gama and those who followed in his wake, the Arabs were replaced as the major trading power in the region by the Portuguese. They proved to be slightly more curious about what lay beyond the coast than their predecessors, perhaps because their primary motives for being there were more colonial than commercial. A vague but once again unmistakable reference to Kilimanjaro can be found in a book, *Suma de Geographia*, published in 1519, an account of a journey to Mombasa by the Spanish cartographer, astronomer and ship's pilot **Fernandes de Encisco**:

West of Mombasa is the Ethiopian Mount Olympus, which is very high, and further off are the Mountains of the Moon in which are the sources of the Nile.

Amazingly, in the fourteen hundred years since Ptolemy this is only the third reference to Kilimanjaro that has been found; with the return of the Arabs in 1699, it was also to be the last for another hundred years or so. Then, just as the eighteenth century was drawing to a close, the Europeans once more cast an avaricious eye on East Africa.

THE 1800s: PIONEERS . . .

With British merchants firmly established on Zanzibar by the 1840s, frequent rumours of a vast mountain situated on the mainland just a few hundred miles from the coast now began to reach European ears. British geographers were especially intrigued by these reports, particularly as it provided a possible solution to one of the oldest riddles of the dark continent: namely, the precise where-abouts of the source of the Nile. Encisco's sixteenth-century reference to *the Mountains of the Moon in which are the sources of the Nile* is in fact a mere echo of the work of Ptolemy, writing fourteen hundred years before Encisco, who also cites the Mountains of the Moon as the true origin of the Nile.

But while these Mountains of the Moon were, for more than a millennium, widely accepted in European academia as the place where the Nile rises, nobody had actually bothered to go and find out if this was so – nor, indeed, if these mountains actually existed at all.

Interest in the 'dark continent' was further aroused by the arrival in London in 1834 of one Khamis bin Uthman: slave dealer, caravan leader, and envoy of the then-ruler of East Africa, Seyyid Said. Uthman met many of Britain's leading dignitaries, including the prime minister, Lord Palmerston. He also met and talked at length with the leading African scholar, **William Desborough Cooley**. A decade after this meeting, Cooley wrote his lengthy essay *The Geography of N'yassi, or the Great Lake of Southern Africa Investigated*, in which he not only provides us with another reference to Kilimanjaro – only the fifth in 1700 years – but also becomes the first author to put a name to the mountain:

The most famous mountain of Eastern Africa is Kirimanjara, which we suppose, from a number of circumstances to be the highest ridge crossed on the road to Monomoezi.

Suddenly Africa, long viewed by the West almost exclusively in terms of the lucrative slave trade, became the centre of a flurry of academic interest, and the quest to find the true origins of the Nile became something of a *cause célèbre* amongst scholars. Long-forgotten manuscripts and journals from Arab traders and Portuguese adventurers were dusted off and scrutinized for clues to the whereabouts of this most enigmatic river source. Most scholars preferred to conduct their research from the comfort of their leather armchairs; there were others, however, who took a more active approach, and pioneering explorers such as Richard Burton and John Hanning Speke set off to find for themselves the source of the Nile, crossing the entire country we now know as Tanzania in 1857. This was also the age of Livingstone and Stanley, the former venturing deep into the heart of Africa in search of both knowledge and potential converts to Christianity, the latter in search of the former.

David Livingstone preaching near Lake Tanganyika. (HG Adams, 1873)

. . . AND PREACHERS

Yet for all their brave endeavours, it was not these Victorian action men but one of the humble Christian missionaries who followed in their wake who became the first European to set eyes on Kilimanjaro. **Johannes Rebmann** was a young Swiss-German missionary who arrived in Mombasa in 1846 with an umbrella, a suitcase, and a heart full of Christian zeal. His brief was to help **Dr Johann Ludwig Krapf**, a doctor of divinity from Tubingen, in his efforts to spread the Christian faith among East Africa's heathen. Krapf was something of a veteran in the missionary field, having previously worked for the London-based Church Missionary Society in Abyssinia. Following the closure of that mission, Krapf sailed down the East African coast to Zanzibar, and from there to Mombasa, where he hoped to found a new mission and continue his evangelical work.

Instead, his life fell apart. His wife succumbed to malaria and died on the 9 July 1884. His daughter, born just three days previously, died five days after the death of her mother from the same disease, while Krapf too fell gravely ill with the same; and though he alone recovered, throughout the rest of his life he suffered from sporadic attacks that would lay him low for weeks at a time.

But though his body grew weak with malaria, his spirit remained strong, and over the next six months following the death of his wife, Krapf both translated the New Testament into Swahili and devised a plan for spreading the gospel throughout the interior of Africa. Estimating that the continent could be crossed on foot from east to west in a matter of 900 hours, Krapf believed that establishing a chain of missions at intervals of one hundred hours right across the continent, each staffed by six 'messengers of peace', would be the best way to promulgate the Christian religion on the dark continent.

Unfortunately for Krapf, Islam had got there first, which made his job rather tougher; indeed, in the six months following his arrival in Mombasa, the total number of successful conversions made by Krapf stood at zero. Clearly, if the faith was to make any inroads in Africa, fresh impetus was required.

That impetus was provided by the arrival of Rebmann in 1846. Having recovered from the obligatory bout of malaria that wiped him out for his first month in Africa, Rebmann set about helping Krapf to establish a new mission at Rabai-mpia (New Rabai), just outside Mombasa. The station lay in the heart of Wanika territory, a tribe who from the first had proved resistant to conversion. Even the founding of a mission in their midst did little to persuade the Wanika to listen to Krapf's preaching: by 1859, 14 years after Krapf first arrived, just seven converts had been made.

It was clear early on that they would have little success in persuading the Wanika to convert, and so from almost the start the proselyting pair began to look to pastures new to find potential members for their flock. In 1847 they founded a second mission station at Mt Kasigau, three days' walk from Rabai-mpia – the first in their proposed chain of such stations across the African continent – and later that same year they began to plan the establishment of the next link, at a place called **Jagga** (now spelt Chagga). Rebmann and Krapf had already heard a lot about Jagga from the caravan leaders who earned their money transferring goods between the interior and the markets on the eastern shore, and who often called into Rabai-mpia on the way. A source of and market for slaves, Jagga was renowned locally for suffering from extremely cold temperatures at times, a reputation that led Krapf to deduce that Jagga was probably at a much higher altitude than the lands that surrounded it. This hypothesis was confirmed by renowned caravan leader Bwana Kheri, who spoke to Krapf of a great mountain called 'Kilimansharo' (this, incidentally, being the sixth definite reference to Kilimanjaro). From other sources Krapf and Rebmann also learnt that the mountain was protected by evil spirits (known in the Islamic faith as *djinns*) who had been responsible for many deaths, and that it was crowned with a strange white substance that resembled silver, but which the locals simply called 'cold'.

Following protracted negotiations, Bwana Kheri was eventually persuaded to take Rebmann to Chagga in 1848 (Krapf, being too ill to travel, remained in Rabai-mpia). The parting caused great distress to both parties, as detailed in Krapf's diary:

Here we are in the midst of African heathenism, among wilful liars and trickish men, who desire only our property... The only earthly friend whom I have, and whom he has, does at once disappear, each of us setting our face towards our respective destinations while our friends at home do not know where we are, whither we go and what we are doing.

Rebmann's journey and the discovery of snow

And so, armed with only his trusty umbrella – along a route where caravans typically travelled under armed escort – Rebmann, accompanied by Bwana Kheri and eight porters, set out for Chagga, on 27 April 1848. A fortnight later, on the morning of 11 May, he came across the most marvellous sight:

*At about ten o'clock, (I had no watch with me) I observed something remarkably white on the top of a high mountain, and first supposed that it was a very white cloud, in which supposition my guide also confirmed me, but having gone a few paces more I could no more rest satisfied with that explanation; and while I was asking my guide a second time whether that white thing was indeed a cloud and scarcely listening to his answer that **yonder** was a cloud but what that white was he did not know, but supposed it was **coldness** – the most delightful recognition took place in my mind, of an old well-known European guest called **snow**. All the strange stories we had so often heard about the gold and silver mountain*

Kilimandjaro in Jagga, supposed to be inaccessible on account of evil spirits, which had killed a great many of those who had attempted to ascend it, were now at once rendered intelligible to me, as of course the extreme cold, to which poor Natives are perfect strangers, would soon chill and kill the half-naked visitors. I endeavoured to explain to my people the nature of that 'white thing' for which no name exists even in the language of Jagga itself... **Johannes Rebmann** from his account of his journey, published in Volume I of the *Church Missionary Intelligencer*, May 1849

An extract from the next edition of the same journal continues the theme:

The cold temperature of the higher regions constituted a limit beyond which they dared not venture. This natural disinclination, existing most strongly in the case of the great mountain, on account of its intenser cold, and the popular traditions respecting the fate of the only expedition which had ever attempted to ascend its heights, had of course prevented them from exploring it, and left them in utter ignorance of such a thing as 'snow', although not in ignorance of that which they so greatly dreaded, 'coldness'.

WD Faulty? – The Snow Debate

The most relentless critic was a redoubtable person, for long years a terror to real explorers, Mr. Desborough Cooley, a kind of geographical ogre, who used to sit in his study in England, shaping and planning out the map of Africa (basing his arrangements of rivers, lakes and mountains on ridiculous and fantastic linguistic coincidences and resemblances of his own imagination), and who rushed out and tore in pieces all unheeding explorers in the field who brought to light actual facts which upset his elaborate schemes. **HH Johnston** *The Kilima-njaro Expedition – A Record of Scientific Exploration in Eastern Equatorial Africa*

Though Rebmann's accounts of Kilimanjaro caused a minor sensation amongst the wider reading public when first published in the *Church Missionary Intelligencer* of May 1849, the response it elicited from academic circles back in Europe was initially as cool as the top of Kibo itself. Leading the sceptics was one **William Desborough (WD) Cooley**. Cooley was widely regarded in his day as one of Britain's leading geographers, and something of an expert on Africa (though he never actually ventured near the continent throughout his entire life). Indeed, Cooley had already added to the stock of knowledge about the mountain way back in 1845, a full four years before Rebmann's essay was published, by providing the world with a description of Kilimanjaro that he had managed to construct from details furnished to him by the slave dealer-cum-ambassador Khamis bin Uthman (see p76).

But if he is remembered at all today it is as the man who refused to believe that Kilimanjaro could be topped with snow, as this response to Rebmann's first account makes clear:

I deny altogether the existence of snow on Mount Kilimanjaro. It rests entirely on the testimony of Mr Rebmann... and he ascertained it, not with his eyes, but by inference and in the visions of his imagination. Athenaeum, May 1849

Absurd as it seems now, Cooley's reputation in intellectual circles at that time was as high as Kili itself, and such was the reverence with which his every pronouncement was received in the mid-nineteenth century that it was his version of reality that was the more widely accepted: as far as people in Europe were concerned, if Cooley said Kili did not have snow on it, then it didn't have snow on it. *(Continued overleaf)*

Still bent on spreading Christianity, and undeterred (or perhaps ignorant) of the scepticism with which his reports in the *Intelligencer* had been met back in Europe (about which, see the box on p79), Rebmann returned to Rabai-mpia but continued to visit and write about Kilimanjaro and the Chagga region for a few more years. His second trip, made in November of the same year, was blessed by favourable weather conditions, providing Rebmann with his clearest view of Kilimanjaro, and the outside world with the most accurate and comprehensive description of the mountain that had yet been written:

There are two main peaks which arise from a common base measuring some twenty-five miles long by as many broad. They are separated by a saddle-shaped depression, running east and west for a distance of about eight or ten miles. The eastern peak is the lower of the two, and is conical in shape. The western and higher presents the appearance of a magnificent dome, and is covered with snow throughout the year, unlike its eastern neighbour, which loses its snowy mantle during the hot season.

❏ **WD Faulty? – The Snow Debate**

(Continued from p79). A second report by Rebmann, following his trip to the Chagga lands in November 1848, did little to stem the scepticism, even though he – perhaps now aware of the controversy his first account had caused back home – went to great lengths to back up his earlier report:

.. during the night, I felt the cold as severely as in Europe in November; and had I been obliged to remain in the open-air, I could not have fallen to sleep for a single moment: neither was this to be wondered at, for so near was I now to the snow-mountain Kilimandjaro (Kilima dja-aro, mountain of greatness), that even at night, by only the dim light of the moon, I could perfectly well distinguish it.

If Rebmann hoped to persuade his critics, however, he was sadly mistaken: if he was capable of making a mistake once, they countered, then surely he could be wrong a second and third time too.

And so for much of the next two years Rebmann's account of his time on Kili was treated with equal parts suspicion and derision. Indeed, it wasn't until 1850 and the publication of an account by Rebmann's friend and mentor, Dr Krapf, that doubts began to be cast on Cooley's ideas. In an edition of the *Church Missionary Intelligencer* in which he recounts his own experiences working in the Ukamba region immediately to the north of Kilimanjaro, Krapf baldly states that:

All the arguments which Mr Cooley has adduced against the existence of such a snow mountain, and against the accuracy of Rebmann's report, dwindle into nothing when one has the evidence of one's own eyes before one; so that they are scarcely worth refuting.

Suddenly it became that much harder to deny the existence of snow on Kili: after all, there were now two Europeans who had seen the mountain for themselves – and both of them had insisted that they'd seen snow there.

Yet Cooley remained adamant in his convictions, and thanks to the support of some pretty influential friends to back up his arguments, enjoyed popular public support. No less a figure than the President of the Royal Geographical Society, **Sir Roderick Murchison**, said that the idea of a snow-capped mountain under the equator was to *'a great degree incredulous'*, (even though there are other snow-capped mountains in the Andes and Papua New Guinea that fall 'under the equator', and which were already known about by the mid-nineteenth century). *(Continued opposite).*

On this second trip Rebmann was also able to correct an error made in his first account of Kilimanjaro: that the local 'Jagga' tribe were indeed familiar with snow and did have a name for it – that name being 'Kibo'!

A third and much more organized expedition in April 1849 – at the same time as the account of his first visits of Kilimanjaro was rolling off the presses in Europe – enabled Rebmann, accompanied by a caravan of 30 porters (and, of course, his trusty umbrella), to ascend to such a height that he was later to boast that he had come 'so close to the snow-line that, supposing no impassable abyss to intervene, I could have reached it in three or four hours'. After Rebmann's pioneering work it was the turn of his friend Krapf, now risen from his sickbed, to see the snowy mountain his friend had described in such detail. In November 1849 he visited the Ukamba district to the north of Kilimanjaro, and during a protracted stay in the area Krapf became the first white man to see Mount Kenya. Perhaps more impor-

---

❏ WD Faulty? – The Snow Debate

(Continued from p80). Even those who *had* been to Africa for themselves had serious reservations about the missionaries' claims. The esteemed explorer **Richard Burton**, for example, having listened to Krapf give a talk on Kilimanjaro in Cairo, declared that *'These stories reminded one of a de Lunatico'*; while **David Livingstone**, recently returned from his latest adventures in Africa, lent further weight to Cooley's arguments during an address to the Royal Geographical Society. In it, Livingstone related a story about some mountains in the Zambezi Valley, which were described to him by locals as being of a *'glistening whiteness'*. Livingstone initially believed that these mountains must be covered by snow, until, having seen the mountains for himself, he realized that they were in fact composed of *'masses of white rock, somewhat like quartz'*. As if to drum home the point of the tale, Sir Roderick Murchison later declared at the same meeting that Livingstone's account

... may prove that the missionaries, who believed that they saw snowy mountains under the equator, have been deceived by the glittering aspect of rocks under a tropical sun.

The next broadside fired by either side occurred in 1852 and the publication of Cooley's grandly (but inaccurately) titled *Inner Africa Laid Open*. This, Cooley clearly hoped, was to be his masterpiece: the culmination of a lifetime's armchair studying, this was the work that would secure his reputation during his lifetime, and ensure his name lived on in perpetuity as one of the great intellectual heavyweights of the nineteenth century. As it transpired, the book did indeed serve to preserve Cooley's name for posterity – though, presumably, not quite in the way that Cooley had hoped.

To read the book now, it is clear that Cooley hoped it would once and for all dismiss all this nonsense about snow on Kilimanjaro. Within the first few pages almost every part of Rebmann's account is called into question, with the claim of snow on Kilimanjaro being treated with particularly vehement derision:

... it is obvious that the discovery of snow rests much more on 'a delightful mental recognition' than on the evidence of the senses..... But in his mind the wish was father to the thought, the 'delightful recognition' developed with amazing rapidity, and in a few minutes the cloudy object, or 'something white,' became a 'beautiful snow mountain', so near to the equator.

(Continued overleaf).

tantly, he was also afforded wonderful views of Kilimanjaro, and was able to back up Rebmann's assertion that the mountain really was adorned with snow.

FIRST ATTEMPTS AT THE SUMMIT

Baron von der Decken and Charles New

After the missionaries came the mountaineers. In August 1861 Baron Carl Claus von der Decken, a Hanoverian naturalist and traveller who had been

---

❏ **WD Faulty? – The Snow Debate**
(Continued from p81). Later on in the book Cooley forgets the conduct becoming to a 19th-century English gentleman, and the attacks on Rebmann border on the personal:

Various and inconsistent reasons have been assigned for this failure [by Rebmann to see Kilimanjaro from a nearby hill], *but the only true explanation of it is contained in Mr Rebmann's confession that he is very short-sighted. He was unable to perceive, with the aid of a small telescope, Lake Ibe, three days distant to the south, which his follow-ers could discern with the naked eye; nor could he even see the rhinoceroses in his path.*

And he goes on to finish his onslaught with this rather uncompromising, hysterical summary of Rebmann's accounts:

... betraying weak powers of observation, strong fancy, an eager craving for wonders, and childish reasoning, could not fail to awaken mistrust by their intrinsic demerits, even if there were no testimony opposed to them.

To further back up his argument, Cooley was able to point out a number of inconsistencies between Rebmann's and Krapf's accounts, such as the postulation by Krapf that the mountain is 12,500 feet (3800m) high – this after Rebmann had estimated the height to be closer to 20,000 feet (6000m, a remarkable guess by the myopic Rebmann).

Cooley's desire to prove Rebmann wrong was fuelled by more than just a desire to crush a young upstart in a field in which he considered himself the ultimate authority. He was also frightened that the existence of snow on Kilimanjaro would provide support for his rivals' theories at the expense of his own. In the big debate that raged in academic circles in the mid-1800s on the exact location of the source of the Nile, Cooley was firmly of the opinion that the river started from a large lake in Central Africa called Lake N'yassi. (Indeed, in the 1830s he even organized an expedition to prove his theory, though unfortunately it failed abysmally for reasons that remain rather obscure.) Aligned against him, Cooley's opponents, such as the geographer **Charles Beke**, preferred the idea that the Nile had its source in a range of mountains in the interior – possibly, as Encisco had stated in the sixteenth century, the legendary Mountains of the Moon – and looked upon the discovery of snow on an East African mountain as evidence to back up their theories. Indeed, when Rebmann and Krapf's accounts first reached Britain Beke was only too keen to accept their every word as the gospel truth, and even went so far as to suggest that Kilimanjaro was now the most likely source of the Nile.

And that, for the next decade or so, was that: Rebmann and Krapf continued to visit Kilimanjaro, and continued to see snow there, while Cooley and the gang back in England continued to refute their every utterance and enjoy the majority of public opinion. Then in 1862, **Baron Carl von der Decken** visited Kilimanjaro. Travelling with Richard Thornton, the baron was the first European to have another European with him to back up his account.   *(Continued opposite).*

residing in Zanzibar, accompanied by young English geologist Richard Thornton, himself an explorer of some renown who had accompanied (and been sacked by) Livingstone during the latter's exploration of the Zambezi, made the first serious attempt on Kilimanjaro's summit. Initially, despite an entourage of over fifty porters, a manservant for von der Decken and a personal slave for Thornton, their efforts proved to be rather dismal and they had to turn back after just three days due to bad weather, having reached the rather puny height of just

---

❏ WD Faulty? – The Snow Debate

(Continued from p82). In trying to climb the mountain, the baron also came as close to the snow as any European ever had. His account of the expedition exploded Cooley's theories once and for all. As the brave baron wrote in his report:

During the night it snowed heavily and next morning the ground lay white all around us. Surely the obstinate Cooley will be satisfied now.

There was now a third eyewitness claiming to have seen snow on Kilimanjaro, and a baron at that; Cooley's position as a result began to look increasingly untenable, and his support began to ebb quietly away. If the baron really believed his testimony alone would persuade Cooley, however, he was much mistaken:

So the Baron says it snowed during the night....In December with the sun standing vertically overhead! The Baron is to be congratulated on the opportuneness of the storm. But it is easier to believe in the misrepresentations of man than in such an unheard-of eccentricity on the part of nature. This description of a snowstorm at the equator during the hottest season of the year, and at an elevation of only 13,000 feet, is too obviously a 'traveller's tale', invented to support Krapf's marvellous story of a mountain 12,500 feet high covered with perpetual snow.

But the redoubtable Cooley was fighting a lonely battle now. The Royal Geographical Society withdrew their backing, with Sir Roderick Murchison – presumably between mouthfuls of humble pie – finally admitting that Rebmann and Krapf were probably right after all. As if to add insult to Cooley's injured pride, the Society even awarded their Gold Medal in 1863 to von der Decken for his contributions to the sum of geographical knowledge of Africa. Fourteen years after Rebmann had first announced that there was snow on the equator, the world was finally listening to him. Cooley meanwhile, resolutely refused to believe in the existence of snow on Kilimanjaro, carrying his scepticism with him to the grave and leaving behind a reputation for stubbornness and ignorance that has survived to this day.

In his defence, one has to remember just how little was known about the 'dark continent' at that time: few people from Europe had ever visited Africa; fewer still had penetrated beyond the coast; and of those who had, even fewer had survived to tell the tale. So the armchair scholars of Europe were forced to rely upon the sketchy mentions of Kili in historical records for their information; and of those descriptions, none since Ptolemy mentions anything about snow. As some compensation, perhaps, Cooley at least had the satisfaction of knowing that, while defeated in this particular battle, he gained at least a partial victory in the wider war: in 1858 a large body of water in the heart of central Africa was discovered, and was named **Lake Victoria** after Britain's sovereign. This lake would later be proved to be the source of the Nile. Cooley may have got the name and location of this body of water wrong, but his supposition that the Nile had a lake as its source, and not a mountain, had been proved correct after all.

8200ft (2460m). Proceeding to the west side of the mountain, however, the pioneering baron did at least enjoy an unobstructed view of Kibo peak on the way:

Bathed in a flood of rosy light, the cap that crowns the mountain's noble brow gleamed in the dazzling glory of the setting sun... Beyond appeared the jagged outlines of the eastern peak, which rises abruptly from a gently inclined plain, forming, as it were, a rough, almost horizontal platform. Three thousand feet lower, like the trough between two mighty waves, is the saddle which separates the sister peaks one from the other.

Von der Decken also provided the most accurate estimate yet for the height of both Kibo – which he guessed was between 19,812 and 20,655 feet (5943.6m to 6196.5m) – and Mawenzi (17,257–17,453 feet, or 5177.1–5235.9m). Thornton, for his part, correctly surmised that the mountain was volcanic, with Kibo the youngest and Shira the oldest parts of the mountain.

The following year, without Thornton, von der Decken reached a much more respectable 14,200ft (4260m) and furthermore reported being caught up in a snow storm. On his return to Europe, the baron described Kibo as a 'mighty dome, rising to a height of about 20,000 feet, of which the last three thousand are covered in snow'.

Following this second attempt, von der Decken urged Charles New (1840–75), a London-born missionary with the United Free Methodist Church in Mombasa, to tackle the mountain, and in 1871 New made a laudable attempt to reach the summit. That attempt failed, as did a second attempt in August of the same year; nevertheless, by choosing on the latter occasion to climb on the south-eastern face of Kibo where the ice cap at that time stretched almost to the base of the cone, New inadvertently wrote himself into the history books as the first European to cross the snow-line at the African Equator:

The gulf was all that now lay between myself and it, but what an all! The snow was on a level with my eye, but my arm was too short to reach it. My heart sank, but before I had time fairly to scan the position my eyes rested upon snows at my very feet! There it lay upon the rocks below me in shining masses, looking like newly washed and sleeping sheep! Hurrah! I cannot describe the sensations that thrilled my heart at that moment. Hurrah!

On this second expedition New also discovered the crater lake of Jala the mountain's only volcanic lake, at Kilimanjaro's foot to the south-east of Mawenzi.

New's experiences on Kilimanjaro fanned his passion for the mountain, and two years later he was back preparing for another assault on the still-unconquered peak. Unfortunately, the volatile tribes living at the foot of the mountain had other ideas, and before New had even reached Kilimanjaro he was forced to return to the coast, having been stripped of all his possessions by the followers of the Chief of 'Moji' (Moshi), a highly unpleasant man by the name of Mandara (see p176). Broken in both health and spirits, the unfortunate New died soon after the attack.

As rumours of New's demise trickled back to Europe, enthusiasm among explorers for the still unconquered Kilimanjaro understandably waned, and for ten years the mountain saw few foreign faces. Those that did visit usually did so on their way to somewhere else; people such as **Dr Gustav A Fischer** in 1883, who stopped in Arusha and visited Mount Meru on his journey to Lake

Naivasha, and declared Kilimanjaro to be fit for 'European settlement', a statement that would have greater resonance later on in the century; and the Scottish geologist, Joseph Thompson, who became one of the first to examine properly the northern side of mountain during an attempt to cross the Masai territories. He also attempted a climb of Kili, though having allowed himself only one day in which to complete the task his attempt was always doomed to failure, and in the end he reached no higher than the tree-line at about 2700m. (Failure though he may have been in this instance, his name lives on as a species of gazelle.)

The first European to venture back to the region with the specific intention of visiting Kilimanjaro arrived in the same year, 1883. In an expedition organized by the Royal Geographical Society, **Harry Johnston** arrived in East Africa with the aim of discovering and documenting the flora and fauna of Kilimanjaro. Though his work did little to further our understanding of the mountain, Johnston's trip is of anecdotal interest in that he later claimed in his biography that he was actually working undercover for the British Secret Service. No documentary evidence has ever turned up to back this claim (though there is a letter written by him to the foreign office in which he asks for 40 men and £5000 for the purpose of colonizing Kilimanjaro). Much doubt has been cast, too, upon his boast that he reached almost 5000m during his time on the mountain; while his suggestion that Kilimanjaro was 'a mountain that can be climbed even without the aid of a walking stick' was widely ridiculed when first broadcast later that year. But whatever the inaccuracies and falsehoods of Johnston's recollections, his journey did at least assure other would-be Kilimanjaro visitors from Europe that the region was once again safe to visit. His visit also served to bring the mountain to the attention of European powers...

COLONIZATION

... a country as large as Switzerland enjoying a singularly fertile soil and healthy climate, ... within a few years it must be either English, French or German ... I am on the spot, the first in the field, and able to make Kilima-njaro as completely English as Ceylon
H H Johnston *The Kilima-njaro Expedition – A Record of Scientific Exploration in Eastern Equatorial Africa*

In describing the mountain thus, HH Johnston brought the mountain to the attention of the world's leading powers. Soon the two great colonizers in East Africa, Germany and Britain, were jockeying for position in the region. British missionaries were accused of putting the temporal interests of their country over the spiritual affairs of their flock, while for their part certain German nationals made no secret of the fact they wished to colonize Kilimanjaro. In 1884, the **Gesellschaft fur Deutsche Kolonisation** (GDK), a political party founded by the 28-year old **Dr Carl Peters** with the ultimate goal of colonizing East Africa, persuaded a dozen local chiefs to throw off the rule of the (British controlled) **Sultan of Zanzibar** and, furthermore, to cede large sections of their territory to the German cause; one of Dr Peters' envoys, Dr Juhlke, even managed to establish a protectorate over Kilimanjaro in 1885. The British fought fire with fire in

---

> **The biggest present ever?**
> There is a widely held belief that the kink in the border between Kenya and Tanzania was created to satisfy the whim of Britain's reigning monarch at the time the border was first defined, Queen Victoria. According to the story, she magnanimously decided to give Kilimanjaro to her grandson, the future Wilhelm II, as a birthday present, following a complaint from him that while Britain had two snowy mountains in her East African territories (mounts Kili and Kenya), Germany was left with none. In order to effect the transfer of such a generous gift, the border had to be redrawn so that Kili fell to the south of the boundary in German territory, which is why the border has a strange kink in it to the east of the mountain.
>
> Alas, however poetic the story, it is simply not true. The kink is there not because of Victoria's largesse, but as part of the agreement struck between Germany and Britain, and it exists not because of Kili, but Mombasa. Britain's territories in East Africa needed a port: the German's already had Dar, and if the border between the two was to continue on the same bearing as it had taken to the west of Kilimanjaro, the Germans were going to end up with Mombasa too. So a kink was placed in the border to allow Mombasa to fall in British territory.

---

response, forcing two dozen chiefs (including some of those who had sided with the Germans) to swear allegiance to the sultan – and therefore indirectly to them. The situation was becoming dangerously volatile and war was starting to look increasingly likely. After further bouts of political manoeuvring, in October 1886 the two sides met in London and Berlin to define once and for all the boundary between British- and German-controlled East Africa and head off the possibility of war: the border between British-controlled Kenya and German East Africa was now in place.

The first period of German rule over Kilimanjaro proved to be exceptionally harsh, and many Germans soon felt uneasy about the excesses of Dr Peters and his followers. In 1906 an enquiry opened in the Reichstag into the conduct of Dr Peters and his men, in which an open letter was read out to the court; its contents give an idea of the hatred that the doctor and his men aroused in the locals:

What have you achieved by perpetual fights, by acts of violence and oppression? You have achieved, Herr Doctor, I have it from your own mouth in the presence of witnesses – that you and the gentlemen of your staff cannot go five minutes' distance from the fort without military escort. My policy enables me to make extensive journeys and shooting trips in Kilimanjaro and the whole surrounding country with never more than four soldiers. You have cut the knot with the sword and achieved that this most beautiful country has become a scene of war. Before God and man you are responsible for the devastation of flourishing districts, you are responsible for the deaths of our comrades Bulow and Wolfram, of our brave soldiers and of hundreds of Wachagga. And now I bring a supreme charge against you: Necessity did not compel you to this. You required deeds only in order that your name might not be forgotten in Europe.

Soon German soldiers were being attacked and killed, and with opposition to their rule growing stronger and more organized by the day, the Germans under General von Bulow suffered a massive defeat at Moshi at the hands of the Chagga, led by Meli, Mandara's son (see p176). Though the Germans regained control, it was now clear to them that a more benevolent style of government was required if they were to continue ruling over their East African territories. This new 'caring colonialism' paid off, and for the last decade or so of their rule the Germans lived largely at peace with their subjects, and even forged a useful alliance with the Chaggas during the German's push against the rebellious Masai tribes. The Germans also started the practice of hut-building on Kilimanjaro, establishing one at 8500ft (2550m), known as **Bismarck Hut**, and at one at 11,500ft (3450m) known as **Peters's Hut**, after Dr Karl.

KILIMANJARO CONQUERED

While all this was going on, attempts to be the first to conquer Kilimanjaro continued apace. In 1887, **Count Samuel Teleki** of the Austro-Hungarian Empire made the most serious assault on Kibo so far, before 'a certain straining of the membrane of the tympanum of the ear' forced him to turn back. Then the American naturalist, **Dr Abbott**, who had primarily come to investigate the fauna and flora of the mountain slopes, made a rather reckless attempt. Abbott was struck down by illness fairly early on in the climb, but his climbing companion, Otto Ehlers of the German East African Company, pushed on, reaching (according to him) 19,680ft (5904m). Not for the first time in the history of climbing Kilimanjaro, however, this figure has been sceptically received by others – particularly as it is at least 8m above the highest point on the mountain!

Both of these men played a part in the success of the eventual conqueror of Kilimanjaro, **Dr Hans Meyer**: Teleki, by providing information about the ascent to Meyer in a chance encounter during Meyer's first trip to the region in 1887 when he managed to reach 18,000ft (5400m); Abbott, by providing accommodation in Moshi for Meyer and his party during their successful expedition of 1889.

Hans Meyer was a geology professor and the son of a wealthy editor from Leipzig (he himself later joined the editorial board and became its director, retiring in 1888, one year before the conquest of Kili, to become professor of Colonial Geography at Leipzig University). In all he made four trips to Kilimanjaro. Following the partial success of his first attempt in 1887, Meyer returned the following year for a second assault with experienced African traveller and friend Dr Oscar Baumann. Unfortunately, his timing couldn't have been worse: the **Abushiri War** had just broken out, and Meyer and his friend Baumann were captured, clapped into chains and held hostage by Sheikh Abushiri himself. In the end, both escaped with their lives, but only after a ransom of ten thousand rupees was paid. (Those who visit the National Museum in Dar es Salaam can see the original note Meyer sent to the German representative in Zanzibar begging him to pay off the chief.)

However, on his third attempt, in 1889, Meyer finally covered himself in glory. Though no doubt a skilful and determined climber, Meyer's success can largely be attributed to his recognition that the biggest obstacle to a successful assault was the lack of food available at the top. Meyer solved this by establishing camps at various points along the route that he had chosen for his attempt, including one at 12,980ft (3894m; Abbott's camp); one, Kibo camp, 'by a conspicuous rock' at 14,210ft (4263m); and, finally, a small encampment by a lava cave and just below the glacier line at 15,260ft (4578m). Thanks to these intermediary camps, Meyer was able to conduct a number of attempts on the summit without having to return to the foot of Kili to replenish supplies after each; instead, food was brought to the camps by the porters every few days.

He also had a considerable back-up party with him, including his friend and climbing companion, Herr Ludwig Purtscheller – a gymnastics teacher and alpine expert from Salzburg – two local headmen, nine porters, three other

Meyer's route to the top and the modern trails: a comparison

While no modern path precisely retraces Hans Meyer's original route to the summit, some of today's paths do occasionally coincide with the trail he blazed. For instance, Meyer and his climbing partner, Purtscheller, began their assault on the summit, on 28 September, 1889, from **Marangu** village. From there they headed due north up through the trees, arriving two days later at the very upper limits of the forest, where they made camp. Trekkers on the Marangu trail follow a similar itinerary today, though their starting point is a good deal higher than Meyer's at Marangu Gate, rather than Marangu village – which explains why trekkers today need only one day to reach the edge of the forest, while Meyer took two. It is also worth noting that, according to the beautifully drawn maps by Dr Bruno Hassenstein in Meyer's book *Across East African Glaciers*, his camp on this second night lay to the south-west of Kifunika Hill at an altitude of 8710ft (2613m), whereas the Mandara Huts lie a couple of hours' walk to the east of Kifunika, situated at a loftier 2743m.

On the third day, Meyer struck a westerly course, crossing the Mdogo (lesser) and Mkuba (greater) streams before making camp at an altitude of 9480ft (2844m). This was the all-important **Halfway Camp**, the intermediate station that Meyer would use as his base for tackling Kibo. In the history of climbing Kibo, no single spot on the entire mountain, save Uhuru Peak itself, has played a more prominent role: Harry Johnston had built some huts nearby during his reconnaissance mission of 1883; Meyer himself had camped here during his first expedition on the mountain, with Baron von Eberstein in 1887, and Abbott and Ehlers had also camped nearby in 1889, just a few months before Meyer and Purtscheller arrived. There's even evidence to suggest Count Teleki had also stopped here in 1887; in his account of their attempt on Kili in *Discovery by Count Teleki of Lakes Rudolf and Stefanie*, Lieutenant Ludwig von Höhnel speaks of making camp at 9390ft by a brook, near some old huts built originally by HH Johnston.

So where is this spot? There are plenty of clues. It is no coincidence, for example, that all these different parties chose to make camp at this site. Then, as now, campsites would have been chosen largely for their proximity to water and other amenities, so we can guess that a mountain stream or brook must run nearby. We also know that Meyer headed almost due west from his camp of the night before, and that the spot lies at around 2844m, above the tree-line. No modern campsite exactly fits this description – the Horombo Huts, the second night's accommodation on the Marangu trail, are too high up at 3657m. Rau Campsite, however, on the Alternative Mweka/Kidia Route, seems a more plausible candidate: though this campsite is too high at 3260m, just below it is a glorious stretch of grasslands bordering the forest and near a mountain stream (described on p219) that would appear to fit the description given by Meyer. If the nineteenth-century explorers really did camp around there, they are to be congratulated on choosing one of the most beautiful places on the mountain. *(cont'd opposite)* locals who would act as supervisors, one cook and one guide supplied by the local chief, Mareale, whom he had befriended during his first trip to the region. These men would help to carry the equipment and man the camps, with each kept in order by Meyer's strict code of discipline, where minor miscreants received ten lashes, and serious wrongdoers twenty.

The size of his entourage, however, shouldn't detract from the magnitude of Meyer's achievement: as well as the usual hardships associated with climbing Kilimanjaro, Meyer also had to contend along the way with deserters from his

---

❑ Meyer's route to the top and the modern trails: a comparison

(Continued from p88) Leaving most of his porters behind at this site – it would be their duty from now on to ferry supplies up to the camp from Marangu – Meyer then struck due north up to the Saddle, past the **Spring in the Snow**, or Schneequell (12910ft, 3873m) and on to **Abbott's Camp** at 12,980ft (3894m), so-called by Meyer because he found an empty Irish stew tin and a sheet of the Salvation Army newspaper *En Avant* at this spot, and guessed that this must have been where his missionary friend Dr Abbott had camped a few months previously. As to their location, according to the maps in Meyer's book the Schneequell lies almost exactly due south of the East Lava Hill, the easternmost of the parasitic cones on the Saddle, and would seem to tie in fairly neatly with the Last Water Point, the Mua River, that lies below the Zebra Rocks on the Marangu Route (see p213). Abbott's Camp, meanwhile, lies to the north-north-west of here, at a point between the two Marangu Route paths to the Saddle.

From here, Meyer's path and the Marangu Route diverge for good. Where Marangu trekkers today head north across the Saddle, keeping Kibo to their left, in 1889 Meyer and his two companions, the alpine expert Purtscheller and Mwini Amani, their guide, set off directly for the summit in a more westerly direction, stopping for the night by a prominent rock at 14,200ft (4260m). This is **Viermannstein**, the Rock of Four Men, a place popular with Kili explorers in the nineteenth century. Unfortunately, because it lies far from any trail today, the site rarely features on modern trekking maps; for an approximate location, draw a line running east from the Barafu Campsite, and a second due south from the easternmost Triplet: the rock stands near to where they coincide.

Meyer's aim in 1889 was the **Ratzel Glacier**, on the south-eastern rim of Kibo. The glacier, though much reduced in size, is still there today: those walking up to the summit from the Barafu Campsite will see it on their right as they approach Stella Point. In Meyer's day the glacier covered the entire south-eastern lip of Kibo, and it was into this glacier that Meyer and Purtscheller, on 3 October, carved a series of steps that led all the way up to the crater rim and a height of 19,260ft (5778m).

On this occasion, considerations of time and weather forced them to withdraw back down to camp, having seen – but not scaled – the highest point on Kibo. After a day's rest and contemplation, however, and having decided to bivouac at **Lava Cave** on the slopes of Kibo at 15,960ft (4788m), the duo were ready for another assault on the summit. From there, at 3am on a cold October morning, they set off. At dawn they were at the foot of the glacier where, to their delight, they found the glacial stairway that they'd built two days previously was still there. By 8am they had reached and crossed a large crevasse, the only serious obstacle on the way to the summit. Just 45 minutes later they were back standing on the crater rim, the limit of their achievements two days previously. On this occasion, however, both time and weather were on their side. Walking around the southern rim of Kibo, they climbed three small hillocks, the middle of which they found by aneroid to be the highest by some forty feet or more. *(cont'd overleaf)*

❏ **Meyer's route to the top and the modern trails: a comparison**
(Cont'd from p89) At 10.30am on 6 October 1889, Meyer and Purtscheller wrote themselves into the history books as the first people to make it to the highest point in Africa.

So where exactly did they gain **access to the crater**? According to Dr Hassenstein's maps, the Lava Cave lies at the northern end of the large South East Valley, due west of the middle of the three triplets. That puts it somewhere to the north-east of the Barafu Campsite, and more than 150m higher, on one of the rocky spurs that run south-east down from Kibo. Where it certainly is *not*, though many a guide will tell you otherwise, is the Hans Meyer Cave on the Marangu Route, which at 5151m is simply too high and too far north. The notch by which they gained access to the crater lay almost exactly north-west of this Lava Cave Camp. Though again this is pure guesswork, all the evidence does seem to point to the fact that Meyer and Purtscheller on this particular occasion passed into the crater rim from a spot very near to **Stella Point** (5745m); the difference in height (Meyer estimated the height at this point on the crater to be 5778m) can possibly be ascribed to the fact that Meyer's estimates tend to be over-estimates (his height for Uhuru Peak, for example, is over 6000m) – perhaps because in Meyer's day there was a lot more ice at the summit, which would have raised the altitudes.

Having christened the summit after their Kaiser and taken the topmost stone from the summit as a souvenir (a stone that Meyer later gave to the Kaiser, who used it as a paperweight), the pair then hurried back to Abbott's camp on the Saddle. The next few days were spent trying to conquer **Mawenzi**, but with no success, the mountain peak defeating them wholly on the first occasion on 13 October, and an attack of colic brought on by some over-ripe bananas stalling their second attempt two days later. Before returning to civilization, however, they spent five more days revisiting Kibo: on 17 October they headed to the crater's northern side, where they reached 5572m before confronting a sheer wall of ice that forced them to retreat; and then finally, on the 18th, they approached the crater from the east.

The path Meyer took up to the crater on this occasion is not too dissimilar to the trail up to Gillman's from the Kibo Huts. Meyer and Purtscheller on this final climb bivouacked at a location they called **Old Fireplace** because, to their considerable surprise, they found the remains of a recent campfire there, along with the bones of an eland and some pieces of banana matting. This camp, according to Meyer, sat at an altitude of 15,390ft (4617m). It's just possible, therefore, that the Old Fireplace is in fact the site that we now call **Jiwe Lainkoyo**, which many local mountain guides insist was once a popular hunters' campsite. From the Old Fireplace, Meyer and Purtscheller climbed up the snow-clad slopes of Kibo once more, gaining access into the crater via a cleft in the rim that is now known as **Hans Meyer Notch**, and which lies just a few hundred metres to the north of Gillman's Point. Though they failed in their attempts to reach the inner cone of the volcano, they were at least able to confirm that the floor of the crater was made up of a mixture of mud and ashes. They were also startled when, peering into the first cone, they came across the carcass of an antelope (which possibly explains what the leopard, whose frozen body was found up here many years later, was doing at this altitude).

After one more unsuccessful attempt on Mawenzi, Meyer and Purtscheller finally decided to call it a day, and on 22 October they said goodbye to the Saddle for the last time. The pair had spent 16 days between 15,000 and 20,000 feet. During this time they had made four ascents of Kibo, reaching the crater three times and the summit once, and three sorties on Mawenzi, reaching the 5049m summit of Purtscheller's Spitze, but failing to reach the very top.

party, a lack of any clear path, elephant traps (large pits dug by locals and concealed by ferns to trap the unwary pachyderm), as well as the unpleasant, rapacious chief of Moshi, Mandara (see p176). It is also worth noting here that Meyer did not begin his walk at the foot of the mountain, as today's visitors do, but in Mombasa, 14 days by foot, according to Meyer, from the Kilimanjaro town of Taveta!

Then there was the snow and ice, so much more prevalent in the late 1800s on Kili than it is today. Above 4500m Meyer had to trek upon snow for virtually the whole day, even though his route up Kibo from the Saddle is not too dissimilar to that taken by the vast majority of the thousands of trekkers every year – and today there is no snow on the route. The added difficulties caused by the snow are well described in Meyer's book *Across East African Glaciers*. Rising at 2.30am for their first assault on the summit, Meyer and Purtscheller spent most of the morning carving a stairway out of a sheer ice-cliff, every stair laboriously hewn with an average of twenty blows of the ice axe. (The cliff formed part of the Ratzel Glacier, named by Meyer after a geography professor in his native Leipzig.) As a result, by the time they reached the eastern lip of the crater, the light was fading fast and the approach of inclement weather forced them to return before they could reach the highest point of that lip.

The conquest of Kilimanjaro
Taking out a small German flag, which I had brought with me for the purpose in my knapsack, I planted it on the weather-beaten lava summit with three ringing cheers, and in virtue of my right as its discoverer christened this hitherto unknown and unnamed mountain peak – the loftiest spot in Africa and the German Empire – Kaiser Wilhelm's Peak [now known as Uhuru Peak]. Then we gave three cheers more for the Emperor, and shook hands in mutual congratulation. **Hans Meyer** Across East African Glaciers

On their second attempt, however, three days later on 6 October 1889, and with the stairs still intact in the ice from the first ascent, they were able to gain the eastern side of the rim by mid-morning; from there it was but a straightforward march to the three small tumescences situated on the higher, southern lip of the crater, the middle one of which was also the highest point of the mountain.

AFTER MEYER

Mawenzi, Pastor Reusch and a frozen leopard

In the decades following Meyer's successful assault on Kili, few followed in his footsteps. Meyer himself climbed again in 1898, though this time he got only as far as the crater rim. In 1909 surveyor M Lange climbed all the way to Uhuru Peak, and in doing so became only the second to reach the summit of Kilimanjaro – a full twenty years after the first. The conquest of the last peak on

Kilimanjaro, that of the summit of Mawenzi (called, somewhat perversely, Hans Meyer Peak), was achieved by the climbers **Edward Oehler** and **Fritz Klute** on 29 July 1912. Thus, 64 years after the first European had clapped eyes on Kilimanjaro, both of its main peaks had been successfully climbed. As an encore, Oehler and Klute made the third successful attempt on Kibo, and the first from the western side. In the same year, **Walter Furtwangler** and **Ziegfried Koenig** achieved the fourth successful climb, and became the first to use skis to descend. Two more successful assaults occurred before the outbreak of World War One, and **Frau von Ruckteschell** kept up the German's impressive record on Kilimanjaro by becoming the first woman to reach Gillman's Point.

Fresh attempts on Kilimanjaro were suspended for a while during World War One. The countryside around Kilimanjaro became the scene of some vicious fighting, including Moshi itself, which was attacked by British forces in March 1916. Paul von Lettow Vorbeck, the German commander, went down in military history at this time as the man who led the longest tactical retreat ever. With the German's defeat, however, Kilimanjaro, along with the rest of German East Africa, reverted to British rule.

After the war, attention turned away from Kibo to the lesser-known Mawenzi. In 1924 **George Londt** of South Africa became, by accident, the first to climb South Peak (he was aiming for Hans Meyer Peak but got lost); the peak (4958m), was named after him. Three years later three English mountaineers climbed Mawenzi, including **Sheila MacDonald**, the first woman to do so; the trio then climbed Kibo, with Ms MacDonald writing her name into the record books again as the first woman to complete the ascent to Uhuru Peak. In 1930 two famous British mountaineers, HW Tilman and Eric Shipton, names more usually associated with Everest, climbed Mawenzi's Nordecke Peak – again, by accident.

While all this was happening on Mawenzi, over on Kibo another man was writing himself into the history of Kili: **Pastor Richard Reusch**. Missionary for the Lutheran Church, former officer in the Cossack army and long-time Marangu resident, Reusch climbed the mountain on no less than 40 different occasions. During his first assault on the summit in 1926 he discovered the frozen leopard on the crater rim that would later inspire Hemingway (Reusch

Kilimanjaro as a national park

Kilimanjaro has enjoyed some form of protection since the early years of the twentieth century under German rule, when the mountain and surrounding area were designated as a game preserve. In 1921 this status was upgraded to become a forest and game preserve, thereby protecting the precious cloud forest that beards Kili's lower slopes.

Another change in 1957 saw the Tanganyika National Parks Authority propose that the mountain become a national park, though this wasn't actually realized until 1973, when Kilimanjaro National Park (KINAPA) was formed; a park that, for simplicity's sake, the authorities decided would include all land above 2700m. KINAPA didn't actually officially open until 1977; twelve years later, in 1989, the park was declared a World Heritage Site by UNESCO.

cut off part of an ear as a souvenir), while on another sortie the following year he became the first to gaze down into the inner crater, a crater that he was later to give his name to. Later work by mountaineer **HW Tilman** and vulcanologist **JJ Richard** led to confirmation, in 1942, that Kilimanjaro was still active, and while this led to some local panic, in 1957 the Tanganyika Geological Survey and the University of Sheffield were able to allay fears by declaring the volcano to be dormant and almost extinct.

KILIMANJARO TODAY

The twentieth century witnessed the inevitable but gradual shift away from exploration towards tourism. The most significant change occurred in 1932 with the building of Kibo Hut; name plates and signs were put up too, as the mountain was gradually made more tourist-friendly. With a ready base for summit assaults now established, tourists began to trickle into Tanzania to make their own attempt on Africa's greatest mountain.

In 1959 the mountain became the focus for nationalist feelings and a symbol of the Tanganyikan's independence aspirations following Julius Nyerere's speech to the Tanganyika Legislative Assembly (see p53 for quote). Nyerere eventually got his wish, and after independence was granted in 1961, a torch was indeed placed on the summit of Kilimanjaro. Independence also provided Tanganyika with the chance to rename many of the features of the mountain; in particular, the very summit, named Kaiser Wilhelm Peak by Hans Meyer, was renamed Uhuru Peak – Uhuru meaning, appropriately, 'Freedom' in Swahili.

Since this mountain's moment of patriotic glory, the story of Kilimanjaro has largely been about tourism. The early trickle of tourists of fifty years ago is nowadays more akin to a flood, with visitor numbers still increasing exponentially today, from less than a thousand in the late 1950s to 11,000 in the mid-1990s to more than 20,000 each year since 2000. Indeed, the turn of the new millennium saw seven thousand attempting to conquer it in that one week alone, with over a thousand on New Year's Day itself.

What has been an economic boon to the people of Kilimanjaro, however, has brought little of benefit to the mountain itself. With these increases come commensurately greater numbers of pressures and problems. Its soil is being eroded, its vegetation is being burnt or chopped, its wildlife is disappearing and its glaciers are melting. Along with these environmental pressures come challenges to its dignity, as climbers dream up ever more bizarre ways of climbing to the top.

Yet no matter how many glaciers melt or how many people climb to the summit in rubber rhino suits, Kilimanjaro continues to inspire both awe and respect in all who gaze upon it. And while man will continue to visit in droves and in his clumsy, careless way will carry on defacing and demeaning Africa's most charismatic place, the mountain itself remains essentially the same powerful, ineffably beautiful sight it always was; perhaps because, while we throw all that we can at it, the Roof of Africa does what it always has done – and what it does best: it simply rises above it all.

Flora and fauna

FLORA

It is said that to climb up Kilimanjaro is to walk through **four seasons in four days**. It is true, of course, and nowhere is this phenomenon more apparent than in its flora. The variety of flora found on Kilimanjaro can be ascribed in part to the mountain's tremendous height and in part to its proximity to both the equator and the Indian Ocean. Add to this the variations in climate, solar radiation and temperature from the top of the mountain to the bottom (temperatures are estimated to drop by 1°C for every 200m gain in altitude), and you end up with the ideal conditions for highly differentiated and distinctive vegetation zones. In all, Kilimanjaro is said to have between four and six distinctive zones depending on who you read. A description of each follows, while a picture chart of the more common species of flower can be found opposite p96.

Cultivated zone and forest (800m–2800m)

The forest zone, along with the cultivated zone that lies below it, together receive the most rainfall – about 2300mm per year – of any part of the mountain. The forest zone also houses the greatest variety of both fauna (see below) and flora.

Enormous **camphorwoods** flourish at this altitude, as do **fig** and, around Marangu Gate, the grey-barked **podocarpus**. Giant ferns enjoy these damp conditions too, as, clearly, does *Usnea* sp., or **old man's beard**, which lies draped over most of the branches, particularly at the upper limit of the forest zone. Also hanging from the trees is the *Begonia meyeri johannis*, with sweet smelling white and pink flowers. On the drier northern and western slopes **juniper** and **olive trees** proliferate, with one species, *Olea kilimandscharica*, indigenous to the mountain. Back on the southern side, towards the upper limit of the zone the smooth grey *Ilex mitis*, with its characteristic red and yellow fruit, becomes the dominant tree, before finally giving way to the first of the giant heathers as the forest zone comes to an end.

The star of the montane forest zone is the beautiful flower *Impatiens kilimanjari*, an endemic splash of dazzling red and yellow in the shape of an inch-long tuba. You'll see them by the side of the path on the southern side of the mountain. Vying for the prime piece of real estate that exists between the roots of the trees are other, equally elegant flowers including the beautiful violet *Viola eminii* and *Impatiens pseudoviola*.

Perhaps the most unusual aspect of Kilimanjaro's forest zone, however, is not the plants and trees that it does have, as one that it doesn't. Kili is almost unique in East Africa in not having any bamboo at the upper limit of the forest zone, possibly because it is one of the driest mountains and cannot support

> ### Kilimanjaro ablaze
> In February 1999 a huge fire swept across the upper slopes of Kilimanjaro. The fires were first discovered on February 6 and over the next five days 70 hectares were destroyed in the blaze. Thanks to the combined efforts of 347 villagers, park rangers and 40 soldiers of the 39th Squadron of the Tanzanian People's Defence Force, the main blaze was eventually brought under control, though not before considerable damage had been done to the mountain. Evidence of fire can still be seen in places on Kili, particularly in the moorland zone where new plants now grow between the charred remains of branches and shrubs.
> Depressingly but unsurprisingly, human activity is believed to have been behind the fires. Twenty-two men from the Kamwanga and Rongai districts were arrested, having been identified as the culprits by six hundred villagers in a secret ballot. The men were all squatters living illegally in the protected areas of the national park; according to one minister who visited the scene of the devastation, there were up to ten thousand such squatters living in Kilimanjaro's forests, most of whom made their living by collecting honey. It is believed that a cigarette butt discarded by one of them started the blaze, though others have pointed an accusing finger at local farmers who like to clear their farms by fire before the start of the annual rains the following month.

bamboo stands the way other African mountains can. As a result, the forest zone ends suddenly, with little warning, throwing us immediately into the less shady trails of the ...

Heath and moorland (2800m–4000m)

These two zones overlap, and together occupy the area immediately above the forest from around 2800m to 4000m – known as the **low alpine zone**. Temperatures can drop below 0°C at this altitude, and most of the precipitation that does fall here comes from the fog and mist that are almost permanent fixtures at this height.

Immediately above the forest zone is the **alpine heath**. Rainfall here is around 1300mm per year. The giant heather *Erica excelsa* and the similar but less bushy *Erica arborea* both grow in abundance. The latter also exists in the upper part of the forest zone, where it can grow to ten metres or more; the higher you go, however, the less impressive the specimens, with many refusing to grow beyond 2.5–3m. Grasses now dominate the mountain slopes, too, picked out here and there with some splendid wild flowers including the yellow-flowered *Protea kilimandscharica*, an indigenous rarity that can be seen on the Mweka trail and, so I've been told, around Maundi Crater – the best place for botanists to spot wild flowers. Another favourite, and one most readers will recognize instantly, is the back-garden favourite *Kniphofia thomsonii*, better known to most as the **red-hot poker**. A whole raft of *Helichrysum* species – some yellow, daisy-like flowers, others looking grey and shiny like living potpourri – make their first appearance here too, though certainly not their last! (See opposite p97.) Climbing higher, you'll begin to come across **sedges** such as *Mariscus kerstenii*.

The shrubs are shrinking now: *Philippia trimera* is the most common of them, along with the gorse-like *Adenocarpus* which it often grows beside; the prettiest shrub in the upper reaches of the heath zone is the pink-flowered *Blaeria filago*.

Climbing ever further, you'll soon reach the imperceptible boundary of the moorland zone, which tends to have clearer skies but an even cooler climate. Average per annum precipitation is now down to 525mm. The most distinctive plant in this area – indeed, on the entire mountain – is the senecio, or **giant** or **tree groundsel**, of which there are two different species thriving on Kilimanjaro: the *Senecio kilimanjari* occurs between 2450 and 4000m, can grow up to 5m high, and on the rare occasion it flowers the petals themselves are yellow and grow from a one-metre-long spike; while the *Senecio johnstonii cottonii* is found only above 3600m, and has duller, mustard-coloured flowers. Groundsels tend to favour the damper, more sheltered parts of the mountain, which is why you'll see them in abundance near the Barranco Campsite as well as other, smaller valleys and ravines.

Sharing roughly the same kind of environment is the strange *lobelia deckenii*, another endemic species, and one that bears no resemblance to the lobelias that you'll find in your back garden. These strange, either phallic or cabbage-shaped plants take eight years to flower (the blue flowers are hidden inside the leaves to protect them from frost), and are a favourite with the *Nectarinia johnstoni*, the dazzling green malachite sunbird.

Alpine desert (4000m–5000m)
By the time you reach the Saddle, only three species of tussock grass and a few everlastings can withstand the extreme conditions. This is the **alpine desert**, where plants have to survive in drought conditions (precipitation here is less than 200mm per year), and put up with both inordinate cold and intense sun, usually in the same day. Up to about 4700m you'll also find the *Asteraceae*, a bright yellow daisy-like flower and the most cheerful-looking organism at this height.

Ice cap (5000m–5895m)
On Kibo, almost nothing lives. There is virtually no water. On the rare occasions that precipitation occurs, most of the moisture instantly disappears into the porous rock or is locked away in the glaciers.

That said, specimens of *Helichrysum newii* – an everlasting that truly deserves its name – have been found near a fumarole in the Reusch Crater, a good 5760m above sea level, and mosses and lichens are said to exist all the way up to the summit. While these lichen may not be the most spectacular of plants, it may interest you to know that their growth rate on the upper reaches of Kilimanjaro is estimated to be just 0.5mm in diameter per year; for this reason, scientists have concluded that the larger lichen on Kilimanjaro could be amongst the oldest living things on earth, being hundreds, and possibly thousands of years old!

*Lantana
camara*

Canna

*Cassia
didymobotrya*

*Impatiens
pseudoviola*

*Impatiens
kilimanjari*

*Parochaetus
communis*

*Desmodium
repandum*

*Begonia
meyeri johannis*

Cycnium

Bearded lichen

Hypericum revolutum

Bidens kilimandsharica

Crotalaria lebrunii

Trifolium usambarensis

Gladiolus watsonioides

Kniphofia thomsonii (Red hot poker)

Leonotis nepetifolia

Protea kilimandsharica

*Thunbergia alata
(Black-eyed Susan)*

*Dierama
pendulum*

*Hebenstretia
kilimandscharium*

*Stoebe
kilimandsharica*

*Senecio
kilimanjari*

*Carduus
keniensis*

Lichen

Lobelia deckenii

Lobelia deckenii

There are numerous varieties of *Helichrysum*, better known as 'everlastings', on Kilimanjaro.

FAUNA

In order to see much in the way of fauna, you have to be either very lucky or, it would seem, an author of a book on Kilimanjaro. When Hans Meyer was coming down from the mountain in 1889, he spotted an elephant on the slopes. In 1926 a leopard was found frozen in the ice at a place we now call Leopard Point – providing Hemingway with the inspiration for *The Snows of Kilimanjaro*. The mountaineer, HW Tilman, saw 27 eland on the Saddle when he passed this way in 1937, with each, according to him, especially adapted for the freezing conditions with thicker fur. In 1962, renowned travel writer Wilfred Thesiger and two companions were accompanied to the summit by five African hunting dogs. Though the dogs then turned round and disappeared after the three men made the summit, paw-prints in the ice proved that this wasn't the first time they had climbed to the top.

More recently, Rick Ridgeway claimed he saw a leopard on his ascent, as did Geoffrey Salisbury while leading his group of blind climbers to the summit; and in 1979 a local guide called David was savaged by a pack of African hunting dogs above the Mandara Huts and lost a finger. Even today, around the north side of Kibo, there are buffalo carcasses near Lava Tower and an elephant skeleton to the north of Shark's Tooth.

I mention these stories to demonstrate that the more exotic fauna of East Africa does occasionally venture onto the mountain. It just doesn't happen very often, with most animals preferring to be somewhere where there aren't 20,000 people marching around every year. So in all probability, you will see virtually nothing during your time on the mountain beyond the occasional monkey or mouse. Nevertheless, keep your mouth shut and your eyes open and you never know ...

Forest and cultivated zones

Animals are more numerous down in the forest zone than anywhere else on the mountain; unfortunately, so is the cover provided by trees and bushes, so sightings remain rare. As with the four-striped grass mice of Horombo (see p178), it tends to be those few species for whom the arrival of man has been a boon rather than a curse that are the easiest to spot, including the **blue monkeys**, which appear daily near the Mandara Huts, and which are not actually blue, but grey or black with a white throat. These, however, are merely the poor relatives of the beautiful **colobus monkey**, with the most enviable tail in the animal kingdom; you can see a troop of these at the start of the forest zone on the Rongai Route. **Olive baboons**, **civets**, **leopards**, **mongooses** and **servals** are said to live in the mountain's forest as well, though sightings are extremely rare; here, too, lives the bush pig with its distinctive white stripe running along its back from head to tail.

Then there's the **honey badger**. Don't be fooled by the rather cute name. As well as being blessed with a face only a mother could love, these are the most powerful and fearless carnivores for their size in Africa. Even lions give them a wide berth. You should too: not only can they kill, but the thought of having to tell your friends that, of all the bloodthirsty creatures that roam the

African plains, you got savaged by a badger, is too shaming to contemplate. Of a similar size, the **aardvark** has enormous claws, but unlike the honey badger this nocturnal, long-snouted anteater is entirely benign. So fear not: as the old adage goes, aardvark never killed anyone. Both aardvarks and honey badgers are rarely, if ever, seen on the mountain, as are **porcupines**, Africa's largest rodents. Though also present in this zone, they are both shy and nocturnal and your best chances of seeing one is as road-kill on the way to Dar es Salaam.

Further down, near or just above the cultivated zone, **bushbabies** are more easily heard than seen as they come out at night and jump on the roof of the hut. Here, too, is the **small-spotted genet** with its distinctive black-and-white tail, and the noisy, chipmunk-like **tree hyrax**.

One creature you definitely won't see at any altitude is the rhinoceros. Although a **black rhinoceros** was seen a few years ago on the north side of the mountain, it is now believed that over-hunting has finally taken its toll of this most majestic of creatures; Count Teleki (see p87) is said to have shot 89 of them during his time in East Africa, including four in one day, and there are none on or anywhere near Kilimanjaro today.

Baboons in the branches of a Dum palm
(from *Across East African Glaciers,* Hans Meyer, 1891)

Heath, moorland and above

Just as plant-life struggles to survive much above 2800m, so animals too find it difficult to live on the barren upper slopes. Yet though we may see little, there are a few creatures living on Kilimanjaro's higher reaches.

Above the treeline you'll be lucky to see much. The one obvious exception to this rule is the **four-striped grass mouse**, which clearly doesn't find it a problem eking (or should that be eeking?) out an existence at high altitude; indeed, if you're staying in the Horombo Huts on the Marangu Route, one is probably running under your table while you read this. Other rodents present at this level include the **harsh-furred** and **climbing mouse** and the **mole rat**, though all are far more difficult to spot.

For anything bigger than a mouse, your best chance above 2800m is either on the Shira Plateau, where **lions** are said to roam occasionally, or on the northern side of the mountain on the Rongai Route. Kenya's Amboseli National Park lies at the foot of the mountain on this side and many animals, particularly **elephants**, amble up the slopes from time to time. **Grey** and **red duikers**, **elands** and **bushbucks** are perhaps the most commonly seen animals at this altitude, though sightings are still extremely rare. None of these larger creatures live above the tree-line of Kilimanjaro permanently, however, and as with the **leopards**, **wild dogs**, **giraffes** and **buffaloes** that occasionally make their way up the slopes, they are, like us, no more than day-trippers.

On **Kibo** itself the entymologist George Salt found a species of **spider** that was living in the **alpine zone** at altitudes of up to 5500m. What exactly these high-altitude arachnids live on up there is unknown – though Salt himself reckoned it was probably the flies that blew in on the wind, of which he found a few, and which appeared to be unwilling or unable to fly. What is known is that the spiders live underground, better to escape the rigours of the weather.

Avifauna

Kilimanjaro is great for birdwatchers. The cultivated fields on the lower slopes provide plenty of food, the forest zone provides shelter and plenty of nesting sites, while the barren upper slopes are the ideal hunting grounds for raptors.

In the **forest**, look out for the noisy dark green **Ross's turacao** (there was one nesting near the first-day lunch stop on the Machame Route), easy to distinguish when it flies because of its bright red underwings. The **silvery-cheeked hornbills** and **speckled mousebirds** hang around the fruit trees in the forest, particularly the fig trees. There's also the **trogon** which, despite a red belly, is difficult to see because it remains motionless in the branches.

Hornbill

Smaller birds include the **white-browed robin chat** (black and white head, grey top, orange lower half) and the **common bulbul**, with a black crest and yellow beneath the tail.

Further up the slopes, the noisy, scavenging, garrulous **white-necked raven** is a constant presence on the heath and moorland zones, eternally hovering on the breeze around the huts and lunch-stops for any scraps. Smaller but just as ubiquitous is the **alpine chat**, a small brown bird with white side feathers in its tail, and the **streaky seed-eater**, another brown bird that can usually be seen hanging around the Horombo Huts. The **alpine swift**

White-necked raven

also enjoys these misty, cold conditions. The prize for the most beautiful bird on the mountain, however, goes to the dazzling **scarlet-tufted malachite sunbird**. Metallic green save for a small scarlet patch on either side of its chest, this

Augur buzzard

delightful bird can often be seen hovering above the grass, hooking its long beak in to reach the nectar from the giant lobelias.

Climbing further, and we come to raptor territory. You will rarely see these birds up close, for they spend most of the day gliding on the currents looking for prey. The **mountain** and **augur buzzards** are regularly spotted hovering above the Saddle (a specimen of the former also hangs about the School Huts when it's quiet); these are impressive birds in themselves – especially if you're lucky enough to see one up close – though neither is as large as the enormous **crowned eagle**, and the rare **lammergeyer**, a giant vulture with long wings and a wedge tail.

The People of Kilimanjaro: The Chagga

With regard to the Chagga people, they are a fine, well-built race. Their full development of bone and muscle being probably due to the exercise they all have to take in moving about on steep hills: they seem intellectually superior to the general run of coast Natives, and despite their objectionable traits (almost always present in the uneducated Native), such as lying, dirty habits, thieving, &c., they are certainly a very nice and attractive race.
Rev A Downes Shaw in 1924 in his book *To Chagga and Back — An Account of a Journey to Moshi, the Capital of Chagga, Eastern Equatorial Africa.*

It is fair to say that when you are in Moshi, Marangu or Machame, there is little indication that you are in a 'Chagga town'. Yet in the smaller villages, though waning year by year, traditional Chagga culture remains fairly strong, and occasionally a reminder of the past is uncovered by today's tourist, particularly when passing through the smaller villages on the little-visited eastern and western sides of Kilimanjaro. Such finds make visits to these villages truly fascinating.

Do not, however, come to Kilimanjaro expecting to witness some of the more extreme practices described below. This point needs emphasizing: the Chaggas' traditional way of life has been eroded by the depredations of Western culture and, as far as we know, is now largely extinct. Indeed, much of the material on which the following account is based is provided by the reports of the eighteenth-century and early nineteenth-century Europeans who visited the area; in particular, Charles Dundas' comprehensive tome, *Kilimanjaro and its People*, which was first published way back in 1924.

This, of course, begs the question: why have we included in a modern guide to Kilimanjaro descriptions of obsolete Chagga practices and beliefs that were largely wiped out almost 100 years ago? Research revealed the relevance of this inclusion since there are still faint echoes of their traditional way of life that have survived into the present day. Reading this admittedly detailed account of the Chagga and how they lived and thought could provide you with a better understanding of them and thereby some insight into the mind of the people who live in Kilimanjaro's shadow today. In addition to these two reasons for including this section, it was a fascinating subject to research and we hope that at least some readers will find it as interesting to read.

ORIGINS

Mount Kilimanjaro is the homeland of the **Chagga** people, one of Tanzania's largest ethnic groups. They are believed to have arrived between 250 and 400 years ago from the north-east, following local upheaval in that area. Logically, therefore, the eastern side of the mountain would have been the first to have been settled. Upon their arrival these new immigrants would have found that the mountain was already inhabited. An aboriginal people known as the Wakonyingo, who were possibly pygmies, were already living here, as indeed were the Wangassa, a tribe similar to the Masai, and the Umbo of the Usambara mountains. All of these groups were either driven out or absorbed by the Chagga.

Initially, these new immigrants were a disparate bunch, with different beliefs, customs and even languages. With no feelings of kinship or loyalty to their neighbour, they instead settled into family groups known as **clans**. According to Dundas, in his day some 732 clans existed on Kilimanjaro; by 1924, however, when his book was published, some of these clans were already down to just a single member.

These family ties were gradually cut and lost over time as people moved away to settle on other parts of the mountain. In place of these blood ties with the clan, people developed new loyalties to the region in which they were living and the neighbours with whom they shared the land. Out of this emerged twenty or so states or chiefdoms, most of them on a permanent war footing with the other nineteen. Wars between the tribes, and indeed between villages in the same tribe, were commonplace, though they usually took the form of organized raids by one village on another rather than actual pitched battles. Slaves would be taken during these raids, cattle rustled, and huts burned down, though there was often little bloodshed — the weaker party would merely withdraw at the first sign of approaching hostilities, and might even try to negotiate a price for peace.

Eventually the number of different groups was whittled down to just six tribes, or states, with each named after one of the mountain's rivers. So, for example, there are the Wamoshi Chaggas (after the Moshi River) and the Wamachame Chaggas who settled near the Machame River. With all this intermingling going on, a few words inevitably became used by all the people living on the mountain — and from this unlikely start grew a common language, of which each tribe had its own dialect. Similar customs developed between the tribes, though as with the language they differed in the detail. However, it was only when the Germans controlled the region during the latter part of the nineteenth century and the local people put aside their differences to present a united front in disputes with their colonial overlords that a single ethnic group was identified and named the Chagga. From this evolved a single, collective Chagga consciousness.

Today the Chaggas, despite their diverse origins, are renowned for having a strong sense of identity and pride. They are also amongst the most powerful and richest people in Tanzania, thanks in part to the fertile soils of Kilimanjaro, and in part to the Western education that they have been receiving for longer than almost any other tribe in Africa, Kilimanjaro being one of the first places to accept missionaries from Europe.

SOCIAL STRUCTURE AND VILLAGE LIFE

Hans Meyer notes in his book that the biggest Chagga settlement when he visited in 1889 was Machame, with 8000 people. 'Moji' (modern-day Moshi) had

Traditional Chagga beehive hut
(from *The Kilima-njaro Expedition*, HH Johnston, 1886)

3000, as did Marangu. Each family unit, according to him, lived in two or three extremely simple thatched huts in the shape of beehives, with a granary and small courtyard attached. There are still numerous examples of these **'beehive' huts** dotted around Kilimanjaro's slopes. Only the **chief**, the head of village society and its lawmaker, lived in anything more extensive. The chief of every village was often venerated by his subjects and even to meet him required going through an elaborate ceremony first. According to his report in the *Church Missionary Intelligencer*, Johannes Rebmann, the first white man to see Kilimanjaro, had to be sprinkled with goat's blood and the juice of a plant and was then left waiting for four days before being granted an audience with Masaki, the chief of Moshi. While modern society has reduced his role to a largely ceremonial one, the chief is still a widely respected person in village life today — though thankfully there is much less ceremony involved when paying him a visit.

There are other similarities between the Chagga society of yesterday and today. The economy was, then as now, largely agricultural, using the environmentally destructive slash-and-burn technique for clearing land. **Bananas** were once the most common crop, and though banana bushes were largely replaced by **coffee** plantations in the early twentieth century, both are still grown today.

When it came to trading these bananas and coffee in former times, instead of the Tanzanian shilling, people used red and blue glass beads as currency, or lengths of cloth known as *doti*. One hundred beads were equal to one *doti*, with which you could buy, for example, twenty unripe bananas; twelve *doti* would get you a cow.

RELIGION AND CEREMONIES

Unsurprisingly, for a people that has been subjected to some pretty relentless missionary work for over a century, the majority of the Chagga are today

Christian. Traditional beliefs are still held by some in rural areas, though the intensity of the beliefs and the excesses of many of the rituals have largely disappeared. Superstition played a central role in traditional Chagga religion: witchcraft (*wusari* in Chagga) played a major part, **rainmakers** and rain-preventers were important members of society, and dreams were infallible oracles of the future: indeed, many Chagga were said to have dreamt of the coming of the white man to Kilimanjaro.

The traditional faith was based around belief in a god called **Ruwa**. Ruwa was a tolerant god who, though not the creator of the universe or men, nevertheless set the latter free from some sort of unspecified incarceration. Ruwa had little to do with man following this episode, however, so the Chagga instead **worshipped their ancestors**, whom they believed could influence events on earth.

Chagga mythology had many parallels with stories from the Bible, including one concerning the fall of man (though in the Chagga version, a sweet potato was the forbidden fruit, and it was a stranger rather than a serpent that persuaded the first man to take a bite); there are also stories that bear a resemblance to the tales of Cain and Abel, and the great flood.

The Chagga faith also had its own **concept of sin**, and their own version of the Catholic practice of confession. In the Chagga religion, however, it is not the sinner but the person who is sinned against who must be purified, in order that the negative force does not remain with him or her. This purification would be performed by the local medicine man, with the victim bringing along the necessary ingredients for performing the 'cleansing'. These included the skin, dung and stomach contents of a hyrax; the shell and blood of a snail; the rainwater from a hollow tree and, as with all Chagga ceremonies, a large quantity of banana beer for the medicine man. All of this would then be put into a hole in the ground lined with banana leaves and with a gate or archway built above, which the victim would then have to pass through. This done, the victim would be painted by the medicine man using the mixture in the hole. This entire ceremony would be performed twice daily over four days.

Medicine men did more than care only for one's spiritual health; they also looked after one's physical well-being. For the price of one goat and, of course, more banana beer, the medicine man would be able to cure any affliction using a whole host of methods – including spitting. If you were suffering from a fever, for instance, you could expect to be spat upon up to 80 times by the medicine man, who would finish off his performance by expectorating up your nostrils and then blowing hard up each to ensure the saliva reached its target. For this particular method, the traditional payment was one pot of honey – and probably banana beer.

Traditional Chagga society also practised preventative medicine, and not just in matters of health. If, for example, a prominent man in the village was for some reason worried about his own safety, the medicine man would order him to lie with his favourite wife in a pit dug in the ground. With the man and wife still inside, the hole would then be decked with poles and covered with banana leaves. They would remain there until evening, while the man's friends above would cook food.

Chagga warriors
(from *Across East African Glaciers*, Hans Meyer, 1891)

Medicine men also performed the vital role of **removing curses**. Curses took many forms: a cheated wife, for example, might curse her husband by turning her back on him, bowing four times and praying for his death. The most feared curse, however, was that of the deathbed curse, issued by somebody shortly before they expired. These were widely held to be the most difficult to reverse, for to have any hope of removing it the medicine man would require the victim to get hold of a piece of the curser's corpse.

Funerals

If the medicine man's efforts at lifting the curse proved to be in vain, a funeral would be the most likely outcome. As with most Chagga ceremonies, this would vary slightly from place to place and from tribe to tribe, and also depended on the status of the deceased. Only married people with children, for example, would be buried: dead youths and girls would be wrapped in banana leaves and left in a banana grove, while babies were merely covered in cow dung and left out for jackals and hyaenas. (It is said that this practice was stopped after a jackal dropped the severed head of a small baby at the feet of the local chief.)

For married adults, the corpse would be stripped and bent double, with the head and legs tied together; **animal sacrifices** would take place on the day of the burial, with the hide of a sacrificed bull used to cover the grave. Interestingly, the corpse would face Kibo in the grave – as if the Chagga believed that the summit of Kilimanjaro was in some way connected with the afterlife. A lot of beer-drinking was also involved. Sacrifices would continue for the next nine days until, it was believed, the soul had finally crossed the harsh desert separating the earthly world from the spirit world. The afterlife, incidentally, was said to be very like our temporal world, only not as good, with food less tasty and the scenery less majestic.

The Ngasi

One of the occasions in which children frequently died was during the initiation ceremony known as **Ngasi**. This was a brutal rite of passage ceremony to mark the passing of boys into adulthood. The ceremony was presided over by the so-called King of Ngasi, a man who had the authority to viciously flog any boy taking part in the ceremony who displeased him.

Before the Ngasi proper started, the boys who were to take part were summoned from their houses by the singing of lugubrious songs at the gate of their homes. From there, they were taken to the place of ceremony deep in the forest,

Chagga language — a quick introduction
The following is a very brief introduction to the Vunjo dialect of Chagga, taken from the book by Bernard Leeman (see p227), to whom I am indebted. The Vunjo district covers Kirua, Kilema, Marangu, Mamba and Mwika. Attempt to speak a little Chagga, and you'll have the porters eating out of the palm of your hand. Or laughing at you. Please note that there are different dialects of Chagga, and as such your Chagga friend may not understand this particular one ... nevertheless, it's worth a try.

Yes	Yee
No	Ote
Please	Tafadhali
Thank you	Aika
Good morning, how are you?	Shimbonyi sha ngamenwi?
Very well, thank you, and how are you?	Nashica kapisa, aika, ungiwie shapfo?

and the ceremony started. **Hunting** formed a large part of the Ngasi; boys were tested on their ability to track down and kill game, the animals caught being smeared with the novices' excrement. Another test they had to undergo was to climb a tree on the riverbank and cross the river by clambering along its branches to where they intertwined with the branches of the trees on the other side. After this, a chicken would be sacrificed and the boys ordered to lick the blood.

The final part of the initial stage was the most brutal, however: orders were secretly given to the boys to slay a crippled or deformed youth amongst their number. Traditionally, the victim was killed in the night. The parents were never actually told what had happened to their son, and as all present at the Ngasi ceremony were sworn to silence, they never did find out the whole story.

The boys then moved to a new camp. They were now called Mbora, and were free to collect their clothes (one set of clothes, of course, was left unclaimed). They then repaired to the chief's house for a feast, from where they headed home. After the tribulations of the ceremony, the boys were allowed a month's holiday, before they returned to the chief's house to participate in the sacrificing of a bull. They were then free to head back to their homes, raping any young women they chanced to meet on way; the poor women themselves had no redress. The Ngasi was now at an end, and the boys who had entered into the ceremony were now men.

Matrimony

Ver hard on Wachaga to get wife, but when he get her she can make do plant corn, she make wash and cook and make do work for him. Ingreza [English] man very much money to spend. She wife no can wash, no plant corn, herd goats or cook. All money, much merkani (cloth), heap money, big dinner. She eat much posho. She no can cook dinner. She only make 'Safari' and look. Porr, porr Ingreza man. A local's view of matrimony as recorded in
Peter MacQueen's book *In Wildest Africa*, written in 1910

After the Ngasi, boys were free to marry. **Marriage** was arranged by the parents, though the boy and girl involved were allowed to voice their opinions –

The Chagga view of Kilimanjaro

The summit of Kilimanjaro is and always has been as enchanting to the Chagga as it has been to visitors. According to Dundas, the Chagga view the Kibo summit as something beautiful, eternal and strengthening, its snows providing streams that support life, while the clouds that gather on its slopes provide precious rainfall. By comparison, the plains that lie in the opposite direction are seen as oppressively hot, where famine stalks, drought and malaria are rife and large creatures such as crocodiles and leopards prey on man. Indeed, so venerated is Kilimanjaro that the Chagga dead are traditionally buried facing towards Kibo, and the side of the village facing the summit is known to be the honourable side, where meetings and feasts are held and chiefs are buried. Furthermore, when meeting somebody, he who comes from higher up the slopes of Kilimanjaro should traditionally greet the other first, for it is he who is coming from the lucky side.

Intriguingly, some Chagga myths about Kilimanjaro are remarkably accurate. In particular, the Chagga traditionally believed that the mountain was formed by a volcano – even though the main eruption that formed Kibo occurred around half a million years ago, way before the arrival of man. What's more, there is a story in Chagga folklore concerning the twin peaks of Mawenzi and Kibo, in which Mawenzi's fire burns out first, and the Mawenzi peak is forced to go to Kibo whose fire was still burning. Parallels between this story and what scientists now believe really happened – with Kibo continuing to erupt long after Mawenzi expired – are remarkable.

But the question remains: did the Chagga ever actually climb all the way to the top of Kilimanjaro before the Europeans? The answer is, probably not. True, their belief that Kibo was covered in a magic silver which melted on the way down does suggest that they had at least reached the snow-line before. Furthermore, Rebmann's guide refers to the snowy summit of Kilimanjaro as 'cold' (see p78), and Meyer found traces of a hunting expedition on the Saddle, both of which seem to confirm this idea. But the fact that Charles New's entourage of porters and guides were buck naked when they climbed up to the snow-line suggests that they were, on the whole, unused to the conditions on Kibo; that, and the fact that the name Kilimanjaro, if it is of Chagga origin (about which, see p74), roughly translates as 'That which is impossible for birds', suggests that they thought that it was therefore impossible for man to reach the top.

Charles Dundas is equally sceptical of the notion that the Chagga climbed Kilimanjaro before Meyer:

It is inconceivable that natives can ever have ascended to the crater rim, for apart from cold, altitude and superstitious fears, it is a sheer impossibility that they could have negotiated the ice. Nor is there any tradition among the natives that anyone went up as high.... Rebmann tells us that Rengwa, great-grandfather of the present chief of Machame, sent an expedition to investigate the nature of the ice, which descends very low above Machame, but is impossible to scale. Only one of the party survived, his hands and feet frozen and crippled for life; all the rest were destroyed by the cold, or by evil spirits, as the survivor reported.

and unless the parents were particularly inflexible, these opinions would count for something. Furthermore, in order for the boy to stand a chance with his potential suitor, he had to woo her. The Chaggas' courtship process involved, as elsewhere in the world, a lot of gift-giving, though the gifts followed a restrictive set of rules: spontaneity played little part in this process. The first gift, for example, from the man to the woman, was always a necklace. In return, the Chagga male would be well rewarded, for traditionally in return the girl would dance naked all day with bells attached to her legs by her mother. Over the following days other gifts were exchanged until at one point the girl, having visited all her relatives, would be shut away for three months. No work would be done by the girl during this time, but instead she would given fattening food, and kept in a cage. At the end of this period a **dowry** would be paid, the marriage ceremony performed and the bride would be carried on the back of the Mkara (the traditional Chagga equivalent of the best man) to her new husband's house.

KILIMANJARO ECONOMY

Tourism is now the biggest earner in the region, though agriculture, as you will discover, is still very much part of the local economy. The volcanic soil of the mountain slopes, so rich with nutrients, is amongst the most fertile in East Africa. Thanks to the regular and reliable rainfall blown in from the Indian Ocean (see p71), and the proliferation of springs trickling forth from the bare rock, Kilimanjaro is also one of the damper parts of the region, and the south-eastern slopes particularly so, thus increasing still further the agricultural fecundity of the mountain.

On the lower slopes of Kilimanjaro annual staple crops such as beans, maize and millet are grown, while cash-crops such as Arabica coffee are planted in the *kihamba* land further up the mountainside. Bananas are also grown at this altitude, their leaves and stems providing both a nutrient-rich mulch for the coffee trees and fodder for the livestock that are traditionally grazed at this height. In Chagga society it is customary for a farmer's land to be divided between his sons on his death; whilst this may seem a fair way of dividing land, it also means that farmer's landholdings diminish in size with every generation, and many farms are now less than a hectare in size.

The Chagga are also keen bee-keepers, the hives being hollow sections of a tree trunk closed at both ends by bungs and left to hang in the trees; you may well see these trunks in the forest zone of Kilimanjaro. Once the swarm has taken possession and completed the combs the bees are smoked out, the bung removed and the honey collected.

PART 4: DAR ES SALAAM AND NAIROBI

The following chapter is devoted to the two cities that you are most likely to fly into for a trek up Kilimanjaro — namely Dar es Salaam and Nairobi. The guides to these two places are deliberately rather brief but they should be adequate for finding your way around the cities, and for finding somewhere to sleep and eat as well to experience something of urban Africa. We also explain, at the end of each city, how to get to Kilimanjaro.

With the opening of Kilimanjaro International Airport there is, of course, now a third, and much more convenient place to touch down in East Africa. Details of this airport are given on p128.

Dar es Salaam

Dar es Salaam is a city with an identity crisis: a large metropolis (population two million-plus) which behaves as if it were a small and sleepy seaside town; a city that was at the forefront of the country's struggle for independence in the 1950s and yet still contains the finest collection of dusty old colonial buildings in possibly the whole of East Africa; and a place that everybody thinks is the capital of Tanzania but isn't. It *is* the commercial heart of the country, however, and has been almost since its inception in the 1860s by Sultan Sayyid Majid of Zanzibar. Intended as a mainland port for many of the goods and spices being traded on his island, the sultan, a man of poetic bent, named his new city Dar es Salaam (Haven of Peace). And peacefully was how it spent its first few years as the sultan died soon after founding the city, allowing Bagamoyo, a dhow port to the north, to emerge as the pre-eminent harbour on this particular stretch of the east coast. Missionaries from Europe added fresh impetus to Dar with their arrival in the 1880s, but it was the coming of the Germans in 1891 that really gave this city a fillip, the colonials feeling that the harbour here was more suitable to their steam-powered craft than Bagamoyo. Having made Dar their seat of power, it remained the capital until 1973 when the Tanzanian government decided to move the legislature to Dodoma, smack in the geometric heart of the country – which probably seemed like a good idea at the time, until somebody pointed out the lack of available water and other basic amenities there.

So while the legislature may meet in Dodoma, most of the politicking and indeed everything else of importance takes place here in Dar. For tourists, there's nothing particularly special to warrant a long stay in this city; but by the same token, don't fret too much if you do have to spend some time in Dar: it's pleasant, it's laid back and, compared to Nairobi, it's a whole lot saner too.

ARRIVAL

Though safer than arriving in Nairobi, it still pays to be on your guard when landing in Dar: like a recently hatched turtle taking to the ocean for the first time, you are at your most vulnerable when you land in a new country – and even in The Haven of Peace there are plenty of sharks out there. There are two terminals at Dar airport, about 700m apart from each other. Arriving from overseas, you will land at **Terminal Two**, the busier of the two, about 12km out from the town centre to the west. A **taxi** into town will set you back about Ts5000 during the day, and about half as much again at night; ignore or haggle with those drivers who quote you a price significantly higher than this. Better still, and certainly cheaper, are the **shuttle buses** (daytime only, Ts1000) that meet most international flights and offer a door-to-door service to your hotel, though check with the driver first that he is going your way. A third option is to take a **dalla-dalla** into town for Ts150. Going **to the airport**, look for the dalla-dalla signed U/Ndege that departs from the New Posta transport stand; leave in plenty of time – it can take well over an hour.

ORIENTATION AND GETTING AROUND

Navigating your way around central Dar is no easy task. Things are fairly straighforward on the coast, where the Kivukoni Front/Ocean Road follows the shore from the train station to the Ocean Road Hospital and beyond. But step back from the shore and you find yourself in a labyrinth of small streets, many of which curve imperceptibly but dramatically enough to confuse and disorientate. Keep the map on p113 with you, using it first to help you find your way to the tourist office (see below) where they have a more detailed and extensive map of the city. They will also be able to help you out with the city's **public transport** system, which can also be rather confusing. Buses and dalla-dallas ply all the main routes, though finding where they start and stop can be difficult. Ask locals, your hotel, or take a cab. Fortunately, central Dar is compact enough to walk around

SERVICES

Tourist office

There's a tourist office on Samora Avenue (Mon–Fri 8am–4pm; Sat 8am–12.30pm; ☎ 213 1555) whose knowledge of the city is rather patchy, but they may well have a copy of the free bi-monthly *Dar Guide* magazine, the most useful rundown of the city, and they smile a lot, too, which is nice.

Banks

There are **cashpoints** at Standard Chartered (Visa only) on Garden Avenue and Sokoine Drive, and a Barclays **ATM** (Visa and MasterCard) opposite the Royal Palm Hotel. The moneychanger in Coastal Travels on Upanga Road allows you to take dollars out on your credit card (Visa and MasterCard). They charge a hefty 7% plus US$2 per transaction though were also recently offering a free

❑ **Embassies and consulates in Dar es Salaam**
If you can't find the address you need in the following list, or for the latest addresses and phone numbers, check the *Dar Guide*.

Belgium Plot 5, Ocean Rd, Sea View, ☎ 2112688
Burundi Plot 1007, Lugalo Rd, Upanga, ☎ 2117615
Canada Plot 38, Mirambo St/Garden Ave, ☎ 2112831
Denmark Ghana Ave, ☎ 2113887
Egypt Plot 24, Garden Ave, ☎ 2113591
Finland Mirambo St/Garden Ave, ☎ 2119170
France AH Mwinyi Rd, Kinondoni, ☎ 2666021
Germany 10th Floor, Investment House, Samora Ave, ☎ 2117409
Ireland Plot 1131, Msasani Rd, Oysterbay, ☎ 2602355
Italy Plot 316, Lugalo Rd, Upanga, ☎ 2115935
Japan Plot 1018, AH Mwinyi Rd, Upanga, ☎ 2115827
Kenya 12th Floor, Investment House, Samora Ave, ☎ 2112811
Malawi Plot 38, AH Mwinyi Rd, Oysterbay, ☎ 2666284
Mozambique Plot 25, Garden Ave, ☎ 2116502
Netherlands ATC House, Ohio St/Garden Ave, ☎ 2130428
Norway Mirambo St/Garden Ave, ☎ 2118807
Rwanda Plot 32, AH Mwinyi Rd, Upanga, ☎ 2117631
South Africa Mwaya Rd, Masaki, Msasani Peninsula, ☎ 2601800
Spain Plot 99B, Kinondoni Rd, Kinondoni, ☎ 2666018
Sweden MiramboSt/Garden Ave, ☎ 2111235
Switzerland Plot 79, Kinondoni Rd, Kinondoni, ☎ 2666008
Uganda Plot 25, Msasani Rd, Oysterbay, ☎ 2666730
United Kingdom Hifadhi Hse, Samora Ave/Azikiwe St, ☎ 2112953
United States Plot 140, Msese Rd, off Kinondoni Rd, ☎ 2666010
Zimbabwe Plot 297, East Upanga, off AH Mwinyi Rd, ☎ 2118481

three-minute phone call to anywhere in the world to those who change money
with them. For cashing **travellers' cheques**, visit the banks; the best rates in
Tanzania are usually those offered by NBC, whose main office is on the corner
opposite the Azania Front Lutheran Church and the New Africa Hotel; for later
opening hours, try the moneychangers down Samora Avenue.

Communications

The main **post office** is on Maktaba Street (Mon-Fri 8am–4.30pm, Sat
9am–noon). The **telephone office** is on Bridge Street, and is open 7.45am–midnight on weekdays, and 8.30am–midnight at weekends. There are as yet no
unofficial offices of the type found in Nairobi, though phonecard phones, currently the cheapest option, are popping up all over the city. You won't have any
trouble finding an **Internet** café in Dar; they are everywhere. Most tourists head
for the one in the Safari, though this is because of its convenient location rather
than anything to do with the service provided.

❑ Dar's area code is ☎ 022. If phoning from outside Tanzania dial ☎ +255-22.

Car hire

Hertz (☎ 2112967, 🖹 2112954; 💻 www.hertz.com) are based in the Royal Palm Hotel. For a big four-wheel drive (4WD) suitable for four people they charge US$120 per day plus 20% VAT; the first 100km per day are free; thereafter it's US$0.90 per km. For a smaller car suitable for two people, it's the same rules, but the fee is US$80 per day plus 20%, and the excess over 100km is US$0.80. Curiously, it is not much more expensive if you actually hire a driver with your rental vehicle. Though this puts the price up to US$130 per day plus 20%, it does include both the fuel and, of course, the driver (though you still have to pay the US$0.90 excess after 100km).

Far cheaper, if a little less reliable, are the automobiles supplied by Evergreen Car Rental (☎ 2183345, 🖹 2183348; 💻 evergreen@raha.com) on Nkrumah St, with self-drive 4WDs from US$45 per day, plus US$10 if taken out of town, and an extra US$0.50 for every kilometre over 120km. They also offer a driver-hire service. As with all rental vehicles, check its condition carefully before setting out.

Trekking agencies

You *can* organize your Kili trek from here, though unless there are mitigating circumstances you'd be daft to do so, it being far easier and a lot cheaper to catch a bus to Moshi and arrange it from there. The average price in Dar is about US$750, though transport to the mountain from Dar is included in this. Recommended companies include:

● **Coastal Travels** Upanga Road, (PO Box 3052, ☎ 2117959, 🖹 2118647; 💻 safari @coastal.cc, aviation@coastal.cc). The most established agent in the city with offices in both Dar es Salaam and Zanzibar airports.

● **Easy** On the front to the east of the car park, on the first floor of Avalon House, Zanaki St, (PO Box 1428, ☎ 2123526, 🖹 2113842; 💻 easytrav el@raha.com). Claim to do all the routes up Kili.

● **JMT African Heart Expeditions** at the Safari Inn (☎/🖹 2124503; 💻 www. africanheart.com). Do the Marangu, Machame and Umbwe routes.

● **Rickshaw Travels** in the Royal Palm Hotel (☎ 2114094, 🖹 2115110). Expensive but trustworthy.

WHERE TO STAY

Those who came to Dar with the intention of **camping** will, if they do so, find themselves at least 25km out of town on the northern beaches at either the Rungwe or Silver Sands hotels, which both offer camping facilities for about Ts1000 per person. Though a shuttle bus runs three times a day from Silver Sands to the New Africa Hotel in central Dar, it is our considered opinion that you're far better off staying in a hostel or hotel in town. The following are listed in **price order**, with the **cheapest first**.

● *Jambo Inn* (☎ 2110711, 🖹 2110686 – though signs say that advance bookings are not allowed!) Libya St; en suite sgl/dbl Ts7200/12,000, or Ts18,000 for air-conditioned 'executive' room. Just a few doors down from the Safari (see p112)

❏ **Abbreviations**

Throughout this book we have used the following abbreviations when writing about accommodation: **s/c** is short for self-contained, a local term meaning that the room comes with a bathroom (ie the room is en suite or attached); **sgl/dbl/tpl** means single/double/triple rooms.

For example, where we have written 's/c sgl/dbl/tpl US$35/40/45', we mean that a self-contained single room costs US$35 per night, a self-contained double costs US$40, and a self-contained triple costs US$45.

---

on Libya Street, the Jambo is a scruffy but very welcoming hotel, slightly cheaper than its neighbour but way friendlier. The restaurant serves Indian, English, Chinese and Pakistani food, and there's a buffet lunch for Ts3000.
● *Safari Inn* (☎ 2138101; 🖳 safari-inn@mailcity.com) Band St, off Libya Street; sgl/dbl Ts7800/9000 to Ts18,000. The budget favourite, despite the best efforts of the miserable staff to frighten travellers away. All the rooms are en suite, though some are a bit gloomy. There's a popular Internet café here too. The room rates include something that resembles a breakfast, only smaller.
● *Econolodge* (☎ 2116048, 🖺 2116053; 🖳 econolodge@raha.com), Libya St; s/c sgl/dbl/tpl Ts10,000/15,000/18,000 up to Ts27,000 for double with air-con. Not quite as 'Econo' as it makes out, though still pretty good value by the standards of Dar. Singles, doubles and triples are all spacious, and all come with bathroom.
● *Lutheran Hostel* (☎ 2126247/2120734) behind Swiss Air on Sokoine Drive; sgl/dbl US$18/21 up to US$30 for an executive room. Hostel occupying a prime slice of real estate in downtown Dar, and with a reasonable Chinese restaurant on the ground floor, though there are better value places in town.
● *Starlight Hotel* (☎ 2119387, 🖺 2119389; 🖳 www.hotelguide.com) Bibi Titi Mohamed St; Ts30,000/36,000 sgl/dbl. Another hotel, like the Peacock below, that seems to cater mainly for local businessmen and warrants a mention largely due to its position in the mid-range price bracket. Impersonal looking but friendly, central and – with all 150 rooms equipped with air-con, hot water, TV and fridge – fair value too.

MAP KEY				
	Ⓢ	Bank	Λ	Camping Site
	🏛	Museum	☆	Police
⌂ Place to stay	📖	Library / Bookstore	☾	Mosque
○ Place to eat	✝	Church	●	Other
✉ Post office	✝	Cathedral	⊘	Bus Station
ⓘ Tourist information	✗	Internet	⛴	Ferry Service

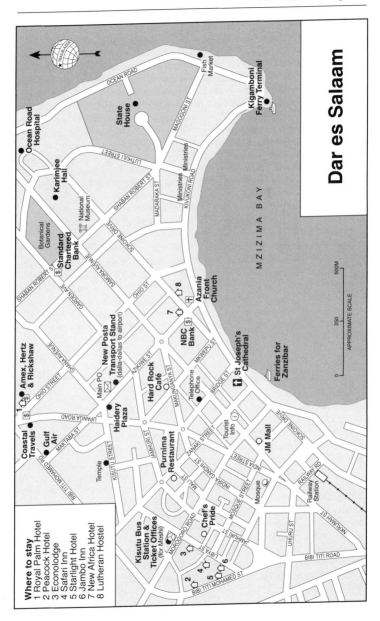

Dar es Salaam

Where to stay
1 Royal Palm Hotel
2 Peacock Hotel
3 Econolodge
4 Safari Inn
5 Starlight Hotel
6 Jambo Inn
7 New Africa Hotel
8 Lutheran Hostel

● *Peacock Hotel* (☎ 2114126, 🖹 2117962; 🖳 www.peacock-hotel.co.tz) Bibi Titi Mohamed St; sgl/dbl/tpl US$70/80/125; bigger dbl rooms (with sofas!) US$15 extra. Refreshingly free of any pretension, an ugly but friendly establishment that sees few tourists, reaping its custom instead from local businessmen. It's OK, with all the facilities you'd expect from a hotel of this class, but to be honest is probably only getting a mention here because of the shortage of other mid-range hotels in Dar – and it's a tad overpriced too.

● *New Africa Hotel* (☎ 2117050, 🖹 2116731; 🖳 reservations@raha.com) corner of Azikiwe/Sokoine Drive; sgl/dbl US$140/165 up to US$200. In a better location than the Royal Palm, though not with quite the same level of sophistication, the New Africa stands on the site of the Germans' original Kaiserhoff. Home to Dar's main casino, as well as a host of bars and restaurants, the New Africa's rooms have everything you'd expect from a hotel of this calibre, including mini-bar, satellite TV, telephones with Internet hook-up and so on. If you're willing to pay over a hundred dollars for all this, you may as well pay the extra US$10 for one of the rooms with a sea view. A courtesy airport shuttle is available to passengers on certain flights.

● *Royal Palm Hotel* (☎ 2112416, 🖹 2113981) Ohio Street; sgl/dbl US$225/250 up to US$1500/1525 for the president suite. Formerly the Sheraton, this is *the* top place in town, with a swimming pool, gym and all mod-cons, as well as being the base for Dar's AMEX representatives, Hertz, Rickshaw Travels and a Bureau de Change that stays open from 8am to 8pm. Even if you're not staying here, do call in to have a peek at the photos of Kili's summit by John Cleare that adorn the shopping walkway, or simply to take advantage of their fierce air-con.

WHERE TO EAT

Many eateries in Dar close on Sundays. One that doesn't, and which is currently the most popular place in town amongst travellers – and indeed, amongst many locals too – is *Chef's Pride* on Chagga Street. It is a popularity that is well deserved: tasty, huge portions of food, very reasonable prices, a location close to the cheaper hotels and English football on the telly is a combination that for some is hard to resist, and many travellers, having tried the food once, venture nowhere else in the city.

If you can tear yourself away from there, for alternative cheap-eats the Indian quarter of central Dar, particularly around the junction of Indira Gandhi and Zanaki streets, is as good a place as any to start looking. *Purnima* on Zanaki Street is a great little place, where a plate of bhajias with various sauces and curds will make you poorer by only Ts500 or so. There are other similar places around here – follow your nose to find them. For the unadventurous there are fast food snack stands at the JM Mall on the corner of Mission St and Samora Avenue, including *Nando's*, *Pizza Inn*, *Chick Inn* and the *Creamy Inn* ice-cream parlour. There's also an Italian-orientated *Hard Rock Café* on Makunganya Street.

For more refined cuisine in plusher surroundings, try the restaurants in the upmarket hotels, including the *Sawasdee Thai* at the New Africa, and the *Raj* at the Royal Palm. Your bank manager won't thank you for dining here, but your stomach certainly will.

A TOUR OF THE CITY

None of Dar's attractions is going to make your eyes pop out on springs from their sockets, but the following tour is fine for those with time to kill in the city and a cursory interest in the place. For those in a hurry, the National Museum at least is worth seeing (see box below), being the most absorbing and, for Kili-bound trekkers, the most relevant attraction in Dar. If you'd prefer to join an **organized walking tour**, call in at the New Africa Hotel and pick up a brochure (☎ 0811 605109). The two-and-a-half-hour tours include many of the attractions described below, with some food-tasting thrown in as well. One word of

National Museum

Open 9.30am–6pm daily; US$3, or US$2 for students, or you can pay in Tanzanian shillings at a rate of US$1=Ts900. Tanzania's National Museum fares badly when compared to Kenya's version, but is still mildly diverting at times, and a cool escape from the heat of the day. And if you manage to avoid the marauding school parties, you may well have the entire complex to yourself, with only the cleaner for occasional company.

Begin your tour by walking through the back door to a small courtyard, home to an even smaller **memorial garden** to the twelve victims who perished in the US Embassy bombing in Dar on 7 August 1998. Similar in style to the one in Nairobi, the **sculpture** here includes twisted metal and a window pane shattered by the blast, as well as a face emerging from concrete, presumably recalling those who were buried in the rubble.

The **original museum building** that stands beyond is of little relevant interest to those heading to Kilimanjaro, nor indeed to anyone with its rather lame displays of marine and ethnographic items. If you hunt around in the latter you'll find a couple of old Chagga storage baskets and some interesting old photos of tribal customs, but nothing really to keep you in this musty old building for too long.

The main building, however, is a different story. Here you'll find a number of absorbing displays including the **Hall of Man**, which describes our evolution with the help of some apposite objects from Leakey's discoveries at **Olduvai Gorge**, as well as a few items of particular interest to those climbing Kili in the **History Gallery** upstairs, which maps out in concise and thorough detail the story of Tanzania. Take your time wandering around, looking in particular for the following items of Kiliphernalia: Hans Meyer's original **letter** to the German representative in Zanzibar, begging for a ransom of ten thousand rupees to be paid to Chief Abushiri, by whom he had been taken hostage during his second expedition to Kilimanjaro; and a **map** of 1856 which was based on the testimonies of Erhardt and Rebmann, in which 'Kilimanjaro' (sic) is clearly shown along with the label *montagne couverte de neige* ('mountain covered with snow') – a neat riposte to Cooley and his ilk who were still denying the existence of snow in this part of the world (see p79). Overall, an hour or two well spent.

warning: if any of the streets listed below seem unhealthily deserted – the lanes around State House and Ocean Road in particular can be a little *too* quiet at times – consider taking an alternative and safer route.

Your tour begins around the back of the **Azania Front Lutheran Church**, built on the seafront at the turn of the century by German missionaries. Heading east along the promenade past many old colonial buildings now used by the Tanzanian authorities to house various ministries, walk round the south-eastern tip of the peninsula and on to the **fish market**, Tanzania's most vibrant attraction. Having ensured all money and valuables are securely tucked away, feel free to take a wander around – it's at its best early in the morning – and see what the local fishermen have managed to catch overnight. Retracing your steps for a few metres, take the first turning on the right (west) up Magogoni Street. Surrounded by spacious grounds, **State House**, built by the British in the years following World War One, stands to your right; you will get your best view of the house itself at the very end of the road at the junction with Luthuli St. Crossing this junction and continuing straight on along Shaban Robert St, to your right is the **National Museum** (see the box on p115); a right turn after that will land you on one of the prettier streets in central Dar, the eastern end of Samora Avenue, with the **botanical gardens** to your left and, on the opposite side towards the end of the street, steeple-topped **Karimjee Hall**, where Nyerere (see p53) was sworn in as Tanzania's first president. Facing the end of the street and hidden behind high walls is the now-defunct **Ocean Road Hospital**, another German building dating back to the last years of the nineteenth century. Stroll round to the sea-facing front of the hospital to study the rather curious architecture, a hybrid of Arabic and European styles, and to view the curious spiked mace that sits atop the hospital roof.

From here you have two choices: one is to continue your walk along the coast road back to the fish market and on to the church; the other is to return to the junction behind the hospital, press on for another hundred metres or so southwards, then take a right and amble along attractive, tree-shaded Sokoine Drive back to the Lutheran church.

MOVING ON – TO KILIMANJARO

Buses

The **bus** station and most of the ticket offices are conveniently located in the Kisutu terminal right in the heart of downtown on Libya Street, although a new terminal has just opened up out of town that may in future be the main station. Choose your bus company carefully: despite the presence of speed ramps and traffic police along certain stretches, the Dar to Moshi highway is notorious for the number of accidents that occur along it and often it's the same few bus companies that are involved.

One to recommend is Fresh Ya Shamba, whose buses do take a little longer to travel between the two cities than their competitors but that's simply because their drivers are alert to road signs, other road users, pedestrians and so forth.

Their buses leave at 7.30am to Moshi (Ts9500), 9am to Arusha (Ts12,500). Other recommended companies include Scandinavia (two buses to Arusha, at 7am and 8.30am) and Dar Express (7am, Ts7500).

Flights
Air Tanzania flies daily to **Kilimanjaro airport** at a different time everyday. The flight takes fifty minutes. Air Excel have a daily flight to **Arusha airport** at 4.20pm (1hr 50min; US$180), while Coastal Aviation on Upanga Road have daily flights from Dar via Zanzibar to Arusha at 9am, arriving at 11.30am at Arusha (US$190). Precision Air also have daily flights to Arusha via Zanzibar, as well as direct flights on Tuesdays, Fridays and Sundays (direct service US$165).

Nairobi

Rough as a lion's tongue, East Africa's largest city has come quite a long way since its inception in May 1899 as a humble railway supply depot on the Mombasa to Kampala line. It is a city that has suffered much from plagues, fire and reconstruction – and that was just in its first ten years – yet it has continued obstinately to prosper and grow, rising from a population of exactly zero in 1898

❏ **Nine useful things to know about Kenya**

● Most countries need a **visa** for Kenya, including Britain and the US. Get your visa before leaving home. You can buy your visa at Nairobi's Jomo Kenyatta Airport, though this takes time and it is not unknown for officials to request bribes before issuing them. Welcome to Kenya.

● One thing to remember: as long as you remain in East Africa, there is no need to buy a multiple-entry Kenya visa if you are flying into Kenya but wish to visit Tanzania or Uganda too, as long as you stay in those countries for less than two weeks, and providing, of course, your Kenyan visa has not expired by the time you return to Kenya.

● The official **language** of Kenya is Swahili. For a quick guide to Swahili, see p230. In addition, many Kenyans speak both their own tribal language and English, which is widely spoken everywhere.

● As with Tanzania, Kenya is **three hours ahead of GMT**. Note that, in addition to Kenya time, many locals use **Swahili time**, which runs from dawn to dusk (or 6am to 6pm to be precise). See p62 for details on how to convert between GMT and Swahili time.

● The Kenyan **currency** is the shilling (Ks). At the time of writing, US$1=Ks78.58, UK£1=Ks121.81. Don't change money on the street.

● Kenya's **electricity supply** uses the British-style three-pin plugs on 220-240V.

● The **international dialling code** for calling Kenya is ☎ 254; Nairobi's code is ☎ 02.

● The **emergency telephone number** is ☎ 999.

● The **opening hours** in Kenya are typically 8am to 5 or 6pm.

to between 1.5 and 3 million today. Official recognition of the city's increasing importance arrived in 1907 when the British made it the capital of their East African territories, and you can still find the occasional colonial relic in the city today, from the Indian-influenced architecture of a few downtown buildings (shipped over from the subcontinent, the Indians supplied much of the labour force used in building the railway) to some distinctly elegant hotels and orderly public gardens (including one, just to the north of Kenyatta Avenue, which still bears a statue of Queen Victoria). But if you came with the specific purpose of seeing a faded colonial relic you'll be disappointed: because as the capital of the Kenyan republic and the UN's fourth official 'World Centre', Nairobi is East Africa's most modern, prosperous and glamourous metropolis. It is also, first and foremost, black Africa at its loudest and proudest.

SECURITY

A few years back some genius dubbed Kenya's capital 'Nairobberi', and lesser geniuses have been retreading that joke ever since. Tired as the gag may be, however, it does still have relevance, for Nairobi's reputation as East Africa's Capital of Crime is well founded. The most notorious hotspot is the area immediately to the **east of Moi Avenue**, including **River Road**, a popular location with travellers because of the cheap hotels there. During daytime violent robbery is rare though certainly not unheard of, simply because it's so packed with people; pickpocketing, on the other hand, is rife at this time, probably for the same reason. At night, both techniques are common. The **airport**, from the immigration counter and passport control to the arrivals' hall, is also a favourite with the local law-breakers as is the **bus into town**.

To avoid being another victim, be vigilant, leave valuables with the hotel (having first checked their security procedures); make sure that they give you a receipt for any goods deposited too. Tuck moneybelts under your clothing. Furthermore, don't walk around at night but take a taxi, even if it's for just a few hundred metres. This last piece of advice is particularly true of the area around River Road: I've heard of people being attacked even as they made their way back to the Iqbal Hotel from the Taj restaurant, a walk of some twenty yards!

It can only be to your advantage if you are over-cautious for your first couple of days in the capital. After that, if you're still staying here, you can begin to appreciate Nairobi's charms – which do exist, and are not entirely inconsiderable – and can begin to moan, like the rest of the travellers here, about how unfair guidebook writers are about Kenya's capital.

ARRIVAL

Before landing at Nairobi's Jomo Kenyatta International Airport read the section about crime and security in the capital. Heed the advice about being vigilant, and from the moment your foot hits the runway tarmac be on your guard against malefactors, and not only among your fellow passengers: signs above your head on the way to passport control warn against the giving and receiving of bribes, proving that some airport staff aren't above a little corruption. Arriving in Kenya without a **visa** does give crooked officials an opportunity to extort a little extra cash, so do try to arrange this before you arrive. If you haven't got a visa you should get one before passing through passport control, from the glass booth to the right of the hall (payment in US dollars or pounds sterling only). Passing through **immigration**, **luggage collection** is straight down the stairs. Once again be vigilant and having retrieved your bags check that nothing is missing: when climbing Kilimanjaro, there are few things more annoying than finding that your thermally insulated mountain hat that you thought was safely tucked away in the side-pocket of your rucksack, had in fact been taken by a light-fingered baggage handler and is now being used as a makeshift tea cosy in the staffroom of Jomo Kenyatta Airport.

Having walked through **customs** to the arrivals' hall, to your right is a **moneychanger** offering, as moneychangers are wont to do at airports worldwide, dismal rates, and an **ATM** that accepts Visa cards – your best bet for a fair rate at the airport, though you could pay for your cab in dollars and wait to change money in town.

You have a number of choices in tackling the 15km from the airport to the centre of Nairobi. Taxis cost about Ks700 with bargaining, or Ks1000 (a fixed rate in this case) in one of the capacious London-style black cabs. Or before 8pm you can take the number 34 bus that runs down River Road (Ks25). Remember to be careful of pickpockets on this route. Incidentally, on the way into town, you pass the huge new US Embassy being built to the left of the main road. For details on what happened to the old one, see p125.

ORIENTATION AND GETTING AROUND

Despite decades of unplanned growth, a mass of sprawling suburbs and a wholesale aversion to street numbers, central Nairobi is actually very easy to navigate, with nearly everything of interest to the traveller within walking distance of Kenyatta Avenue. A couple of obvious landmarks are the enormous **KANU Tower**, to the south of City Hall, and the even more enormous **Nation Centre**, a red Meccano-type structure nestling between two giant cylindrical towers just off the eastern end of the avenue. Central Nairobi is fairly compact and the fit will be able to walk everywhere. Buses and matatus run from early morning to late at night, though we strongly advise you to take taxis after dark. During the day things are much safer, though keep your wits about you. In the text we give the numbers of some of the buses you may need.

SERVICES

Banks

Banks and foreign exchange bureaux tend to share roughly the same opening hours: Mon–Fri 9am–3pm, Sat 9–11am (noon for private exchange bureaux). Many of the banks have **ATM**s (cash machines) too, with most accepting Visa cards. Be on your guard when withdrawing money from an ATM.

❏ **Embassies, consulates and high commissions in Nairobi**
Austria City House, 2nd floor, Wabera St, ☎ 228281
Australia Box 39341, Icipe House, Riverside Drive, ☎ 445034
Belgium Box 30461, Muthaiga, Limuru Rd, ☎ 741564
Canada Box 30481, Comcraft House, 6th floor, ☎ 214804
Denmark Box 40412, HFCK Building, 11th floor, Kenyatta Ave, ☎ 331088
Finland Box 30379, International House, 2nd floor, Mama Ngina St, ☎ 334408
France Box 41784, Barclays Plaza, 9th floor, Loita St, ☎ 339783
Germany Box 30180, Williamson House, 8th floor, 4th Ngong Ave, ☎ 712527
Israel Box 30354, Bishops Road, ☎ 722182
Italy Box 30107, International Life House, 9th floor, Mama Ngina St, ☎ 2115935
Spain Box 48868, Bruce House, 5th floor, Standard St, off Ngecha Rd, ☎ 582944
Uganda Box 60853, Uganda House, 5th floor, Kenyatta Ave, ☎ 330975
United Kingdom Box 30465, Upper Hill Road, ☎ 714699
Zambia Box 48741, Nyerere Road, ☎ 724796
Zimbabwe Box 30806, Minet ICDC House, 6th floor,Mamlaka Road, ☎ 721071

Communications

Big, bright and gleaming, the new **post office** (Mon–Fri 8am–6pm, Sat 9am–noon) occupies a fairly large slice of valuable real estate at the western end of Kenyatta Avenue. Registered, recorded and normal deliveries can be made here, and there's a poste restante counter. Extelcom, 100m west down Haile Selassie Avenue from the American Embassy Remembrance Garden, is the main **telephone** exchange, but they're not particularly cheap, with a minute to Britain costing a whopping Ks200; buying a phonecard from them and using the booths outside (the only booths from which you can make international calls) is a slightly less pricey alternative.

Cheapest of all, however, are the unofficial – and very possibly illegal – phone exchanges that have sprung up all over town, usually in dingy offices above or behind shops. These places are usually pretty chaotic, noisy (there are rarely any private booths) and the delay on the line can often be rather large, constituting a significant obstacle to free-flowing social intercourse. They are, however, very, very cheap, though rates do vary widely; Kashifnet, up the stairs between the Jamboree and Trendwear shops on Muindi Mbingu, is currently the cheapest, charging Ks25 per minute to Britain. To help you find these places, the touts who come up to you on the street and then stick to you like chewing gum on the sole of your shoe usually know the cheapest exchange *du jour*; in return, be sure to give them a small tip or agree to visit their handicraft shop/safari agency afterwards.

Opposite the Iqbal Hotel on Taveta Road, up the stairs between the shops, is a string of three or four **Internet places**, all with fairly quick connections and all charging a very reasonable Ks2 per minute (Ks1 at weekends), or Ks100 per hour, with some extra time free for long stints at the keyboard. If you don't wish to venture into the River Road area, there should be an Internet café near you, though around Kenyatta Avenue they tend to be a bit more expensive at about Ks3 per minute.

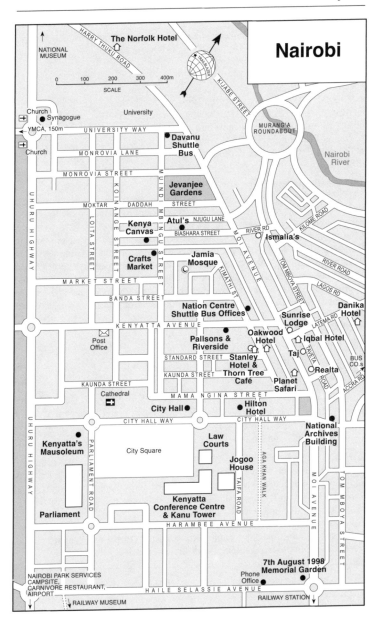

Trekking agencies

It's a lot cheaper to book your trek in Tanzania, though booking in Nairobi may be worthwhile if you intend to climb via the Rongai Route, which starts at the border between the two countries.

● **Kibo Slopes Safaris** (PO Box 58064; ☎ 717373, 🖹 716028; 🖳 www.kibosl opessafaris.com). Agent specializing in climbing Kilimanjaro from the northern side up the Rongai Route. Partner of Snow Cap in Moshi (see p153) and the German company Hauser Exkursionen (see p21). Prices start at US$1279 per person (for a group of six or more) for a Rongai trek including a side-trip up to Mawenzi Tarn Hut (or US$1124 without the side-trip).

● **Tropical Trekking** (see Tropical Trekking in Arusha, p142) have a branch office at Wilson Airport; contact 🖳 hoopoe@swiftkenya.com.

Camping equipment

Nairobi has the only trekking shop in the whole of East Africa; indeed it has two, both within 100 yards of each other, so this is your last chance to buy specialist camping equipment (though remember that you can rent everything you need from the trekking agencies in Arusha and Moshi, or from the stall at Marangu Gate; see p173). **Atul's** (☎ 228064) on Biashara St, more a haberdashery than anything else, is the only place in the city that rents out camping gear, though they're not cheap: Ks180 per day for a down sleeping bag for example. On the opposite side of the same street, though just over the other side of Muindi Mbingu, is **Kenya Canvas** (☎ 333509), with a smaller selection for sale only.

WHERE TO STAY

The following list of hostels and hotels is arranged with the cheapest first. Those intending to **camp** should check out the Nairobi Park Services Campsite on Magadi Road, just past Langata gate to the south of town, on the western perimeter of the Nairobi National Park. Clean, safe, cheap (Ks200 per person per night camping charge), this campsite has some dormitory beds (Ks300), tents for hire (Ks60 per person per night), a café and even satellite TV. Bus 126 or matatu 125 from the KBS bus station (3km east of town, take a cab to get there) will drop you off nearby. You can also camp at Planet Safari (see below).

● *Planet Safari* (☎ 229799, 🖹 211899; 🖳 www.planetkenyasafaris.com), Sonalux House, 9th Floor, Moi Avenue; dorm beds Ks300. Safari agency with tatty dorms attached, or you can pitch your tent on the roof for the same price. Use of the kitchen is also included as is the balcony café with a great view – well, an extensive one at least – over River Road and beyond. Agree to sign up for a safari (you'll almost feel obliged to if you stay here), and three nights' accommodation in the same tatty dorms are free. Other organizations such as *Prime Time*, in the next building, operate a similar deal.

❏ Nairobi's area code is ☎ 02. If phoning from outside Kenya dial ☎ +254-2.

● *Iqbal Hotel* (☎ 220914) Latema Road, entrance round the corner on Taveta Road; non s/c dorm/sgl/dbl Ks280/400/600. The longest established budget hostel in Nairobi, which for years survived on its reputation as a travellers' Mecca despite declining standards of helpfulness and security. With jolly Jason now guarding the door and helpful Hassan on reception, things have improved considerably – at the very moment that backpackers have started to leave for other hostels.

● *Danika* (☎ 230687) Dubois Road; sgl/dbl Ks500/600. Very secure, pleasant rooms matched by the attitude of the staff. Not exactly atmospheric, but safe; and that, in this neck of the jungle, is a very precious quality. They even have mosquito nets, which is a bonus.

● *YMCA* (☎ 724116) University Way; non s/c dorm/sgl/dbl Ks540/690/1180; s/c dorm/sgl/dbl Ks640/940/1480; add Ks320 half-board, Ks600 full-board. Despite the name, women, atheists and the elderly are all welcome at this friendly, secure hostel, currently the number one destination for those on a budget who don't fancy their chances in the hurly-burly of the River Road area. The real clincher, however, is the pool (Ks50 residents, Ks80 non-residents).

● *Oakwood Hotel* (☎ 220592/3, 🖷 332170) Kimathi Street; s/c sgl/dbl/tpl US$50/60/75 including breakfast. Wooden floors, wooden walls, wooden ceiling and wooden doors – spending a night at the Oakwood can make you feel like Charles II hiding from Parliament. The Oakwood's strengths are its location opposite the Thorn Tree Café, its elegant antique lift, the TV and video in each room, and its vague whiff of colonial charm. Not spectacular, but fine.

● *The Stanley* (☎ 228830/333233, 🖷 229388; 🖳 www.sarovahotels.com) Corner of Kenyatta Avenue and Kimathi Street; s/c sgl/dbl US$195/210. A luxury hotel with a bit of character, the Stanley first opened its doors to the very well-heeled in 1902 – making it just a few years younger than the city itself. Edward, Prince of Wales, Ernest Hemingway and Hollywood's finest from Ava Gardner to Clark Gable have all rested their eminent heads on the Stanley's sumptuously stuffed pillows. Victorian elegance still abounds, though the demands of the modern client have led to the introduction of a shopping arcade, swimming pool and gymnasium. Also plays host to the Thorn Tree Café.

● *The Norfolk* (☎ 216940, 🖷 216796; 🖳 www.lonrhohotels.com) Harry Thuku Road; room only prices: s/c sgl/dbl US$250/US$290; suites US$320–500. Nairobi's *other* historic hotel, and younger by two years, the Norfolk has been oozing class from its premises since it first opened its doors on Christmas Day 1904. Boasts the same facilities as The Stanley plus a fine collection of carriages and classic cars in the central courtyard and a more peaceful, out-of-town feel.

WHERE TO EAT

Kenya's cuisine is virtually indistinguishable from Tanzania's, being hearty, meaty and with an emphasis firmly on quantity rather than quality. Embodying this description is the legendary tourist-attraction-cum-restaurant, *Carnivore* (Langata Road, near the Nairobi National Park; take a taxi from the town centre), designed specifically for those people whose thoughts upon seeing the playful gambolling of a young impala for the first time is to wonder what it would taste like coated in a spicy barbecue sauce. Hartebeest, wildebeest, gazelle (Africa's very own fast food) and zebra can be found migrating across the pages of the menu most nights, and there are even a few vegetarian options too. To be honest, some of it – particularly the zebra – is revolting, but it's all good fun – and where else can you legitimately address the staff with that classic old chestnut 'Waiter, bring me some crocodile and make it snappy!'.

Vying with the celebrity of Carnivore is the **Thorn Tree Café**, something of a Mecca for travellers. Now on its third acacia, the original idea behind planting a tree in the middle of the courtyard was so that travellers could leave messages for other travellers on its thorns. Unfortunately, trees being trees, the roots of the previous two eventually started to undermine the building itself and had to be destroyed. As for the food here, it's a great place for a post-climb breakfast feed- up (Ks1000 all-u-can-eat fry-up, or Ks700 for the continental version), while at other times of the day they do a mean chicken dharia (Ks650), a local speciality made with tomatoes and fresh coriander and creamed spinach, all served with rice or ugali.

For cheaper and more mundane fare, the **Taj**, on Taveta Road, one of a host of cheap eateries around River Road, is a reasonable African-style Indian curry house: don't expect hot towels, flock wallpaper and Cobra beer, but do expect fast service, low prices and waiters who bring extra sauce if your rice or chapatis have outlasted your curry.

Other cheap options nearby include **Sunrise Lodge**, a non-too-friendly but very cheap café, **Realta**, a small place serving British-style fish and chips, and **Ismalia's**, a little to the north at the top end of River Road, which serves very cheap no-nonsense local food including a fine vegetarian choice.

National Museum

(Off Ngara Rd, near Uhuru Highway; every day, 9.30am–6pm; Ks200)

East Africa's foremost trove of tribal, troglodytic and taxidermically treated treasures, Kenya's National Museum is well worth an afternoon's browsing. The region's unparalleled fecundity of **wildlife** fills the main hall, with both room and exhibits pretty well stuffed (though why they feel the need to display these moth-eaten corpses when they've got their living descendants on the city's doorstep is a moot point). There's also a model of the nation's favourite pachyderm, Ahmed, an elephant so huge its tusks alone weighed a whopping 65kg each, faithfully cast in fibreglass (there presumably not being enough sawdust in Kenya to stuff the real thing). Perhaps the most interesting sections, however, are the following: the display celebrating Kenya's Asian immigrants, including a run-through of the building of the **Uganda Railway** from Mombasa to Kampala, a project that took over five years (August 1896 to December 1901) and claimed 582 lives; a wonderful collection of Joy Adamson's portraits of **Kenyan tribes** – look out for the depictions of people wearing ear-stretchers, and the priest enveloped in hippo teeth; and the startling prehistoric section, including the **1.6-million-year-old skeleton** of a boy and a couple of amusing and well-rendered 'caveman' dioramas.

A TOUR OF THE CITY

This half- to full-day walking tour is best done on a Sunday morning, when the hassle from safari touts is at its lowest and the gospel choirs are out in force on the streets and in the parks. It begins at the corner of Moi and Haile Selassie avenues, at the former site of the **American Embassy**, blown to smithereens on the 7 August 1998, allegedly by fundamentalist billionaire Osama Bin Laden and his Al-Qaeda gang. The site has now been landscaped into a very small **remembrance garden** (entry Ks20) where a concrete and stone memorial has been erected bearing the names of the Kenyan victims (who constituted all but twelve of the total 263 who perished). At the back of the enclosure is a glass pyramid sculpture containing some of the debris from that day, namely some twisted metal, a lump or two of concrete and a door handle. It's a busy junction, and the Co-op building behind – also badly damaged in the blast – is from the eyesore school of architecture; yet still the park manages to convey an atmosphere of the deepest poignancy.

From here, head north along Moi to the **National Archives Building** – a free art gallery and exhibition centre that's worth a nose around, particularly the African boot sale that is the ethnography section in the middle of the building. Opposite and just slightly to the south is City Hall Way, the **hall** itself lying about 400m along the road on the right. Before that, to your left, is a **statue** of benign old first president Jomo Kenyatta sitting regally overlooking the city square with his back to the **law courts**. To Kenyatta's left, rising imperiously from some stagnant ponds, are the **Kenyatta International Conference Centre**, like a giant crocus bud on the verge of opening, and the vertiginous **KANU Tower**, formerly the tallest building in the city and still one of the ugliest – though most locals would probably take issue with this opinion. (KANU, incidentally, are the most powerful party in Kenya and have dominated the political arena since independence.) Most glorious of all, however, are the marabou storks that are currently nesting in the trees by City Hall, spending their days swooping and gliding above the park.

Continuing along City Hall Way – past the **Holy Family Cathedral**, neatly juxtaposed with the casino directly opposite – to the left of the road, lined with flags and guarded by two black lions and several bored-looking guards in neo-colonial ceremonial livery, is the object of the Kenyatta statue's gaze: his own **mausoleum**. Next door and adorned with a rather quaint clocktower that would not look out of place in a small market town in middle England is the **Parliament**, which can be visited; entry is gained through the entrance on Harambee Avenue, marked by a frieze of what appears to be men in oversized pith helmets.

From this entrance, continue west along Harambee to the Uhuru Highway. You now have two choices: turn right and head towards the national museum; or left, across Haile Selassie Avenue and through the waste ground to the **Railway Museum** (everyday, 8.15am–4.45pm; Ks200/100 adults/students). I would opt for the latter: if it's possible to feel nostalgia for a time that one never knew, and a place that one has never visited before, then this is the museum that will prompt those feelings with its fading photos of British royalty riding in the cow-catcher seats and its old posters advertising the newly-opened Uganda railway. This is truly an endearing little museum, and the rusty locomotive graveyard out front is a fascinating place for a nose around too.

Heading back north along the Uhuru Highway, 15 minutes along you'll come to a large roundabout and the centre of worship in the city, surrounded as it is by a **synagogue** (to the north-east) and no less than **four churches** (St Paul's Catholic Chapel to the north-west, with St Andrews behind it up the hill, the First Church of Christ Scientist further along the same road, and the city's main Lutheran church on the roundabout's south-western edge). From the roundabout you can continue north for fifteen hot and dusty minutes along the highway to the National Museum (see p124), or you can turn east along University Way, taking a right turn south through the business heart of Nairobi along Muindi Mbingu Street. On the way you might wish to take a short detour to visit the **Jamia Mosque** (Nairobi's most impressive mosque but closed to infidels), and the tawdry craft market, before rejoining Kenyatta Avenue. Take a left here, pausing on the way at one of the street vendors to pick up some reading material – a month-old *Newsweek*, say, or a copy of the filthy but ubiquitous *Secret Emotions* – to peruse at your table, and after a couple of hundred metres you'll come to the final port of call on this walk, the Thorn Tree Café, with its overpriced but wonderfully cold beer.

MOVING ON – TO KILIMANJARO

With the sad demise of the **train** service between Voi and Moshi, on the Nairobi to Mombasa line, the only way overlanders can reach the towns and villages around Kilimanjaro now is by **bus**. (It would be worth enquiring at the train station as to whether this service has been resumed, for there can surely be no more splendid a way to travel through East Africa than in the faded colonial grandeur of a carriage belonging to Kenya Railways. The train to **Mombasa**, incidentally, leaves on Mondays, Tuesdays, Thursdays and Fridays at 7pm from the terminus to the south of Haile Selassie Road, arriving, all being well – which it very often isn't – at 8.36am the next morning. Fares are Ks3000 in first class, Ks2100 in second, Ks350 third.)

For the best view of Kilimanjaro as you travel to Arusha, sit on the left-hand side of the bus. Though Arusha Express is, sadly, no longer with us, **Tawfiq** and **Takrim** offer buses to Arusha for around Ks600 (these buses then go on to Dar es Salaam). Their offices are at the northern end of Accra Road; watch your possessions at the station, and don't expect even a hint of luxury with either of these two. It's about seven hours to Arusha.

Far more convenient and comfortable are the **shuttle buses**. There are three main companies operating these little minibuses to Arusha. **Riverside** (☎ 229618, 🖺 241032) 3rd Floor, Pan African House, Kenyatta Avenue, have two buses, at 8.25am (which continues on to Moshi) and 2pm. Officially the fare is US$25 to Arusha, or US$30 to Moshi, but it doesn't take much bargaining to get the

'residents' price of Ks1000 to Arusha (Ks1500 to Moshi). The second company is **Davanu** (☎ 222002, 🖹 216475) 4th floor, Windsor Building, corner of
Muindi Mbingu Street and University Way, which also operates two buses (8am
to Moshi via Arusha and 2pm to Arusha only), though they're a little pricier
(US$30, US$35 to Moshi), and trying to get the residents' price seems more difficult here. Though both of these companies promise to collect you from your
hotel, in reality if you're staying anywhere in the centre of Nairobi they will
probably ask you to go to the Stanley or Norfolk hotels and pick you up there.
These two established companies have been joined by a new outfit, **Pallsons** (☎
708999) at Pan African House, Kenyatta Avenue, which, though they go to
Arusha only, currently offer the best deal. Having been operating only a short
time, their buses are still sparkling new and, because they're still relatively
unknown, are usually fairly empty too, allowing you to stretch out; they are also
fitted with televisions, though this is a debatable bonus. They too charge all passengers the residents' rate of Ks1000.

Crossing the border
Despite the chaos of souvenir hawkers and Masai warriors that surrounds the
Kenya-Tanzania border crossing at Namanga, the border formalities themselves
are straightforward enough. On the Kenyan side you'll doubtless have to queue
to have your passport stamped, and on the Tanzanian side there's usually a little wait while the customs officials cast a cursory eye over your belongings and
draw a little chalk cross on the side of your bag. It is possible to change money
at the border though the crossing is renowned for its charlatans so you're probably better off waiting until Arusha.

Flights
Air Tanzania fly daily to **Kilimanjaro International Airport** from Nairobi on
Mondays, Wednesdays and Fridays at 1.30pm, arriving 50 minutes later.
Precision Air also do the trip on the same days, and just fifteen minutes later at
1.45pm, taking ten minutes more (US$112).

PART 5: ARUSHA, MOSHI AND MARANGU

Kilimanjaro International Airport

Is Kilimanjaro the first mountain to have its own international airport? It is situated equidistant between Moshi and Arusha, to the south of the disused rail-tracks. Arriving is straightforward: the terminal is small and you'll instantly be ushered into the Arrivals Hall. The baggage hall and immigration formalities are easily negotiated – Kilimanjaro is also one of only four places where you can pick up a visa if your own country of residence does not have a Tanzanian consulate or embassy. There is also a cash-only moneychanger here offering reasonable rates for the dollar, though as yet no ATM. To get to Arusha or Moshi, both about 45 minutes away, see pp131-2 and p145.

Departing from Tanzania, things are just as simple. The check-in desks face the door as you walk into the departure lounge. Don't be in too much of a hurry to get through customs, for there's even less to do on that side of the X-ray machine than there is on this side. Instead, go for a beer (Ts1000) in the café to the right of the check-in desks, which isn't as big a rip-off as many airport establishments – and where you can sit and sip while gazing at a stuffed leopard catching a stuffed antelope. The food isn't too nasty either. Drink drunk and sandwich scoffed, you can then peruse the small string of shops separating you from the departure lounge, which some tourists say offer the best-value souvenir shopping in the country. If you have any Tanzanian money you want to change, you can go and see if the cash-only bureau de change in the Arrivals Hall is open (the dollar and Kenya shilling rates are reasonable, but the other rates are a bit stingy). All of these activities should take you less than seven minutes, giving you plenty of time to visit the viewing platform upstairs, call in at the toilets in the basement, and have another beer.

Opposite Top: The snow-cap of Kibo dominates the backdrop of Moshi.
Bottom: Fish market, Dar es Salaam.

Arusha

Arusha may be only Tanzania's sixth largest town but it is, nevertheless, one of considerable consequence. This importance has been rather thrust upon it, and has a lot to do with its location. As a Tanzanian city situated conveniently close to the border with Kenya and reasonably near to Uganda, Arusha was the obvious choice as headquarters of the East African Community when these three nations were part of an economic union in the seventies; it has latterly become the centre for recent attempts to revive this union by the Tripartate Commission for East African Collaboration. By coincidence, Arusha also happens to be almost exactly halfway between Capetown and Cairo, and possibly as a result has become something of a venue for sorting out issues from all over Africa – including the Tanzanian-brokered peace talks on Burundi and, most famously, the Rwanda War Crimes Tribunal, still currently taking place in the Arusha International Conference Centre (AICC).

These momentous deliberations aside, Arusha is largely unremarkable, and it must be said that few visitors leave Arusha with fond memories, simply because of the inordinate amount of hassle that they are subjected to from the safari agents and their touts. This badgering begins the moment you set foot in town, and pretty much continues for each and every moment that you spend outside your room. (It should be stated here, however, that locals who aren't working as touts, and who don't profess to be your best friend when you first meet them, are on the whole very pleasant indeed.) Manage to survive the pestering and stick around for a few days in the town and you will find that it does have its charms, including some decent restaurants and other tourist amenities and a chaotic but occasionally fascinating central market – though with the call of the wild from Kilimanjaro, Ngorongoro and the Serengeti beckoning from the east and west, it's a rare tourist who stays long enough to savour them.

ARRIVAL

Arusha airport lies to the west of the city and serves internal flights only. A taxi into town will set you back about Ts5000, or you can walk to the main junction and wait for a dalla-dalla to pass by (Ts250). Not to be confused with Arusha airport, **Kilimanjaro International Airport** lies to the other (eastern)

Opposite Top: Under the canopy of the cloud forest, Marangu Route.

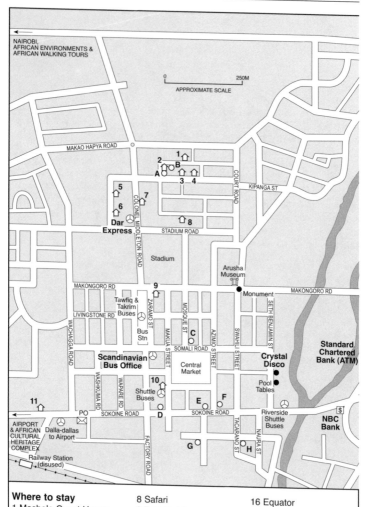

Where to stay

1 Mashele Guest House
2 Casablanca Mini Lodge
3 Monjes
4 Levolosi and Kitundu
5 Williams Inn
6 AM Hotel
7 Golden Rose

8 Safari
9 7-11 Hotel
10 Pallsons
11 Meru House Inn
12 Arusha Naaz
13 Lutheran
14 New Safari
15 YMCA

16 Equator
17 Arusha Vision Campsite
18 Novotel
19 Outpost
20 Impala
21 Jacaranda
22 Herbs and Spices
23 Hotel 77

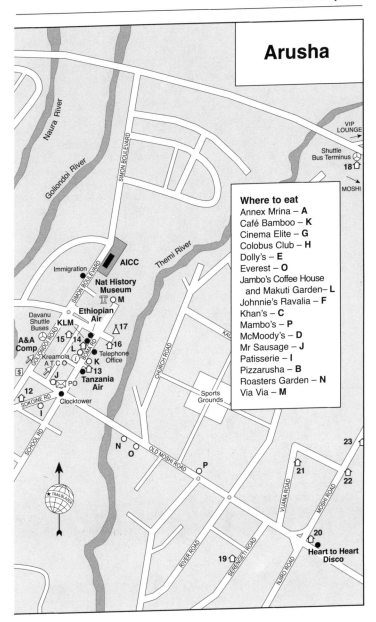

Arusha

VIP LOUNGE

Shuttle Bus Terminus
18

MOSHI

Naura River

Goliondoi River

SIMON BOULEVARD

Themi River

Immigration

AICC

Nat History Museum

M

Ethiopian Air

Davanu Shuttle Buses

KLM

15 14

16

17

L

A&A Comp

Kreamola
A T C O

i

Telephone Office

K

J

PO

13

Tanzania Air

12

SOKOINE RD

$

Clocktower

I

SCHOOL RD

N   O

CHURCH ROAD

Sports Grounds

OLD MOSHI ROAD

P

23

21

22

VIJANA ROAD

MOSHI ROAD

20

Heart to Heart Disco

RIVER ROAD

SERENGETI ROAD

NJIRO ROAD

19

TRAILBLAZER

Where to eat

Annex Mrina – **A**
Café Bamboo – **K**
Cinema Elite – **G**
Colobus Club – **H**
Dolly's – **E**
Everest – **O**
Jambo's Coffee House
  and Makuti Garden– **L**
Johnnie's Ravalia – **F**
Khan's – **C**
Mambo's – **P**
McMoody's – **D**
Mr Sausage – **J**
Patisserie – **I**
Pizzarusha – **B**
Roasters Garden – **N**
Via Via – **M**

side of town, some distance to the south of the road to Moshi. If you flew in with Air Tanzania, a shuttle bus should be waiting to ferry you into Arusha or Moshi (free with an Air Tanzania flight ticket, Ts5000 otherwise). KLM passengers have the chance to catch a shuttle to Arusha with Riverside (US$10), their minibuses officially leaving at 9pm from the airport, though often if they've still got seats they'll wait until every last KLM passenger has passed through customs before setting off. Davanu shuttle are the only other shuttle bus company operating between Kilimanjaro International Airport and Arusha. They have one bus per day in the afternoon, its arrival at the airport conveniently coinciding with the Ethiopian Air flight from Addis Ababa. Precision Air are also said to operate their own shuttle service for their flights from Kenya or Shinyanga. Fly in with any other airline, however, such as Kenya Airways, and you'll probably have to take a cab, there being no public transport to and from the airport. These can be very expensive (at least Ts15,000, more at night), though after a long flight you may not feel inclined to argue. For details on **going to the airports**, see the box on p143.

Arriving by **public bus**, expect to be dumped (sometimes literally) at the station, reasonably close to the budget hostels at the southern end of Colonel Middleton Road, in the western half of town. If you've reached Arusha by **shuttle bus** on the other hand, the chances are you'll be dropped off at the Novotel, in the north-eastern corner of town. From here, any number of drivers will offer to take you, free of charge, to the hotel of your choice. Whether they are working, as they often say they are, for the shuttle companies or whether they are working for one of the safari outfits in town and look upon this drive as a chance to hook another client, I have no idea. Suffice to say they will deliver you to your door without charge and after a long journey, that is a good enough reason to accept their offer.

ORIENTATION AND GETTING AROUND

Arusha is bisected by the Naura River Valley, a narrow and shallow dip in the town's topography. The division is more than just geographical: to the west is downtown, the busier, noisier and more fun part of Arusha, where most of the cheap lodgings can be found. To the east of the valley lies the tourist centre, where most hotels, safari companies and better restaurants are located.

Arusha is not a big place, most things are in walking distance and **getting around** is not a major hassle, though to get from one half of town to the other it's a good idea to take a **dalla-dalla**. They charge Ts150 for short trips around town or Ts250 for destinations further afield. To the west of the post office on Sokoine is the stop for dalla-dallas heading west towards Arusha airport, dropping off passengers by the roundabout near the terminal for Ts250.

❏ Arusha's area code is ☎ 027. If phoning from outside Tanzania dial ☎ +255-27.

SERVICES

Tourist information

The **tourist information** is on Boma Road (Mon–Fri 8am–4pm, Sat 8.30am–1pm). Full of brochures, the office also stocks photocopied maps of the town, but is only moderately helpful when dealing with any enquiries you may have about the city.

Best of all, however, is the list of licensed tour agencies in both Moshi and Arusha that they keep, as well a blacklist of those that have been struck off; as such, they should be your first port of call before you arrange your Kilimanjaro expedition. They also have a noticeboard where some people advertise for trekking companions.

Banks

Standard Chartered at the southern end of Goliondoi Road is currently the only place with a **cashpoint**. A great place to change **travellers' cheques** is the NBC on Sokoine, offering by far the best rates, and commission-free to boot. The **AMEX** agent in Arusha is Rickshaw Travels in the Marshall Building on Sokoine (☎ 2506655).

Communications

The **post office** is by the clocktower (Mon–Fri 8am–4.30pm, Sat 9am–noon). The only place to buy phonecards is from the **ATCO Telecom office** on Boma Road (Mon–Sat 7.30am–10pm, Sun 8am–8pm). Phoning is hideously expensive at Ts3350 per minute to the UK, Europe and the US, or Ts9570 for three minutes. Curiously, it's a little cheaper from the post office on Sokoine, though this might just be temporary. Finding an **Internet** café in Arusha isn't difficult. All charge much the same with Ts500 for thirty minutes being the norm. My favourite is Kreamola ATCO on India Street (Mon–Fri 8am–7pm, Sat and Sun 8am–5pm), which claims to have the fastest service in town and is a friendly little place; A&A on Goliondoi Road is similar, though I found the keyboards to be worryingly sticky here.

Airline offices

- **Ethiopian Air** Boma Road (PO Box 93; ☎ 2504231; Mon–Fri 8am–1pm, 2–5pm, Sat 8.30am–1pm, Sat and Sun 9am–1pm).
- **Air Excel** (PO Box 12731; ☎ 2501597, 🖷 2548429; 🖳 airexcel@arkeoltz.com)
- **KLM and Northwest Airlines** Boma Road (☎ 2506063/8062; Mon–Fri 8.30am–5pm, Sat 9.30am–1pm; 🖳 www.klm.com).
- **Precision Air** New Safari Hotel Building, Boma Road (PO Box 1636; ☎ 2506903, 🖷 2508204; 🖳 www.precisionairtz.com)
- **Air Tanzania** Boma Road (☎ 2503201/02/03; Mon–Fri 8am–12.30pm, 2–5pm, Sat 8.30am–1pm).

Immigration

The immigration office (Mon–Fri 7.30am–3.30pm) is on Simon Boulevard, south and across the road from the AICC.

WHERE TO STAY

As with much of the rest of Tanzania, the hotels in Arusha officially charge different rates for locals and foreigners. But, as usual, it doesn't take too much to persuade some hotels to let you have the cheaper residents' rate. For the prices listed below, however, we have opted to list the **non-residents' rate**; the residents' rate is lower by 50% or more. For those who wish to **camp**, the Masai Camp lies 3km from the centre on the old Moshi Road and charges US$3 per person including hot showers. Arusha Vision on Boma Road opposite the Equator Hotel is the most central campsite, though it is rather noisy and said to be unsafe.

Budget

Most of the cheaper places are gathered a few metres to the east of Col Middleton Rd, in a small cluster of roads that have yet to experience the joys of tarmac. Some of the places around here that are not mentioned below are rather sleazy. As for the rest, we must mention the *Mashele Guest House* first, if only because it is the one most independent travellers migrate to. If the truth be told, however, it stopped trying years ago, and though the rooms are comfortable enough and the water from the showers is hot, there are now enough negative sides to Mashele Guest House – from the owner's permanently wintry expression to the crowds of locals who gather in the courtyard to drink the night away and sell batiks/safaris – to take away the laurels on which it has been resting for far too long. It does remain the best place to meet other travellers, however, and at just Ts3000 for a double with shared facilities, or Ts4000 for those in the quieter block at the back (with new mattresses, though also not en suite), it's fair value.

If meeting travellers is not your primary concern but saving money is you're better off staying at one of the other hostels nearby, in particular the charming *Casablanca Mini Lodge* (☎ 2507062), on the corner of the same street, with self-contained rooms and a manager who has learnt how to smile, or the spartan but acceptable *Kitundu* (☎ 2400466), *Levolosi* and *Monjes* on Kaloleni, the next street south. All of these charge the same tariff as the Mashele, as does the *Safari* (☎ 2507819; includes a pitch for a tent for US$1 a night), one block further south.

Continuing southwards, the *7–11 Hotel* (no phone as yet) by the bus station may not be quite finished yet, but most of the rooms are now available, all are sparklingly spotless, comfy, and best of all are currently going for between Ts7500-8,000, or Ts12,500 with a huge television included. Whether the affable owner, Massawe, will raise prices when the hotel is finally completed remains to be seen; until then, the best thing to do is grab a room while they're still cheap and treat yourself to the best value accommodation in Arusha.

Moving south to commercial Sokoine Street, *Meru House Inn* (☎ 2507803; 🖳 meruhouseinn@hotmail.com; non-s/c sgl/dbl Ts4500/5500, Ts8000/9000 with bathroom) is another hotel often patronized by foreign tourists, which is surprising given that it makes little effort to attract them. Still, it's pleasant and relaxed and there's a good Indian restaurant down below, though avoid the rooms overlooking either the central courtyard or the road if you want a good night's sleep.

Moving to the other side of town, *Arusha Naaz* (☎ 2508893; 🖳 arushanaaz
@yahoo.com) has a fine restaurant (see under Where to Eat and Drink on p136),
eager-to-please staff and spotless sunny rooms; still, it is a touch overpriced at
US$20/25 sgl/dbl. There was also a foul smell when I visited, though I was
assured this was because they happened to be cleaning the drains that day and
in view of its generally high standard I feel fairly sure this is so. Across and up
on Boma Road, the *Lutheran* (☎ 2508855/7; Ts5000/10,000 sgl/dbl) is a dreary
but safe place, while the *YMCA* (☎ 2506907; US$13/15/23 for non-self-con-
tained sgl/dbl/tpl), one block west on India St, is chaotic and a bit of a dump.

Mid-range and upmarket

The major landmark on Col Middleton Road is the *Golden Rose* (☎ 2507959,
🖹 2508862; 🖳 goldenrose@habari.co.tz; sgl/dbl/tpl US$36/48/60 including
English breakfast) a deservedly popular place. The name is apt too, for this is a
hotel with something of a gilt complex, with all the rooms decorated in shiny
golden hues. The restaurant is a bit of a classic as well, with hartebeest and
impala frequently spotted on the menu.

Moving one block west of Col Middleton Road, the towering *AM Hotel*
(☎ 2507873; sgl/dbl/tpl/suite US$40/60/80/100) is one of the older places in
town, having been founded in 1988. Unfortunately, neither the papier-maché
giraffe and elephant in reception nor the surly attitude of the staff does much to
endear. Just above it is *Williams Inn* (☎ 2503578), a place that is run like a
boarding school, with notices everywhere reminding people of the rules of the
house, including orders barring guests from bringing in both alcohol and
'women of immoral turpitude'. Given its location at the seamier side of town,
however, such discipline is no bad thing and the rooms are comfortable, quiet
and pleasant enough, though Ts60,000/80,000 for sgl/dbl including breakfast is
too much. Staying on this side of town, *Hotel Pallsons* (☎/🖹 2548123; 🖳 pall
sonshotel@yahoo.com; sgl/dbl/tpl US$25/30/40 including continental break-
fast), on Makua St, is run by the same enterprise that organizes the shuttle buses
to Nairobi, and is surprisingly clean and comfy considering the location. It
appears their reception has of late become a venue for watching English football matches on the telly, but if you're not a fan you can sneak off to your room
to watch something else, because as well as a bathroom all rooms have TV.

Moving eastwards and occupying the most central location of them all
(though perhaps, given the number of touts right outside the door, not the best),
the *New Safari* on Boma Road (☎ 2503261; sgl/dbl/tpl US$30/50/62) is a dis-
appointment. The smart entrance leads into a gloomy cavernous lobby, while
the tired and threadbare corridors running off it and the standardized rooms
themselves, where charm, character and homeliness are all sadly absent, are
reminiscent of a Stalinist housing estate in central Siberia. Unsurprisingly, I find
on reading the brochure that it was built in 1967, the same year as the socialist-
inspired Arusha Declaration. Still, at least the staff are lovely here, and if you
can get the residents' rate (Ts18,000–32,000) you may rightly consider that
you've got a bargain. Nearby, the smart *Hotel Equator* (☎ 2508409, 🖹 2508085;
🖳 nah@tz2000.com) is now reopened after some extensive renovations. In an

ideal location behind the phone office, and with every room fitted out with a shower, private balcony, satellite TV and phone – some with Internet connection – this is now one of the plushest in the town centre, and the price is fair at sgl/dbl US$55/65 including continental breakfast.

However, our favourite in this price range is the *Jacaranda* (☎ 2544624; 🖳 www.chez.com/jacaranda), set in a quiet street to the north of the Old Moshi Road. This is a great place with fantastic, huge rooms with four-poster beds and massive bathrooms (including bath!) and even a mini-golf course in the garden. The tariff at US$50/55 sgl/dbl represents good value. Also in this neck of the forest is the *Outpost* (☎ 2503908) down Serengeti Road, a district so exclusive that the noise of traffic and touts is replaced by the soothing sound of birdsong and the gentle rhythm of people brushing the dust from the street. Popular with upmarket tour groups, the Outpost has its own Internet and laundry service and a satellite TV in the sumptuous lounge area. B&B here costs US$25/28 for shared/self-contained single, or US$32/36 double: extremely good value indeed. The Ethiopian *Herbs and Spices* restaurant (see p138; ☎ 2502279, 0744-281320; 🖳 axiumspices@hotmail.com) has a few rooms around a central courtyard at the back of their premises. The rooms are clean and airy, but a tad overpriced at US$35/45 for self-contained sgl/dbl, or US$15/25 for rooms with shared facilities (all prices inclusive of breakfast). Further north is the enormous *Hotel 77* (☎ 2548054, 📠 2548407; 🖳 hotel77@tz2000.com; sgl/dbl/tpl US$30/40/45), a huge tourist village, said to be the largest in East Africa, with 120 rooms. It's all rather tatty, however, and while its sheer size has helped it win some custom from conference organizers and the like, few tourists stay here.

Back down at the southern end of the street, one can only guess at the number of woodland creatures that were made homeless in order to supply the *Impala Hotel* (☎ 2508448/49/50/51, 📠 2508680; 🖳 www.impalahotel.com) with its wood-heavy reception. Along with the Novotel it's the main business centre in Arusha, with all the trimmings one would expect – a plethora of restaurants and bars, a pool and conference facilities and colour televisions in every room; there's also the Heart to Heart nightclub next door. Rooms are actually quite reasonably priced at US$65/75/120/190 sgl/dbl/tpl/suite. As for the *Novotel* (☎ 2502711, 📠 2508503), well, if you've seen one of these places before you'll pretty much know what to expect from Arusha's. Rates are US$135/155 for sgl/dbl.

WHERE TO EAT AND DRINK

Arusha is a good place for foodies, with African, Oriental and Indian eating places abounding. Some also advertise Continental food, which basically means any dish that doesn't fit into one of the categories above. Two local hangouts specializing in Tanzania's hearty, cheap and simple brand of cuisine, both of which are worth a visit, are the busy *Annex Mrina*, just east of Col Middleton Road near the cheap guest houses, where a kilo of beef will set you back around Ts2100, and the enduringly popular *VIP Lounge* to the north of the Novotel across the Moshi Road, where a whole roast *kuku* (chicken) can be yours for just

Ts3000. Then there's *Khan's*, another place that has long been a favourite with locals, and which is now winning a whole legion of foreign fans too. Something of a tourist attraction in its own right, Khan's is a garage by day, but transforms itself into a barbecue at night to serve up a variation on the chicken-in-a-basket theme, namely 'chicken-on-a-bonnet'(around Ts4000 for a whole one). It's just to the north of the Central Market on Mosque Street, by Musicland café.

Back up north of the stadium, the *Pizzarusha* to the west of the Mashele Guest House has clearly set out to cater for the travellers staying in the cheap hostels nearby and is doing it rather splendidly too. This is an enduring favourite amongst budget-conscious backpackers and with good reason: a tout-free haven, the pizzas are wonderful and the service excellent.

Moving down to Sokoine, if you thought Tanzanian fast food simply meant impala on the hoof, then think again and pay a visit to *McMoody's* (closed Monday). But while it may look like its high-street counterparts in the West, and the menu is similar too, McMoody's is thankfully a whole lot more civilized, with basic restaurant formalities such as full table service still observed here. The food's OK too. On the same section of Sokoine, *Dolly's* serves a fair – if minuscule – rendition of the Middle Eastern staple shawarma in spotlessly clean surroundings, making this a favourite for Americans and travellers with children, while just to the east is *Johnnie's Ravalia*, a place which seems to have been around since God was a boy and Kilimanjaro no more than a twinkle in His eye. The owner is an affable bloke who serves tasty, no-nonsense subconti-nental vegetarian snacks – samosas, bhajias and the like – at about Ts250 a time. Down the road opposite is the *Elite Cinema*, supplying basic staples served up by a talkative old Indian gentleman with one eye permanently on the telly.

Continuing east along Sokoine, down towards the school you'll come on the finest Mexican in town: every evening upstairs on the roof at the *Colobus Club* they concoct the most authentic and fiery interpretation of Mexican food that will keep your tongue burning long after you've climbed Kilimanjaro, come back down and returned to your home country. Also serving molten-hot fare, *Arusha Naaz*, in the hotel of the same name, is rarely less than wonderful. This is the place to come for barbecues, cooked out on the grill right on the pavement. There are few activities more pleasant in Arusha than to sit outside with the chef and watch the world go by while your tongue slowly melts under a fiery chicken *pilipili* (with chilli).

Moving up past the clock(less)tower, on Boma Road by the tourist office is *Jambo's Coffee House* and *Makuti Garden*. The first is a nice little coffee house serving great coffee, good cake, and copies of *Newsweek*, *Time*, *International Express* and even *Cosmopolitan*; though it's early days yet, we can expect this to feature large in travellers' itineraries in future, particularly as they also organize idiosyncratic tours of Arusha and the surrounding villages (see p139). The latter is more a bar/evening cocktail venue and, like so many places around here, it can be chock-a-block one night, and deadly quiet the next.

Opposite, the *Café Bamboo* with its wooden furniture and check tablecloths looks for all the world like a tearoom in the Cotswolds and curiously has the same genteel air about it, too. Ex-pats and Arusha's élite flock here throughout the day; we recommend you call in for a juice, coffee and egg-on-toast breakfast. Direct competition is provided by *Patisserie* a little way down the hill, a favourite with overland trucks who get special deals in the Internet café there.

With branches in the Honduras, Java and Zanzibar, *Via Via* is a chain of travellers' cafés renowned for the good work they do in introducing travellers to the local cultures. Arusha's branch, in the grounds of the old German Boma, is no different, with dancing displays and music performances held regularly. And if you don't give a cuss about the culture there's always the food, which includes such travellers' staples as banana pancakes and tuna sandwiches. The current managers, Jef and Kathleen, are mines of information too.

To the south on Old Moshi Road there's a number of large-scale restaurants that are perfect as venues for that post-Kili celebration (or commiseration) meal with the trekkers you met on the way. *Roasters Garden* is a huge alfresco place where diners enjoy traditional East African fare (nyama choma Ts2500), or continental, Indian or Chinese if you prefer, under thatched shelters. It's a very pleasant restaurant, though surprisingly it seems to be struggling to break even, with the result that they open only in the daytime now. Next door is *Everest*, the finest Chinese restaurant in town, with delicious, authentic Oriental dishes and friendly staff, including a genuinely Chinese manager. On the other side of the road and down a few hundred metres is *Mambo's*, where a Tanzanian chef attempts to recreate the flavours of Italy with his extensive pizza and pasta-based menu; not a promising marriage, the food is nevertheless very, very tasty indeed. Finally, for something out of the ordinary, a trip to *Herbs and Spices*, the Ethiopian restaurant in the hotel of the same name, could be in order. With vegetarian dishes ranging from Ts2000 to Ts5000 as well as meat dishes (Ts4000–10,000), this place has been garnering praise from hungry travellers for years. Try the lamb in Ethiopian butter, with onions, green peppers and oregano, and you'll see why.

Bars and nightclubs

Arusha is the **nightclub** capital of northern Tanzania, attracting rastas and ravers from far and wide. There are three main venues. **Colobus** (see Where to Eat and Drink, p136; Ts3000) has a disco on the floor below the restaurant on Fridays and Saturdays that spins mainly Western sounds. The **Heart to Heart Club** (Ts3000) next to the **Impala Hotel** is open nightly, though weekends are less sleazy and more popular. Music varies throughout the night, with an hour devoted to Western pop, another to African rhythms and so on. Finally there's **Crystal** on Seth Benjamin St (Ts1500), a much more homely venue playing largely African tunes to a largely African crowd. Once you've done the round of these places, **Mr Sausage** is on hand outside the post office selling hot dogs from his van for your midnight munchies.

WHAT TO DO

Very little is the short answer. There are a couple of museums that could conceivably be worth visiting but only if you're absolutely sure you've finished preparing for your trek, have written all your postcards, bought all your souvenirs, sent all your emails, cut all your toenails and done all your laundry. The better of the two is the **Arusha Museum** (Ts1000, Ts500 students; 9am–6pm daily) by the Arusha Monument. Consisting in the main of a few photos and a number of traditional tools and weapons, perhaps the most interesting part is the building itself, which is where Nyerere and chums met to hammer out the details of the Arusha Declaration (26–29 January 1967); that and the torch which is supposed to be carried around the country every year to promote unity and patriotism among folk. Some might find this place provides a useful précis of Tanzanian history from pre-colonial times to the death of Nyerere, and the authorities are to be commended for trying. Worthy if not exactly worthwhile.

And then there's the **Natural History Museum** (Ts1000) in the old German Boma, which manages the rather difficult feat of making the Arusha Museum seem fascinating. For Ts1000 you have the chance to look at a few incomplete skulls of early hominids, one diorama of a neanderthal sitting in a cave, a fragment or two of a prehistoric rhinoceros skeleton, and ... that's it. The Via Via Café which is located in the grounds is committed to improving the museum, for which we offer both our best wishes and deepest sympathy.

In a similar vein to the above, the **African Cultural Heritage Complex** lies to the west of town on the way to the airport. Once again, perhaps the most interesting exhibit is the actual building, the roof of which is designed to resemble Uhuru Peak. The complex itself, however, is little more than a market for woodcarvings with a couple of recreated Masai dwellings in the courtyard. While there's no denying the artistry that's gone into the sculptures, the designs themselves may be too elaborate to appeal to Western tastes. Nearby, the unfinished **art centre** will perhaps be of more interest when it is finally completed; it aims to be the biggest in East Africa.

Organized tours around Arusha

Jambo's Coffee House on the Boma Road organizes tours around the city and neighbouring hills. Some of the trips they run include visits to Lake Duluti to walk through the banana groves and coffee plantations, a morning at a banana wine factory, a visit to some Masai houses, or a tour around the old churches of Arusha. None of these sights will take your breath away, nor is that their intention: they are simply very pleasant escapes from the city – or, in the case of the Arusha churches tour, a different way to look at it – and a refreshing way of discovering the country that exists outside the national parks.

For tours that take you further afield, the Dutch development organization SNV in association with the Tanzanian Tourist Board have created **Cultural Tourism Programmes**, where you can visit the rural areas of Tanzania and experience 'real' African life, with all profits going towards various development projects. Amongst the many tours they organize country-wide is a trip to Kyalia, near Machame Gate (see p185) to see the environmentally sound 'agro-forestry' practices of the region; from Kyalia, the local people have organized various tours around the area to a number of waterfalls, caves and farms. For details, visit the Cultural Tourism Programme offices in the AICC building, contact them by phone or email (☎ 2507515; 🖥 www.infoj ep.com/culturaltours) or pick up a brochure at the tourist offices in Dar and Arusha.

With such a dearth of formal attractions, perhaps the most educational and entertaining thing you can do in Arusha is visit a **football game**; it will teach you more about Tanzanians (or at least the male half of the population) and what makes them tick than any papier maché diorama or reconstructed Masai dwelling. The next game is usually chalked up on the noticeboard outside the stadium's main entrance on Col Middleton Road. Some of the games are rather low-key, but attend a big league match and you're in for a treat. If football's not your game then you can always **play pool** on one of the two tables in the hall below the Crystal nightclub, or go **swimming** in the pool at the Novotel (Ts2000).

TREKKING AGENCIES

In terms of value for money and choice, you are probably better off organizing your trek in Moshi than Arusha. Agencies in Arusha tend to be more expensive than those in Moshi for three reasons: firstly, some Arusha agencies are just acting as middlemen for those in Moshi, and take their cut; secondly, most of the larger and more expensive companies prefer to base themselves in Arusha and enjoy the greater facilities there; and thirdly, the transport costs to Kilimanjaro are much higher than they are from Moshi: for the trip out to the Machame Gate, for example, I was quoted a ridiculous US$160 return for a ride in a 4WD.

For all these reasons, in this book we have tended to concentrate more on the better-value Moshi-based operators than those in Arusha, though that does not mean you should necessarily dismiss the latter: if there are enough people going to split the transport costs then the difference in price is negligible. Indeed, the cheapest offer we had in Arusha was a reasonable US$540 on the Machame Route with Shidolya (see opposite), mainly because the size of the group was so large that shared costs such as transport at the start and finish of the trek were smaller than normal. The most expensive, incidentally, was over US$2000 with African Environments, though this company is said to be the most accommodating of all the companies in Tanzania – a willingness to please that once included, so it is rumoured, the carting of a proper porcelain Armitage Shanks toilet up Kili for one customer. It's also worth mentioning here that they pay their porters and guides the best rates of all.

To research this section we visited each of the agencies below and asked them about their costs, and what we can expect for our money. This gave us an idea of the price, of course, but little information about the quality of the service they offered. For this we looked at the comments books they kept (and if the company you are negotiating with doesn't keep such a book, be very suspicious) and, most importantly of all, asked other trekkers on Kili their opinion of the agency they were with. In this way a fairly reliable and – we hope – accurate picture of the trekking agency scene in both Arusha and Moshi emerged. We hope you find it useful, and would welcome feedback about any agency, whether listed in this book or not. The prices quoted in the following list are per person. For details of what to look for in an agency, and what questions to ask, see pp24–7. And one other tip: don't be afraid to tell the tour operator that you're shopping around; it's the quickest way to get them to give you a good deal.

● **African Environments** (PO Box 2125; ☎/🖷 2548625; 🖳 www.africanenvi ronments.co.tz). Established in mid-1987, American-owned African Environments are at the very top end of the market. They are renowned for the luxurious quality of their treks and the higher wages that they pay their staff, and are a favourite with many foreign film crews. Their Shira Route is said to boast a 98% success rate. They also run a Machame trail trek. Costs are vague depending on what sort of trek you want but are said to be around US$300 per day.

● **Bobby Camping** PPF Shopping Center NJIRO (PO Box 15152; ☎ 2544057, 🖷 2507842; 🖳 www.habari.co.tz/bobbycamping). Not to be confused with the company below, Bobby Tours offers just the Marangu trail.

● **Bobby Tours** Goliondoi Rd (PO Box 2169; ☎ 503490, 🖷 508176; 🖳 www. bobbytours.com). Established way back in 1976, Bobby are a reasonably upmarket trekking and safari company offering all six routes up Kili.

● **Equatorial Safari** Boma Road (PO Box 2156, ☎ 2501163; 🖳 www.whiteyel low.com/equatorialsafaris). Part of the New Safari Hotel, they offer treks beginning at US$680 for two people on the Machame Route, or US$650 for three people. Unusually, they charge the same for the Marangu Route. Their prices for Levosho and Shira, incidentally, were both US$780.

● **Kibo Express** India Street (PO Box 934, ☎ 2504670; 🖳 www.kiboexpr ess.com). Located in the YMCA and run by Fred Tenu, though we spoke to indefatigable Jiusta. For Machame, they were charging US$650 per person for 6 days (two people), or US$630 (three people); for Marangu, the charges were US$600/580 for five days (2/3 pax), or US$650/630 for six days. They also offered me a price on the Rongai Route, namely US$750/720 (2/3 pax).

● **Moon adventure tours and safaris** Seth Benjamin Street, opp. Meru Primary School (PO Box 12023, ☎/🖷 2504462; 🖳 www.moon-adventure.com). These were one of the cheapest for safaris, though they also do the Marangu and Machame routes. Prices are around US$620 for Marangu, US$680 for Machame.

● **Roys** India Street (☎ 2507057, 🖷 2548892; 🖳 www.roysafaris.com). Not the most helpful, they asked for US$850 for the Machame Route, and tutted when I asked about Marangu, though in their defence this company does have one of the better reputations in Arusha, and we probably just caught them on an off day.

● **Safari makers** India Street (PO Box 12902; ☎ 300817; 🖳 www.safarim akers.com). Popular, efficient and reliable safari company, run jointly by a Tanzanian man and American woman, that also runs treks up Kilimanjaro on all the major routes. A five-day Marangu Trek costs US$785/705 for one/two people; six days on Machame for one/two people costs US$905/825.

● **Shidolya** Room 218, at the end of the corridor on the second floor, Ngorongoro wing, AICC building (PO Box 1436, ☎ 2548506, 🖷 2508242). This lot certainly seem to be one of the more professional outfits, with a busy office and a slick professional style, including computer print-outs of the day-to-day itineraries of each trek. They are also, somewhat surprisingly, relatively cheap by Arusha standards, with six-day two-person Marangu treks for US$630, or ten dollars less if there's three of you. For Machame, the fee is US$600 for three-person six-day treks, or US$620 for two people. Definitely worth investigating.

● **Silver Spear**   (PO Box 706; ☎ 0744-485440; 0744-273184; 🖳 silversp ear@usa.net). If nothing else, Silver Spear wins the award for the most persist-ent touts. They claim to be specialists in wildlife safaris, mountain trekking, ornithological safaris, walking safaris, camping and lodge safaris – which just about covers everything. They used to labour under a bad name. However, they do seem to be pulling their act together at last, and a visit to their offices near KLM may not be such a bad idea – if only to keep the touts happy. Marangu US$550/600 for 5/6 nights; Machame US$600, or US$580 for 3 pax.

● **Sunny Safaris** Col Middleton Rd (PO Box 7267; ☎ 2507145, 🖹 2548037; 🖳 www.sunnysafaris.com). One of the better budget companies in Arusha, rec-ommended time and again. Their prices of US$700 for the Machame Route, (US$660 if three or more people) was definitely at the cheaper end of the scale in Arusha, and your money, furthermore, is protected by Tanzanian Tourist Board and Tanzanian Association of Tour Operators – so if something goes wrong with the company, there's a slight chance somebody will compensate you.

● **Tropical Trekking**   (PO Box 2047, ☎ 2507011; 🖳 www.tropicaltrekking.com) India Street. Branch office of Hoopoe UK and its sister Tropical Trekking; for information on the range of treks offered, see p20. If they have space, it may be possible to book a place on a trek from this office, and it will usually cost a little less than that paid by trekkers who booked abroad – though if you are booking with this company, cost is probably not a major concern anyway.

 Climbing Meru

Mount Meru, the second highest mountain in Tanzania at 4566m, cannot com-pete with the allure of Kili, but it's still an interesting climb to the top of this beautiful volcanic cone, and the perfect preparation for tackling Kili. There is only one route, called the **Momela Route**, a four-day slog through the various vegetation zones.

Meru enjoys a few advantages over its loftier neighbour: for one thing, Meru's location, inside Arusha National Park, and the lack of trekkers who make it here mean that it can boast of a far, far greater variety of wildlife and, just as importantly, a much better chance of seeing it than you would on Kili. Indeed, because of the large popu-lation of buffalo and other fauna that have made the slopes their home, an armed guide or escort is compulsory when climbing Meru; they are provided by the park, though you have to pay for them. Another advantage Meru holds over Kilimanjaro is that it's a lot cheaper to climb: while the rescue fees are the same as on Kilimanjaro (US$20 per person) park fees on Meru are less (US$20 as opposed to US$30 per day), and hut fees are just US$20 per person per night, half the price of Kili's accommo-dation. There are two huts on the way, the Miriakamba Hut at 2470m and the Saddle Hut at 3500m, so camping is not necessary, and each hut is equipped with kerosene stoves for trekkers to use, though you have to bring your own kerosene. Other expenses include a park commission of US$5 per group, and guide fees of approxi-mately US$15 per day. For a porter expect to pay Ts2500–3000 per day, though this is negotiable. Furthermore, while travel agencies in Arusha do offer treks up Mount Meru, this trek *can* be done independently, thereby avoiding the agency's fees. The tourist office in Arusha should be able to provide details of the latest prices and rec-ommend a guide. Happily, tips, while still expected, are not aggressively demanded by the guides, and are traditionally a bit smaller than the tips paid on Kili.

GETTING AWAY

Buses

Moshi and Kilimanjaro Those heading to Kili will find the local buses are the most convenient way to get to **Moshi**. They run throughout the day from the main bus station, with the last one at around 5pm (Ts1000). Buses line up in a queue, with the driver of the first one waiting until every last cubic centimetre within the bus has been filled with passengers, baggage or livestock before setting off for the 90-minute journey.

It's not a particularly pleasant way to travel but other options are thin on the ground, with Moshi ill-served by the **shuttle bus** companies. The best is Riverside (☎ 2502639), with its offices in a chemists on Sokoine, who have just one bus per day at 2pm (Ts5000). Pallsons have none, and while Davanu *do* operate a daily bus to Moshi, this starts in Nairobi and they seem reluctant to allow passengers to board it in Arusha.

Nairobi Of the **bus** companies, Scandinavia, whose offices are just south of Arusha's Central Bus Station, run one bus daily to the Coastal Bus Station in Nairobi at 3.15pm (Ts8000). Tawfiq and Takrim, with offices at the bus station, both do the Nairobi run too (Ts6000), though be warned: most travellers who ride in a Tawfiq bus later swear that they will never to do so again, and Takrim are reputed to be even worse.

The most popular **shuttle bus** company is Riverside on Sokoine Road. They run two shuttles daily to Nairobi, at 8am and 2pm (US$20 for foreign tourists, though you are more likely to be charged the more reasonable residents' price of Ts10,000). Pallsons can be found in the hotel of the same name; they have two buses daily to Nairobi at 8am and 1pm (Ts10,000). As with all shuttles, they should pick you up from your hotel, though you should press

---

Getting to the airports

Air Tanzania charge Ts5000 (free to flight passengers) for their shuttle to **Kilimanjaro International Airport**, their buses leaving from the Air Tanzania office on Boma Road two hours prior to the scheduled departure of their flights, a timetable of which is prominently displayed in the office window. Riverside (☎ 2502639) coincide their shuttle buses to meet KLM flights, their buses currently leaving their offices on Sokoine Road at 6pm – thus allowing passengers who are joining the KLM flight enough time to check-in – and returning at 9pm, for US$10. Davanu (☎ 2501240) buses leave their offices in Goliondoi Road at 2pm. Precision Air have also started a shuttle service to and from KIA for their flights. A taxi to the airport will cost at least Ts15,000, more at night.

For **Arusha airport**, Precision Air charges Ts1000 (free to flight passengers) to travel in one of their shuttle buses which leave about 1hr 15min before the scheduled departure of their flights from their offices in the AICC building. Curiously, for the return journey you pay double (Ts2000). Alternatively, take a dalla-dalla from just west of the post office on Sokoine to the junction near the airport, and walk to the terminal building from there.

home this point when making the booking. The other two companies – Davanu, in the Adventure Centre on Goliondoi Road (☎ 501242), and Serena at the top of Goliondoi Road – both run buses at 8am and 2pm, though both seem curiously reluctant to lower the price from US$20 to the residents' rate.

Dar es Salaam Scandinavia have **buses** to Dar each morning at 7.30am (Ts15,000), two at 8.30am (Ts17,500 and Ts11,000 – the different prices reflecting the quality of the buses) and at 11am (Ts15,000). There are also a couple of companies with booking offices opposite each other on Middleton Road: Dar Express is on the left hand side as you walk up the road, with buses at 6am (Ts8000), 7.15am and 8.15am (both Ts11,000); MSAE is on the right, running buses at 6am, 7.30am and 3pm (all Ts7800). Other bus companies serving Dar can be found around the bus station.

Flights
See p133 for details of the airline offices in Arusha. Bear in mind that the times listed below are subject to frequent change. Remember, too, that there is a **departure tax**, namely Ts5000 for domestic flights, US$30 for international destinations.

Arusha effectively has two airports, with **Kilimanjaro International Airport** being less than an hour away. You may be able to find a direct flight to Dar on one of the international carriers from there, though most refuse or are simply not permitted to board passengers for this short journey. One that does is Air Tanzania – see Appendix C, p232, for details of this service and other flights from Kilimanjaro International Airport.

From **Arusha airport** direct flights to **Dar** are surprisingly limited, with local carriers preferring to go via **Zanzibar**. These include Precision Air who fly daily at 3.25pm (arriving at Zanzibar at 4.35pm and Dar at 5.15pm; US$165 for both destinations from Arusha), and Coastal Aviation, whose 12.15pm flight arrives at Zanzibar at 1.50pm and at Dar at 2.20pm (US$190 for both destinations). This flight, incidentally, then continues on to **Selous** for the big national park, arriving at 3.15pm at the camp of your choice; US$310. Air Excel's Zanzibar flight leaves daily at 2pm, arriving at 3.30pm, then continues on to Dar fifteen minutes later, arriving at 4.05pm (both destinations US$180). ZanAir also fly daily to Zanzibar at 1.45pm (except Mondays at 12.45pm).

Air Excel serve a number of other destinations in Tanzania, including **Grumeti** (daily at 8am, US$170), **Mamire** (8am, US$65), **Manyara** (8am, US$55), **Musoma** (8am, US$190), **Serengeti South** (8am, US$145) and Seronera (daily, 8am, US$145), while Precision Air have a weekly flight to **Mwanza** (Tuesdays at 12.15pm, US$145).

Though Arusha is not an international airport, Precision Air have flights from Arusha via **Kilimanjaro International** (20min; US$25) to two destinations in Kenya: **Nairobi** (departure daily 3.25pm, total travelling time 2hr including a 40-minute stopover; total cost US$120) and a weekly flight to **Mombasa** (currently departing Thursday at 10.30am, total travelling time 1hr 45min including a 25-minute stopover; US$120).

Moshi

Cheaper, quieter, nearer and prettier, Moshi sits in the shadow of Kilimanjaro and, for climbing the mountain, is a superior base to neighbouring Arusha, 80km away to the west. As the unofficial capital of the Chagga world, most visitors find Moshi a little more interesting too. The missionaries who followed in the wake of Rebmann gave the Chaggas the advantage of a Western education and this, combined with the agricultural fecundity of Kilimanjaro's southern slopes, has enabled the Chaggas to become one of the wealthiest, most influential and most securely self-aware groups in the country. Moshi has reaped the benefits too, prospering to the point where it is now one of the smartest towns in Tanzania (though grim poverty is not difficult to find, as anybody who has walked around Moshi at night, stepping over the sleeping bodies of the dispossessed lying on the pavements as they do so, can testify).

While the Chaggas are the dominant force in town, Moshi is still a cosmopolitan place, with a highly visible Indian minority; the colourful ethnic mixture is reflected in the architecture, with a huge Hindu temple abutting an equally striking mosque, and with dozens of small churches and chapels scattered in the streets thereabouts. Moshi cannot boast of the variety of agencies, restaurants and nightclubs of its neighbour Arusha, but after the relentless hassle of Arusha that will come as something of a relief for many visitors – and there are still enough facilities to both enable you to organize a trek from here and enjoy some long nights of celebration at the end.

ARRIVAL

Arriving on an Air Tanzania flight to **Kilimanjaro International Airport**, a shuttle bus should be waiting to take you to their Moshi office by the roundabout (make sure you get on the Moshi-bound shuttle, however, as they also run one from the airport to Arusha). Riverside are supposed to meet the KLM flights, but are not as reliable – the chances are you'll have to take the free shuttle to Arusha and change there. Precision Air also claim to run a shuttle service between KIA and Moshi. Or you'll have to pay for a cab from the airport. Arrive by **bus** and you'll be dropped off at the terminal on Mawenzi Road, 300m south of the clocktower, within walking distance of most hotels.

ORIENTATION AND GETTING AROUND

According to Harry Johnston, Moshi could simply mean town or settlement, though as with everything Johnston wrote, this could well be wrong. What is certain is that Moshi is compact, with almost everything of interest to the holidaying visitor lying on or near the main thoroughfare, **Mawenzi Rd**, and its northern extension, **Kibo Rd** (the two names borrowed from the peaks of Kilimanjaro).

KEY TO MAP OPPOSITE

Trekking and travel agencies

1 CCM (Snowcap Trekking Agency)
2 Akaro Trekking Agency
3 Zara Trekking Agency
4 Air Tanzania
5 Precision Air & Samjoe Tours

6 BA Agent
7 Mauly Tours
8 Shah Tours
9 Serengeti Tours
10 Tanganyika Tours
11 Ahsante Trekking Agency

Where to eat

A The Bakery
B Kibo House
C EK Saturday
D Traffic Police Mess
E Hill Street Café
F Coffee Shop

Together they run all the way from the market, down the hill at the southern end of town, to the roundabout at the northern end which for reasons beyond this author's understanding has a statue of a crocodile chasing an ostrich, a huddle of grazing giraffes and a monkey holding up a billboard; you'll have to see it for yourself to fully appreciate it. Separating Mawenzi from Kibo roads is a second roundabout adorned with a soft-drink sponsored digital clocktower, the centre of town. **Dalla-dallas** drive up and down the main Mawenzi and Market streets for Ts150, though it doesn't take long to walk anywhere, Moshi being compact.

SERVICES

Banks

The NBC bank in Moshi offers the best rates in town just as it does almost everywhere else in Tanzania, though there is a 0.5% commission charge for **travellers' cheques** at this branch. They are open from Monday to Friday between 8.30am and 3pm, and Saturday 8.30am–noon. Before calling in, check with the CRDB Bank in the nearby Kahawa Building, who post their rates on a board outside their offices. **Moneychangers** such as Chase on Rindi Lane stay open later but their rates are inferior. The only **ATM** in town is at the Standard Chartered Bank on Rindi Lane.

Communications

The **post office** is by the clocktower, at the junction with Boma Road. Opening times are Mon–Fri 8am–1pm and 2–4.30pm, Sat 9am–noon. The **Telecom office** is next to the post office (Mon–Fri 7.45am–4.30pm, and Sat 9am–noon); they run an operator-assisted service and also sell phonecards for the phone boxes outside. For **Internet**, Easycom are the fairest, fastest and friendliest. They charge Ts900 per 30 minutes, and gratifyingly add a couple of minutes extra on top for free every time. They can be found in the basement of Kahawa House near the clocktower. Duma Cybercafé next to the Coffee Shop is more convenient for those staying at the southern end of town (Ts1000 for 30min). There are plenty of other places, particularly north of the clocktower on Old Moshi Road and west on Horombo Road.

❑ Moshi's area code is ☎ 027. If phoning from outside Tanzania dial ☎ +255-27.

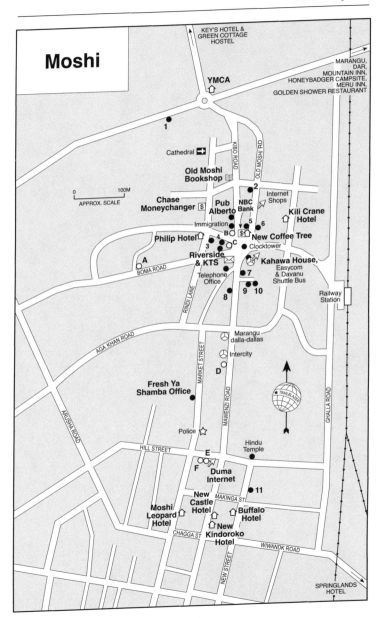

Swimming pool

The YMCA charges non-residents Ts2000 for the use of their swimming pool; guests can use it for free.

Trekking provisions

Your agency should be able to supply you with any major bits of equipment – torches, sleeping bags etc – that you might have forgotten to bring with you. Other items that you may well have overlooked but will find extremely useful include: chapsticks, which can be brought from the chemists on Mawenzi Road, 50m south of the New Kindoroko Hotel; and bin liners, useful for keeping clothing within your rucksack dry, which, strangely, only the 'Hole in the Wall' shop opposite the Buffalo seemed to have in stock the last time we checked. Maps, and books about Kili can be brought from the Old Moshi Bookshop on Rindi Lane at the junction with Kibo or the souvenir shop by Marangu Gate.

WHERE TO STAY

The following is not an exhaustive list, but whilst there are some cheaper places at the southern end of town, many refuse to accept Westerners. Manage to persuade one to let you stay for the night and you can expect to pay around Ts1500–2000 per night, though the chances are it'll be assumed that you want bed and broad rather than bed and board. **Campsites** include the grounds of the *Green Hostels* and *Key's Hotel* (see below), and at the *Golden Shower Restaurant* on the main road to Marangu and Dar. Expect to pay around US$3 per person at the last place, slightly more at the *Key's* and *Green Hostels*.

As for the hotels that definitely do welcome tourists, beginning with the cheapest, the *New Coffee Tree Hotel* (☎ 2755040) is for those for whom every *shilingi* matters. I like this place: I like the staff, I like the location right next to the clocktower, and I like the restaurant on the top floor. Admittedly, the rooms are basic but they're functional, fine and fairly priced at only Ts3500 for a single with shared facilities (Ts4500/6000 for s/c sgl/dbl), all including breakfast.

That may be the cheapest but it's certainly not the most popular, for while the lion may be the king of the jungle, on Moshi's hotel scene it's the Leopard and the Buffalo that rule. Both are wonderful: the *Buffalo* (☎ 2750270) on New Street has clean bright rooms, all en suite and with mosquito nets, and a deservedly popular bar and restaurant downstairs. It's not the cheapest in town that accepts foreigners, but it is perhaps the best value. The only drawback is that some of the female waiting staff in the restaurant can be downright surly: at your peril ask them to change TV channels while their favourite soap is on – but then Joseph the waiter compensates for that by being the nicest man in town. The hotel seemed to be installing cable TV when I was staying, so expect prices to jump when work is complete. Until then, it's Ts7000/10,000 sgl/dbl including breakfast. As for the *Moshi Leopard Hotel* on Market Street (☎ 2750884, 🖺 2751261; 🖳 www.geocities.com/thetropics/lagoon/5659), this is just a rather more upmarket version of the Buffalo, though with an excellent terrace bar – from where, peering through the branches of the nearby tree, you can see Kibo

– and friendlier waitresses. The rooms themselves are also just that little bit better than the Buffalo's, and as well as being en suite, include a fridge, TV, wardrobe, fan and balcony. The non-residents' prices are rather steep at US$30/40 sgl/dbl, but see if you can get the residents' rates of Ts15,000/18,000 sgl/dbl, which represent pretty good value.

Sharing the same block as the Buffalo, the *New Kindoroko* on Mawenzi Road (☎ 2754054, 🖨 2752988; 🖵 www.africaonline.co.tz/kindorokohotel) is the Buffalo's biggest rival when it comes to attracting backpackers, but while the restaurant is good and gives you a rooftop view of Kibo, the room prices are a little higher (Ts10,000/12,000 sgl/dbl including breakfast) and the rooms themselves are rather dingy and come a definite second to those of its neighbour. The fourth member of this cluster of hotels is the *New Castle*, but while it's cheap and has a pool table to pacify the inmates, I could find nothing that warranted any more space in this book than I have already given it.

Moving northwards but staying in the same price bracket as the Leopard, the *Philip Hotel* (☎ 27-2754746, 🖨 2750456; 🖵 www.africaonline.co.tz/philip) boasts a good location in a quiet but convenient corner of town, some pleasant staff and a smart exterior and lobby. Indeed, the only drawbacks are the rooms themselves which, though clean and furnished with amenities such as a TV, hot and cold shower and a balcony, are surprisingly lacking any sort of homely touches: a few pictures on the walls, for instance, wouldn't go amiss. Prices are the same as the Leopard at sgl/dbl US$30/40 for non-residents, Ts15,000/20,000 residents' price, all including continental breakfast. The nearby *Moshi Hotel*, by the way, is currently closed for renovations, with the new management planning to reopen as the *New Livingstone Hotel* sometime in the near future.

Moving to the other side of the clocktower and up a notch in price and quality, *Kilimanjaro Crane Hotel* (☎ 2751114, 🖨 2754876; 🖵 www.geociti es.com/TheTropics/cove/7585) seems to be more of a local businessman's hotel. It's a decent enough place, however, though deathly quiet at times. Singles, which have showers, TV and telephone, are US$30 each; doubles and triples have both bathtubs and showers and are US$40/50, or US$60 for a double with air-con.

North on Uru Road is the *Key's Hotel* (☎ 2752250/2751875, 🖨 2750073; 🖵 www.keys-hotels.com), a traditional-looking, family-run hotel and the smartest address in Moshi. Oozing class and knocking spots off the Leopard in terms of style, in the main building it's doubles only, all coming with TV, telephone, mini-bar, toilet and a shower with hot/cold running water. Those facing the road are fan only (US$50), those overlooking the back garden also have air-conditioning and cost US$60. There are also 15 small thatched cottages in the grounds (dbl/tpl US$50/75) which are quite fun. All rates include continental breakfast. Further north again, the *Green Cottage Hostel* (aka *Green Hostels*) on Nkomo Ave (☎ 2753198) is a quiet balmy retreat hidden down a leafy cul-de-sac, perfect for those who wish to get away from it all; the three non-s/c doubles are fairly priced at US$15, or US$20 en suite, whilst the one single (not self-contained) costs US$10, and the triple is US$20. Prices include breakfast.

The **YMCA** (☎ 2751754) on the main roundabout is still open but a bit rundown now and, despite the continuing popularity of its swimming pool, feels very sleepy too, as if the management has lost interest and can't be bothered anymore. The prices (US$10/13 sgl/dbl shared bathroom, US$18/26 en suite), especially when compared to those at the other end of town, are simply too high too.

Finally, there are two places, both just a little out of town, that are owned and run by trekking agencies. Unless you have booked with these agencies it is highly unlikely you will stay here; if you *have* booked with these agencies, on the other hand, the chances are you will get a night or two free at the hotel before or after your trek. The first is the very comfortable **Mountain Inn**, four kilometres from town on the way to Marangu, which is owned and run by Shah Tours (see p153 for contact details). A pool, sauna and a pretty garden are just some of the attractions here; prices start at US$38/55 for standard sgl/dbl half-board, while the new de luxe rooms are US$45/75 sgl/dbl. The second place is the Zara-run **Springlands Hotel** (☎ 2753105), 1500m to the south of town. Once again a pool and sauna are the main attractions, though the buffet dinners are to be recommended too. Singles/doubles are US$25/35.

WHERE TO EAT AND DRINK

For most of your time in Moshi you'll probably be eating in the restaurant of your hotel, where most of the town's better food can be found. Of these, the **New Coffee Tree Café** on the top floor of the eponymous hotel is a light and airy place with wonderful views towards Moshi in one direction, and Kili in the other – both of which you'll have plenty of time to enjoy while you wait the interminably long time for your food. When it does finally put in an appearance, it's tasty, hearty, and very good value. The restaurant at the **Buffalo** does some wonderful dishes, too, with the chef displaying an impressive degree of finesse in many of his creations; the **Kindoroko** nearby has a similar menu. The **Golden Shower Restaurant**, by the campsite a few kilometres out of town on the way to Marangu, serves great food from an extensive menu (that includes impala) with prices beginning at Ts2500 per dish, but unless you turn up at the weekend when the disco is on you may find it too quiet.

If you're not eating in your hotel, then the chances are you'll find yourself at the **Coffee Shop** on Hill Street instead. The travellers' number one hangout, the food here, including salads, juices, cakes, pies and a wealth of Tanzanian coffees, is simply great, the drinks are cold, and there's heaps of local information on the noticeboards and in the invaluable Moshi guidebook that they have for sale. Perhaps the best thing about this café, however, is the wonderfully tranquil little garden out back. Just down the hill, the **Hill Street Café** serves Indian nibbles – samosas, kebabs and the like – which range from the flavourful and filling to the downright revolting.

The only place that can come close to the Coffee Shop when it comes to baking is **Abbas Ali's Hot Bread Shop** on Boma Road. A bit more of a local hangout (but only a bit), it's very pleasant and they usually have copies of

Western magazines and newspapers for sale. Down the hill towards the clock-tower, *EK Saturdays* (closed evenings) is a very cheap self-service place, and the seats by the big windows are ideal places from which to watch the world go by, while the somewhat dingier *Coffee Bar* at Kibo House serves a few basic snacks with their coffee. Finally, the *Traffic Police Mess* below the bus station is a bit of an eye-opener, if only because it comes as something of a surprise to find that traffic police could be this much fun. The food is standard Tanzanian fare, but the buzzing atmosphere of this place is what makes it special, and every Saturday beginning at 5pm they have live music. Currently it's the most popular restaurant in town.

Finally, for a sleazy but fun end to your time in Moshi, pay a visit to the *Pub Alberto*, Moshi's only nightclub with a couple of pool tables and a lively atmosphere – sometimes too lively, if rival street gangs are in.

TREKKING AGENCIES

Cheaper than both Arusha and Marangu, Moshi captures the lion's share of the Kilimanjaro-trekking business, and some of the trekking companies in this town do a roaring trade. But beware: there is still a fair bit of monkey business going on here too, and you do need to be on your guard against cheetahs (!). For this reason we have compiled the following summary of some of the bigger agencies in town. Before booking with any of them, read the general advice given on pp24-7 about dealing with the agencies.

Please also bear in mind that the following is our opinion only – an opinion that was largely formed by interviewing both the agencies themselves and, more importantly, their customers. By combining the information they imparted with other sources such as the Internet, the opinions of local guides and trekkers, the odd rumour and so on, we hope to have presented a fairly accurate account of the Moshi trekking scene.

Since things change very quickly in this part of the world some of the following will inevitably have altered by the time you reach Moshi. If you have any advice, comments, praise or criticisms about any of the following agencies, or indeed any recommended agencies that I haven't mentioned, please write to me at the email/postal address given at the front of this book.

The prices listed below for the treks are the ones that were quoted to us in the offices in Moshi. For the record, the lowest price quoted for the **Machame Route** was US$450 (Samjoe), though I was too sceptical to believe this and did not take them up on the offer. The lowest I heard for the Machame trek that somebody had actually taken up was US$500, quoted by Ahsante. However, the two English women who managed to get this price had only done so after agreeing to carry their own bags and – perhaps because of the extra effort involved – they suffered altitude sickness and failed to reach the summit as a result. As for **Marangu**, the cheapest trek I heard of was an incredible US$380, offered to an Australian trekker in Marangu town. Perhaps wisely, he didn't take it up – as the cost of his park and accommodation fees alone comes to US$370, and with the cost of portering, transport and food to add on top, this quote sounds decidedly fishy. The cheapest for Marangu that somebody did take up was US$460 for four nights, quoted to me by Samjoe; see opposite.

Agencies

● **Akaro** Shop 6, National Social Security Fund Building, Old Moshi Road (PO Box 8578; ☎ 2752986, 📄 2752249; 💻 www.akarotours.com). Run by the helpful and ambitious Ally, their prices seem unexceptional and their name is not one you hear too often, but they are extremely efficient and reliable and everybody we interviewed who trekked with them seemed well satisfied. They are also to be applauded for their refusal to use touts to drum up trade. Costs: US$600 Marangu for five nights, US$500 for four nights; US$560 per person on the Machame trail.

● **Ahsante** New Street (PO Box 855; ☎/📄 2750479; 💻 www.ahsante.com). In our experience the most responsible and reliable outfit at the budget end of the price spectrum. On the Machame Trek I walked with two girls who had paid just US$500 each for their trek. Admittedly, part of the deal was that both had to carry their own packs, thereby reducing the number of porters they needed by one, but nevertheless this is good value. On my second trek, they quoted me US$500 for the five-day Marangu Route, less if we walked in a group. One point to note, however: it seems that different people in the office quote a different price for the same trek, by as much as US$80. For this reason we recommend you go straight to Cuthbert Swai, the boss, who in our experience quotes the lowest, and he seems the more organized too.

● **Key's** Key's Hotel (see under hotels for contact details). Just like the hotel, a thoroughly professional, highly efficient and very satisfactory outfit with a rock-solid reputation and no pretensions towards being cheap. Costs: Marangu US$750 for five nights if you're alone, or US$700 per person if there are three of you; US$890 for six days on the Machame trail if you're alone, or US$840 if there are three of you.

● **Kilimanjaro Guide Tours & Safaris** Horombo Road, just off the main roundabout (PO Box 210; ☎/📄 2750120; 💻 kiguto@hotmail.com). Sounding very world-weary, the lady we spoke to here, Hilda, though nice enough, was obviously aware that we had little interest in their company, probably because the prices they charged were, according to trekkers who'd used them, a little too high for the service they provide. Costs: US$630 for four nights on the Marangu trail if alone, or US$550 in a group.

● **Kilimanjaro Serengeti Tours and Travel** Mawenzi Road (PO Box 8213; ☎ 2751287, 📄 2751017; 💻 kilimanjaroserengeti@yahoo.com). This agency seemed slightly desperate for custom when we visited, and as they quoted an exorbitant US$690 to join with a group on the Marangu Route, or US$820 if we insisted on walking solo, we can see why. But to be fair they did seem more willing than most to negotiate this fee, and a couple of times they even asked me to name my price. Apparently they are the main Moshi agent for a German tour company, which perhaps explains the higher rates, and it must be said that in town they have a solid reputation for integrity and honesty.

● **Kilimanjaro Travel Service (KTS)** Room 221, Second floor, THB Building, Rengua St (PO Box 1823; ☎ 2752124, 🖨 2750654; 🖳 kilitravel@eoltz.com). Touted by the hardworking, ever-so affable and ubiquitous Dougie, we found this lot, particularly the manager, to be helpful, polite and sincere, and ready to accept defeat gracefully when another company came in with a lower offer. They're certainly worth checking out if you're in the market for a budget tour, and they are one of the few that came in under US$500 for the Marangu trail. Trekkers who completed the Umbwe Route with this agency said that they were on the whole satisfied, although the guide's English was not up to much, which did spoil their experience a little. Costs: US$480 for four nights on Marangu, or US$570 for five nights, with a further discount if there is a group. Other quotes they gave me included Shira/Rongai (US$550), and Umbwe US$500.

● **Mauly** Mawenzi Road (☎ 2750730, 🖨 2753330; 🖳 www.glcom.com/mauly). Nobody can deny that Mauly are a well-run, professional agency. I did find their prices a little – but only a little – steep for a self-professed budget outfit, but then you pay for reliability more than anything else at this end of the market, and Mauly certainly are reliable. My only gripe is the way they continually warn you about charlatans in their industry. This is sound advice, of course, but employed as a sales tactic we found it rather unpleasant. That grumble aside, this lot are fine. Costs: US$630 on the Machame trail; US$580 for five nights on the Marangu trail, US$500 for four nights.

● **Samjoe** KNCU Building (PO Box 1467; ☎ 2751484, 🖨 2751306; samjoetours@yahoo.com). One of the cheapest in town, and if all you wish to do is get to the top of Kili and are not too bothered how pleasant or otherwise the experience is, then this lot are worth looking into. However, my experience of Samjoe was not an entirely happy one: the guide was the worst I had, and the transport to take me back to Moshi at the end of the trek never materialized, so I had to catch a bus instead. As a final knockout blow, when it came to the end of my stay in the Buffalo, the receptionist informed me that Samjoe had failed to pay for a night's accommodation as they had promised, and I was pressed into paying for it myself. Apparently, if you conduct your business with the founder, Betty, you should have no problems. Her staff, however, seem a lot less reliable.

● **Shah Tours** Mawenzi Road (PO Box 1821; ☎ 2752370, 🖨 2751449; 🖳 www.kilimanjaro-shah.com). Owners of the Mountain Inn, Shah are a long established and very reputable firm, and Zara's nearest rivals in Moshi. Agents for many overseas companies, this lot are extremely reliable and their website is one of the best on the net. Costs: Marangu $430 plus park fees (US$275 if three or more in your group), Machame $550 ($380 if three or more) plus park fees.

● **Snow Cap Mountain Climbing Camp** Rooms 404/406, Third Floor, CCM Regional Building (PO Box 8358; ☎ 2752256, 🖨 2750499; 🖳 www.snow-cap.com). There's one reason to contact Snow Cap, and one reason only: to do the Rongai Route, which they concentrate on more than any other company, and which they have done more than any other company to help popularize; indeed, they built and own the rather smart campsite on the Kenyan border by the start of the trek. Most of their business is actually booked in Europe, and as a consequence they expend little effort in trying to drum up trade in Moshi – hence the somewhat obscure location in the CCM building on Taifa Road. Their prices range from US$650 if you plan to do the walk solo, or US$550 if there are more than four of you – though if you are alone and have time to wait, you may just be able to join a larger group.

● **Tanganyika Travels** Mawenzi Road (PO Box 8357; ☎/🖹 2751017). This bunch seemed efficient enough, and the price they offered seemed highly reasonable too, at US$500 for a four-night Marangu Route if trekking solo, or US$480 if other walkers could be found. The only person we found who had trekked with them, however, was not impressed with their service, and said that, if he could have his Kilimanjaro trek again, he'd pay a bit more and go with another agency.

● **Trans-Kibo Travels Limited** YMCA Building, Kilimanjaro Road (PO Box 558; ☎/🖹 2752107; 🖳 www.transkibo.com). One of oldest and more reputable companies, but as far as we could tell from the moribund atmosphere of their offices, the lacklustre efforts of the staff and the fact they seemed so very surprised that we visited, suggests that they have all but given up competing. Their prices were unexceptional too: Machame US$600, or US$580 for three people. Marangu US$520 for four nights, or US$620 for five nights (for two or three people).

● **Zara International** Rindi Lane (PO Box 1990; ☎ 2750011, 🖹 2750233; 🖳 zara@form-net.com; 🖳 www.kilimanjaro.co.tz). They may come last in the Yellow Pages, but in every other aspect this agency comes out either top or very close to it. Simply put, Zara is the doyenne of the agency scene. A quick perusal of the recommendations from satisfied customers that have been posted on the Internet will reassure you of Zara's reliability. True, they are a little more expensive than most other companies in Moshi, but you are paying for peace of mind, quality of service, and tablecloths (you'll see what I mean when you're on your trek). You'll also get one or two nights in their excellent if isolated Springlands Hotel thrown in.

If you do decide to book online, however, one piece of advice: their website is said to be maintained by an Internet 'middleman' company that is reported to take a cut from every online booking, which has resulted in higher prices for those who book through the website. Therefore, if you really do feel confident enough to book online before you've even met anybody (and many do), you'd save yourself a fair wedge of cash if you contact Zara directly at zara@form-net.com rather than going through the address posted on their website. If, on the other hand, you'd rather wait until you reach Moshi before booking, let them know you're coming and what you want to do as it's not inconceivable that they and their guides will be booked out. And when you do reach Moshi, I found it more expeditious to visit the Springlands Hotel and speak to director Zainab Ansell than to call into the office on Rindi Lane and deal with her minions. Costs (if booking direct): US$750 for both Marangu and Machame, including two nights at Springlands; U$700 if you arrange your own accommodation.

WHAT TO BUY

There are plenty of knick-knacks to buy in Moshi, and plenty of places willing to flog them to you. **Our Heritage** next to the Coffee Shop does a nice line in 'I climbed Kili' T-shirts, postcards, jewellery and other gewgaws. **Cranecraft**, in the Kilimanjaro Crane Hotel, has similar stock plus a decent selection of books about the country, its wildlife and, of course, the mountain. **U's Variety** are on the main Mawenzi drag near, but on the opposite side of the road to, the New Kindoroko, and are worth sniffing around, and there are other souvenir places near here too. The **Coffee Shop** itself runs a profitable little trade in neatly wrapped Kilimanjaro coffee, though apparently you can get much the same sort of stuff for half the price at the supermarket.

Finally, **Shah Industries** is a leather workshop-cum-aquarium housed in what used to be a flour mill. It's a strange combination, but a beautiful place, and a worthy one too: over a third of the workers at Shah Industries have some sort of disability. Definitely worth looking around, they lie to the south-east of town across the train tracks on the way to the Springlands Hotel.

GETTING AWAY

Buses

Heading to **Arusha**, buses (Ts1000) leave regularly throughout the day from the terminal on Mawenzi, while travellers wishing to journey to **Marangu** (Ts600) can catch one of the dalla-dallas from the adjacent terminal.

Nairobi Shuttle buses leave from their offices. Davanu (☎ 2753416) are in Kahawa House, and are the most efficient bus office in Moshi. Their Nairobi bus leaves at 11.30am, arriving after dark at 7pm in Nairobi (Ts15,000 residents' price, US$35 otherwise). Riverside are in Room 122, on the first floor of the THB Building (☎ 2750093); their bus to Nairobi also leaves at 11.30am, but they are slightly cheaper than Davanu at US$25 (Ts12,000 residents' rate).

Cheaper still are the big **buses**, though to Nairobi they're not recommended due to lack of comfort, and the fact that they arrive at the bus terminal in Nairobi after dark – and the last place you ever want to be in this world is in a Nairobi bus terminal after dark. If you are determined or stupid, however, Tawfiq operate a couple of buses at 2pm and 5pm for Ts9500.

Dar es Salaam There are plenty of **bus** companies plying the route to Dar. One to recommend is Fresh Ya Shamba, whose offices are a small booth in the garage forecourt on Market Street opposite the bus station. Their daily bus leaves at 10.30am, costs Ts9500, and takes seven-and-a-half hours to reach Dar.

Dar Express have two buses to Dar that start in Moshi, at 6.30am and 9am, as well as others that pass through Moshi on their way to Dar from Arusha. The price of ticket varies from Ts8000 to Ts11,000 depending on the quality of the bus: like many companies, they have started calling in at the big new terminus to the north of Dar, but for the moment at least they are still continuing on to Kisutu in the centre, and even on to the ferry port for those going on to Zanzibar.

Flights

For details of flights out of Kilimanjaro International, see Appendix C p232. The **Air Tanzania** office is by the clocktower on Rengua Road (☎ 2755205; Mon–Fri 8am–5pm, Sat and Sun 8am–2pm). **The Precision Air** representative is Huduma Exim (☎ 2753495; Mon-Sat 8am-5pm, Sun 8am-noon) on Old Moshi Road, part of the Coffee Tree Hotel building. For other airlines, call in at Emslies on Old Moshi Road, (☎ 2752701).

Getting to the airport takes about 45 minutes from Moshi. There is no public transport to Kilimanjaro International, and while you can take an Arusha-bound bus from Moshi and jump off at the junction, that still means you have to hitch down to the airport itself (it's too far to walk). Air Tanzania run shuttles daily (and sometimes twice daily, depending on flight schedule) to the airport to coincide with their flights. The shuttles leave from the Air Tanzania office by the clocktower 2hr and 10min before their flight departure times and are free to those with flight tickets, Ts5000 each way otherwise. Ask at the office the day before to check on departure times and availability.

Riverside are supposed to run shuttles to the airport to tie in with the arrival of KLM flights (US$10 each way), though this service is less reliable than the one from Arusha. Precision Air are also rumoured to run a shuttle service. A **taxi** should cost around Ts15,000, more at night.

Marangu

According to legend, Marangu got its name when the first settlers in this part of Kilimanjaro, astonished by the lush vegetation, well-watered soils and the countless waterfalls they found here, cried out in delight 'Mora ngu, Mora ngu!' ('mora ngu' meaning 'much water'). It remains a verdant and extremely attractive place today, at least once you move away from the small huddle of shops and hustlers by the bus stop and start to climb up the hill towards Marangu Gate. The town is extremely elongated, but is in reality little more than two roads running up the mountain 14km along the Himo-Taveta highway, with a filigree of dusty paths running off both.

Marangu is reached by a Ts600 **dalla-dalla** from Moshi, which takes about an hour. Passengers are normally dropped by the junction next to the bridge, though occasionally they will drive up the hill to drop you off on your doorstep. If not, a ride in the back of a pick-up truck up to Marangu Gate costs Ts300, the pick-ups leaving when full from the bridge.

Nearby there are a number of waterfalls – the nearest being **Kinukamori Falls** (Ts1000 entrance fee), just twenty minutes' walk up from the bridge. You'll often have the place to yourself, except maybe for the occasional villager doing the washing. Ask at the ticket booth here for other attractions nearby, and about walks in the surrounding countryside.

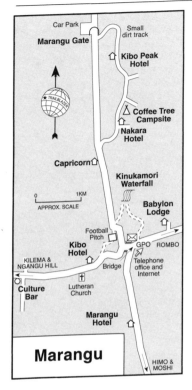

Marangu

Map labels: Car Park · Small dirt track · Marangu Gate · Kibo Peak Hotel · TRAILBLAZER · Coffee Tree Campsite · Nakara Hotel · Capricorn · Kinukamori Waterfall · Babylon Lodge · 0 1KM APPROX. SCALE · Football Pitch · Kibo Hotel · GPO ROMBO · KILEMA & NGANGU HILL · Bridge · Telephone office and Internet · Culture Bar · Lutheran Church · Marangu Hotel · HIMO & MOSHI

PRACTICALITIES

There's a **post office** just to the east of the bridge, and a **telephone office** with **Internet facilities** (though at Ts100 per minute, you'd have to be pretty desperate to want to use it).

Accommodation in Marangu is fairly luxurious and survives by catering to the tour group trade. Note that just about all of the hotels and campsites have some sort of trekking agency attached, and though they are not the cheapest, they are amongst the most reliable. There is a **campsite** in Marangu, though this too is rather luxurious: the *Coffee Tree Campsite* (PO Box 835; ☎ 2754818; 🖥 alpinet rekking@eoltz.com), is an immaculate, manicured place to the east of main road leading up to Marangu Gate where camping alone costs US$8 per person per day, or its US$12 per person per day in one of the chalets (beds for 6 or mattresses for 16) and US$10 in the rondavel (up to four people). Tents can be hired (Ts10,000), as can stoves (Ts6000) and even a fireplace (Ts5000; firewood costs Ts1000). They can also cook for you for around Ts8000. Alpine Tours are based here, arranging trips to waterfalls and other beauty spots around Marangu. Camping is also available at Babylon Lodge and Kibo Hotel (see p158).

The nearest thing to budget **hotel accommodation** in Marangu is the **youth hostel** at Marangu Gate; usually reserved for school groups, they do *occasionally* allow trekkers to stay if it's open and there's room – though whether you'd want to sleep in the same room as a group of over-excited schoolchildren on vacation is another matter. Still, if you are desperate to stay there, or you have a school group of your own, you could give KINAPA a ring (☎ 2756602) to see if there are places available. The cost is US$10 per person per night. Not too far away and also reasonably cheap (US$20 per night), the *Kibo Peak Hotel* is tatty, neglected and nearly always deserted; further down, near the Coffee Tree Campsite is the new *Hotel Nakara* (☎ 2756571, 🖹 2756599; 🖥 www.nak aratz.com), which is clearly aiming to grab its share of the tour group trade, though independent trekkers are welcome if there's space, and rates are negotiable (rack rates US$50 per person per night for B&B, US$60 half-board, or US$70 full board). Down the hill and on the opposite side, rooms at the *Capricorn Hotel* (PO Box 938, ☎ 2751309, 🖹 2752442; 🖳 www.africaonline. co.tz/capricornhotel) look a little tired, particularly the fitted cabinets – which is a little odd considering the hotel is only just six years old – but guests forgive them everything when they see the splendid garden, a real labyrinth of flowers, birds and streams with giant Chagga storage baskets and a traditional Chagga house outside reception. Try to get a room with balcony; the cost is the same as those without.

Two places worth mentioning on the Himo-Taveta road: east of Marangu and just off the main road is the very pleasant *Babylon Lodge* (PO Box 227; ☎/🖹 2751315; 🖳 babylon@africaonline.co.tz), a deceptively large place with 40 unusually-shaped rooms, some of them sunnier and cleaner than others so check them out before checking in (US$25/40/60 sgl/dbl/tpl); they also have a campsite for US$5 per person. The *Marangu Hotel* (☎ 2751307; 🖳 www.ma ranguhotel.com) is an established favourite, standing in 12 acres of gardens (with pool) 4km south of town on the way to Himo. The building used to be a farmhouse, was built in the early 1900s and is absolutely charming. All rooms are self-contained, the food is great, the bread home-baked, and rates vary from US$30–70 per person per night.

Finally, no hotel review of Marangu would be complete without mentioning the *Kibo Hotel* (PO Box 102, ☎/🖹 2751308; 🖳 www.kibohotel.com) which, whilst it cannot compete with most of the other hotels here in terms of luxury or comfort, cannot be beaten when it comes to character and history. A sign welcoming former US president Jimmy Carter still hangs above the door – it's a perfect symbol of the faded yet fascinating grandeur of the place, and of the time-warp it appears to be living in now. Antique German maps and other paraphernalia from the last century (and the one before that) adorn reception; the rooms themselves are overpriced, but it remains an absorbing place to wander around even if you don't intend staying. Prices: US$40/70/88 for sgl/dbl/tpl half board, US$25/40/58 for bed and breakfast. Camping (including a hot shower) costs US$6.

Getting away

Leaving Marangu, there's a bus straight from here to Dar es Salaam: every day at about 1pm the Dar Express drives through on its way to Rombo, further north; ask nicely, and your hotel may send someone to stop it and reserve seats for the return journey that passes by on the way to Dar at around 6am the next day. The cost is Ts7000, with the total travel time about six hours. (Incidentally, the Mombasa Express also drives by, at about 3pm every day.) The only other option to these is to catch a dalla-dalla to Moshi and reserve a seat there; it is in theory possible to stop a Dar-bound bus on the Moshi-Dar highway at Himo, though travellers who have tried this usually end up waiting for hours for one with a spare seat, and eventually most give up.

PART 6: MINIMUM IMPACT AND SAFE TREKKING

Minimum impact trekking

Manya ulanyc upangenyi cha ipfuve – 'Do not foul the cave where you have slept'
(A Chagga proverb that is said to refer to the living habits of the baboon, who do indeed 'foul their caves' until there comes a point where the stench compels them to find alternative accommodation.)

KINAPA have gone to great lengths to clean up Kilimanjaro. At all huts and most campsites, every trekking group must have its rubbish weighed by the ranger and if there's any evidence that some rubbish has been dumped (ie if the rubbish carried weighs less at one campsite than it did at the previous one) then the guide could have his licence temporarily revoked and/or have to pay a heavy fine. It's a system that would appear to have many loopholes, but somehow it seems to work: Kili *is* a very clean mountain, and it remains the only one I know where porters and guides will voluntarily walk fifty yards from the trail to pick up a discarded water bottle or sweet wrapper. And while it can be a little frustrating to have to wait for your guide every morning while the rubbish is weighed, it's a small price to pay for a pristine peak.

Trekkers can also do their bit in keeping Kilimanjaro beautiful by following these simple rules that apply to almost every mountain anywhere in the world:
● **Don't start fires**. For some reason, many trekkers feel that lighting a fire and sitting around it in the evening is an integral part of the trekking and camping experience. But the box on p95 will give you an idea of just how much damage an out-of-control fire can cause. There's absolutely no need to light a fire on Kilimanjaro: for cooking, your guides and porters should use kerosene, while for heat, put another layer of clothes on, or cuddle up to somebody who doesn't mind being cuddled up to.
● **Dispose of litter properly**. On Kili, all you have to do is give your litter to your 'staff': given the stiff punishments they receive for leaving rubbish behind (see above), this should ensure all waste is taken off the mountain. The only exception to this rule is **used batteries**, which you must keep with you and take back to the West where they have the facilities to dispose of them properly.
● **Boil, filter or purify your drinking water**. This will help to reduce the number of non-returnable, non-reusable, non-biodegradable and very non-environmentally friendly plastic mineral water bottles that are used on Kili.
● **Use the purpose-built latrines**. True, some of them could do with emptying (especially the central toilet at the Barranco campsite, which is now so full that the pile of human waste is in danger of developing a snowy cap all of its own), but this is still better than having piles of poo behind all the bushes on the trail and toilet paper hanging from every bough. If the situation is really urgent and

you cannot wait until you reach one of the purpose-built latrines along the way, deliberate before you defecate: firstly, make sure you're at least 20m away from both the path and any streams or rivers – the mountain is still the main source of water for many villages, and the people who live there would prefer it if you didn't crap in their H_2O. Secondly, take a plastic spade or trowel with you so you can dig a hole to squat over, and cover this hole with plenty of earth when you've finished. And finally, dispose of your toilet paper properly, by either burning it (the preferable method) or, if this is not feasible, by putting it in the hole you've just dug and covering it with plenty of soil.

● **Leave the flora and fauna alone**. Kili is home to some beautiful flowers and fascinating wildlife, but the giant groundsels rarely thrive in the soils of Europe and the wild buffalo, though they may look docile when splashing about in the streams of Kili, have an awful temper that makes them quite unsuitable as pets. It's illegal to take the flora or fauna out of the park, so leave it all alone; that way, other trekkers can enjoy them too.

● **Stay on the main trail**. The continued use of shortcuts, particularly steep ones, erodes the slopes. This is particularly true on Kibo: having reached the summit, it's very tempting on your return to slide down on the shale like a skier, and you'll see many people, especially guides, doing just that. There's no doubt that it's a fast, fun and furious way to get to the bottom, but with thousands of trekkers doing likewise every year, the slopes of Kibo are gradually being eroded as all the shale gets pushed further down the mountain. Laborious as it sounds, stick to the same snaking path that you used to ascend.

● **Wash away from streams and rivers**. You wouldn't like to bathe in somebody else's bathwater; nor, probably, would you like to cook with it, do your laundry in it, nor indeed drink it. And neither would the villagers on Kili's lower slopes, so don't pollute their water by washing your hair, body or clothes in the mountain streams, no matter how romantic an idea this sounds. If your guide is halfway decent he will bring some hot water in a bowl at the end of the day's walk for you to wash with. Dispose of it at least 20m away from any streams or rivers.

Opposite Top: Strange cloud patterns above Kifunika Hill, just off the Marangu Route. **Bottom**: The most popular huts on Kili: the Horombo Huts at 3657m.

Safe trekking

Came to cave. Men cold. Passed two corpses of young men who died of exposure, a short time ago. The vultures had pecked out their eyes, the leopards had taken a leg from each.
From the diary of **Peter MacQueen** as recorded in his book *In Wildest Africa*

Because of the number of trekkers who scale Kilimanjaro each year, and the odd ways in which some of them choose to do so, many people are under the mistaken impression that Africa's highest mountain is also a safe mountain. Unfortunately, as any mountaineer will tell you, there's no such thing as a safe mountain, particularly one nearly 6000m tall with extremes of climate near the summit and ferociously carnivorous animals roaming the lower slopes.

Your biggest enemy on Kilimanjaro, however, is likely to be neither the weather nor the wildlife but the altitude. Unsurprisingly, KINAPA are shy about revealing how many trekkers perish on Kili each year but what is known is that, during the millennium celebrations, when the mountain was swamped by more than a thousand trekkers on New Year's Eve alone, three died and thirty-three more had to be rescued. The culprit behind at least one of the fatalities was the condition known as acute mountain sickness, or AMS.

The authorities are doing what they can to minimize the number of deaths: guides are given thorough training in what to do if one of their group is showing signs of AMS and trekkers are required to register each night upon arrival at the campsite and have to pay a US$20 'rescue fee' as part of their park fees. But you too can do your bit, by avoiding AMS in the first place. The following few pages discuss in detail what AMS actually is, how it is caused, the symptoms and, finally, how to avoid it. Read this section carefully: it may well save your life. Following this, on p166 you'll find details of other ailments commonly suffered by trekkers on Kilimanjaro.

WHAT IS AMS?

At Uhuru Peak, the summit of Kilimanjaro, the oxygen present in the atmosphere is only half that found at sea level. In other words, every time you breathe on Kibo, you are taking in only half as much oxygen as you would if you took the same breath in Dar es Salaam.

This can, of course, be seriously detrimental to your health; oxygen is, after all, pretty essential to your physical well-being. All of your vital organs need it, as do your muscles. They receive their oxygen via red blood cells, which are loaded with oxygen by your lungs and then pumped around your body by your heart, delivering oxygen as they go.

Opposite Top: The first night's campsite on the Machame Route, just above the tree-line at 3000m. **Bottom**: Blue monkeys on the trail above the Mandara Huts on the Marangu Route.

Problems arise at altitude when that most vital of organs, the brain, isn't getting enough oxygen and malfunctions as a result; because as the body's central control room, if the brain malfunctions, so does the rest of you, often with fatal consequences.

Fortunately, your body is an adaptable piece of machinery and can adjust to the lower levels of oxygen present at altitude. Unconsciously you will start to breathe deeper and faster, your blood will thicken as your body produces more red blood cells, and your heart will beat faster. As a result, your essential organs will receive the same level of oxygen as they always did. But your body needs time before it can effect all these changes. Though the deeper, faster breathing and heart-quickening happen almost as soon as your body realizes that there is less oxygen available, it takes a few days for the blood to thicken. And with Kilimanjaro, of course, a few days is usually all you have on the mountain, and the changes may simply not happen in time. The result, is AMS.

AMS, or acute mountain sickness (also known as **altitude sickness**), is what happens when the body fails to adapt in time to the lack of oxygen at altitude. There are three levels of AMS: mild, moderate and severe. On Kilimanjaro, it's fair to say that most people will get some symptoms of the illness and will fall into the mild-to-moderate categories. Having symptoms of mild AMS is not *necessarily* a sign that the sufferer should give up climbing Kili and descend immediately. Indeed, most or all of the symptoms suffered by those with **mild AMS** will disappear if the person rests and ascends no further, and assuming the recovery is complete, the assault on the summit can continue. The same goes for **moderate AMS** too, though here the poor individual and his or her symptoms should be monitored far more closely to ensure that they are not getting any worse and developing into **severe AMS**. This is a lot more serious and sufferers with severe AMS should always descend immediately, even if it means going down by torchlight in the middle of the night.

The following describes the symptoms of the various levels of AMS.

What are the symptoms?

The symptoms of **mild AMS** are not dissimilar to the symptoms of a particularly vicious hangover, namely a thumping headache, nausea and a general feeling of lousiness. An AMS headache is generally agreed to be one of the most dreadful headaches you can get, a blinding pain that thuds continuously at ever decreasing intervals; only those who have bungee-jumped from a 99ft building with a 100ft elasticated rope will know the intense, repetitive pain AMS can cause. Thankfully, the usual headache remedies should prove effective against a mild AMS headache.

As with a hangover, mild AMS sufferers often have trouble sleeping and, when they do, that sleep can be light and intermittent. They can also suffer from a lack of appetite. Given the energy you've expended getting to altitude in the first place, both of these symptoms can seem surprising if you're not aware of AMS.

Moderate AMS is more serious and requires careful monitoring of the sufferer to ensure that it does not progress to severe AMS. With moderate AMS,

Other effects of altitude

There are other symptoms suffered by people at high altitude that are not in themselves usually cause for any concern. The first is the phenomenon of **periodic breathing**. What happens is that, during sleep, the breathing of a person becomes less and less deep, until it appears that he or she has stopped breathing altogether for a few seconds — to the obvious consternation of those sharing the person's tent. The person will then breathe or snore deeply a couple of times to recover, causing relief all round. Another phenomenon is that of **swollen hands and feet**, more common amongst women than men. Once again, this is no cause for concern unless the swelling is particularly severe. Another one that is far more common among women than men, is **irregular periods**. The need to **urinate** and **break wind** frequently are also typical of high altitude living, and far from being something to be concerned about, are actually positive indications that your body is adapting well to the conditions. As is written on an ancient tombstone in Dorset:

Let your wind go free, where e'er you be,
For holding it in, was the death of me.

the sufferer's nausea will lead to vomiting, the headache will not go away even after pain-relief remedies, and in addition the sufferer will appear to be permanently out of breath, even when doing nothing.

With moderate AMS, it is possible to continue to the summit, but only after a prolonged period of relaxation that will enable the sufferer to make a complete recovery. Unfortunately, treks run to tight schedules and cannot change their itineraries mid-trek. Whether you, as a victim of moderate AMS, will be given time to recover will depend largely upon how fortunate you are, and whether the onset of your illness happens to coincide with a scheduled rest day or not.

With **severe AMS**, on the other hand, there should be no debate about whether or not to continue: if anybody is showing symptoms of severe AMS it is imperative that they **descend immediately**. These symptoms include a lack of coordination and balance, a symptom known as **ataxia**. A quick and easy way to check for ataxia is to draw a 10m line in the sand and ask the person to walk along it. If they clearly struggle to complete this simple test, suspect ataxia and descend. (Note, however, that ataxia can also be caused by hypothermia or extreme fatigue. As such, ensure that the sufferer is suitably dressed in warm clothing and has eaten well before ascertaining whether or not he or she is suffering from ataxia, and what to do about it). Other symptoms of severe AMS include mental confusion, slurred or incoherent speech, and an inability to stay awake. There may also be a gurgling, liquid sound in the lungs combined with a persistent watery cough which may produce a clear liquid, a pinky phlegm or possibly even blood. There may also be a marked blueness around the face and lips, and a heartbeat that, even at rest, may be over 130 beats per minute. These are the symptoms of either HACO and HAPO, as outlined below.

Other ways of dealing with somebody with AMS are given on p165.

HACO AND HAPO

Poor Mapandi, a carrier whom I had noticed shivering with fever for the last day or two, stiffened, grew cold and died beside me in the mud. **Peter MacQueen** *In Wildest Africa*

HACO (High Altitude Cerebral Oedema) is a build-up of fluid around the brain. It's as serious as it sounds. It is HACO that is causing the persistent headache, vomiting, ataxia and the lack of consciousness. If not treated, death could follow in as little as 24 hours, less if the victim continues ascending.

Just as serious, **HAPO** (High Altitude Pulmonary Oedema) is the accumulation of fluid around the lungs. It is this condition that is causing the persistent cough and pinkish phlegm. Once again, the only sensible option is to descend as fast as possible. In addition, one of the treatments outlined on p165 should also be considered.

HOW TO AVOID IT

Haraka haraka haina baraka 'Great haste has no blessing' – a common Swahili saying.

AMS is easily avoided. The only surefire way to to do is to **take your time**. Opting to save money by climbing the mountain as quickly as possible is a false economy: the chances are you will have to turn back because of AMS, and all your efforts (and money) will be wasted.

According to the Expedition Advisory Committee at the Royal Geographical Society, the recommended acclimatization period for any altitude greater than 2500m is to sleep no more than 300m higher than your previous night's camp, and to spend an extra night at every third camp. But if you were to follow this on the Kilimanjaro's Marangu Route, for example, from Mandara Huts you would have to take a further *eight* nights in order to safely adjust to the Kibo Huts' altitude of 4700m – whereas most trekkers take just two days to walk between the two. The EAC realize that the short distances and high per diem cost of climbing Kilimanjaro make this lengthy itinerary impractical, so instead they recommend a pre-trek acclimatization walk on Mount Meru (see p142) or Mount Kenya (4895m to Point Lenana). This is an excellent idea if you have the time and are feeling fit, and providing you do one of these walks *immediately* before you climb Kili, these treks can be beneficial – and the views towards Kilimanjaro from Meru are delightful too.

But what if you don't have the time or money to do these other climbs? The answer is to plan your walk on Kilimanjaro as carefully as possible. If you have enough money for a 'rest day' or two, take them. These 'rest days' are not actually days of rest at all – on the Marangu trail, for example, guides usually lead their trekkers up from Horombo Huts to the Mawenzi Hut at 4600m before returning that same afternoon. But they do provide trekkers with the chance to experience a higher altitude before returning to below 3000–4000m again, thereby obeying the mountaineers' old maxim about the need to '**climb high, sleep low**' to avoid mountain sickness.

The route you take is also important. Some of the routes – the Machame, Lemosho and Shira trails via the Barafu Huts, for example – obey the moun-

Diamox

Acetazolamide (traded under the brand name Diamox) is the wonder drug that fights AMS, and the first treatment doctors give to somebody suffering from mountain sickness. Indeed, many trekkers use it as a prophylactic, taking it during the walk to prevent AMS.

Diamox works by acidifying the blood, which stimulates breathing, allowing a greater amount of oxygen to enter into the bloodstream. Always consult with your doctor before taking Diamox to discuss the risks and benefits. If you do take it, remember to try it out first back at home to check for allergic reaction, as Diamox is a sulfa derivative, and some people do suffer from side effects, particularly a strange tingling sensation in their hands and feet.

The disadvantage with taking AMS prophylactically, according to one doctor serving on the Annapurna Circuit in Nepal, is that you are using up one possible cure. That is to say, should you begin to suffer from AMS despite taking Diamox, doctors are going to have to look for another form of treatment to ensure your survival. For this reason, a number of trekkers are now buying the drug and taking it up the mountain with them, but are using it only as a last resort when symptoms are persistent. If you are unfamiliar with Diamox and uncertain about the effect it could have on you, this is perhaps the best option.

taineers' maxim on the third or fourth days, when the trail climbs to 4530m before plunging down to an altitude of 3950m at Barranco Camp where you spend the night. Some of the shorter trails, however, do not: for example, it is possible for a trekker walking at an average pace on the Marangu or Rongai trails to reach the Kibo Huts in three days and attempt an assault on the summit for that third night. This sort of schedule is entirely too rapid, allowing insufficient time for trekkers to adapt to the new conditions prevalent at the higher altitude. This is why the majority of people fail on these trails, and it is also the reason why **it is imperative that you take a 'rest day' on the way up**: to give your body more time to acclimatize.

How you approach the walk is important too. Statistically, men are more likely to suffer from AMS than women, with young men the most vulnerable. The reason is obvious. The competitive streak in most young men causes them to walk faster than the group; that, and the mistaken belief that greater fitness and strength (which most men, mistakenly or otherwise, believe they have) will protect them against AMS. But AMS is no respecter of fitness or health. Indeed, many experienced mountaineers believe the reverse is true: the less fit you are, the slower you will want to walk, and thus the greater chance you have of acclimatizing properly. The best advice, then, is to **go as slowly as possible**. Let your guide be the pacemaker: do not be tempted to hare off ahead of him, but stick with him. That way you can keep a sensible pace – and, what's more, can ask him any questions about the mountain that occur to you on the way.

There are other things you can do that may or may not reduce the chance of getting AMS. One is to **eat well**: fatigue is said to be a major contributor to AMS, so try to keep energy levels up by eating as much as you can.

Dehydration can exacerbate AMS too, so it is vital that you **drink every few minutes** when walking; for this reason, one of the new platypus-style water bags which allow you to drink hands-free without breaking stride are invaluable (see p43). **Wearing warm clothes** is very important too, allowing you to conserve energy that would otherwise be spent on maintaining a reasonable body temperature. Although there hasn't been a serious study on this subject, many people swear that carrying your own rucksack increases your chance of succumbing to AMS. Certainly, in my experience, this is true, so, finally, **hire a porter to carry your baggage**.

HOW TO TREAT IT

Sat down beside P.D. in the mud. Gave him one bottle of champagne. Revived him greatly.
Peter MacQueen *In Wildest Africa*

The chances are that on your trek you will see at least one poor sod being wheeled down Kili, surrounded by porters and strapped to the strange unicycle-cum-stretcher device that KINAPA uses for evacuating the sick and suffering from the mountain. Descent is the most effective cure for AMS, but in some severe cases it is not enough. Diamox (see box above) is also usually given, though again, if the victim has been suffering for a while or Diamox is not available, some other treatment may be used such as:

Gamow bag Some of the upmarket trek operators may carry a gamow bag with them. This is a man-sized plastic bag into which the victim is enclosed. The bag is then zipped up and inflated. As it is inflated, the pressure felt by the sufferer inside the bag is increased, thus mimicking the atmospheric conditions present at a lower altitude. The disadvantage with this method is that of inconvenience. The cumbersome bag has to be dragged up the mountain and, worst of all, in order to work effectively once the patient is inside, the bag must be kept at a constant pressure. This means that somebody must pump up the bag every two or three minutes. This is tricky when at least two other people are trying to manoeuvre the body and bag down the slopes.

Oxygen Giving the victim extra oxygen from a bottle or canister does not immediately reverse all the symptoms, though in conjunction with rapid descent it can be most effective.

OTHER POTENTIAL HEALTH PROBLEMS

Coughs and colds

These are common on Kilimanjaro. Aspirin can be taken for a cold; lozenges containing anaesthetic are useful for a sore throat, as is gargling with warm salty water. Drinking plenty helps too. A cough that produces mucus has one of a number of causes; most likely are the common cold or irritation of the bronchi by cold air which produces symptoms that are similar to flu. It could, however, point to AMS. A cough that produces thick green and yellow mucus could indicate bronchitis. If there is also chest pain (most severe when the patient breathes out), a high fever and blood-stained mucus, any of these could indicate pneumonia, requiring a course of antibiotics. Consult a doctor.

Exposure
Also known as hypothermia, this is caused by a combination of not wearing enough warm clothes against the cold, exhaustion, high altitude, dehydration and lack of food. Note that it does not need to be very cold for exposure to occur. Make sure everyone (particularly your porters) is properly equipped.

Symptoms of exposure include a low body temperature (below 34.5°C or 94°F), poor co-ordination, exhaustion and shivering. As the condition deteriorates the shivering ceases, co-ordination gets worse making walking difficult and the patient may start hallucinating. The pulse then slows and unconsciousness and death follow shortly. Treatment involves thoroughly warming the patient quickly. Find shelter as soon as possible. Put the patient, without their clothes, into a sleeping-bag with hot water bottles (use your water bottles); someone else should take their clothes off, too, and get into the sleeping bag with the patient. Nothing like bodily warmth to hasten recovery.

Frostbite
The severe form of frostbite that leads to the loss of fingers and toes rarely happens to trekkers on Kilimanjaro. You could, however, be affected if you get stuck or lost in particularly inclement weather. Ensure that all members of your party are properly kitted out with thick socks, boots, gloves and woolly hats.

The first stage of frostbite is known as 'frostnip'. The fingers or toes first become cold and painful, then numb and white. Heat them up on a warm part of the body (eg an armpit) until the colour comes back. In cases of severe frostbite the affected part of the body becomes frozen. Don't try to warm it up until you reach a lodge/camp. Immersion in warm water (40°C or 100°F) is the treatment. Medical help should then be sought.

Gynaecological problems
If you have had a vaginal infection in the past it would be a good idea to bring a course of treatment in case it recurs.

Haemorrhoids
If you've suffered from these in the past bring the required medication with you since haemorrhoids can flare up on a trek, particularly if you get constipated.

Snowblindness
Though the snows of Kilimanjaro are fast disappearing, you are still strongly advised to wear sunglasses when walking on the summit – particularly if you plan on spending more than just an hour or two up there – to prevent this uncomfortable, though temporary, condition. Ensure everyone in your group, including porters, has eye protection. If you lose your sunglasses a piece of cardboard with two narrow slits (just wide enough to see through) will protect your eyes. The cure for snow-blindness is to keep the eyes closed, and lie down in a dark room. Eye-drops and aspirin can be helpful.

Sunburn

Protect against sunburn by wearing a hat, sunglasses and a shirt with a collar that can be turned up. At altitude you'll also need sunscreen for your face.

Care of feet, ankles and knees

A twisted ankle, swollen knee or a septic blister on your foot could ruin your trek so it's important to take care to avoid these. Choose comfortable boots with good ankle support. Don't carry too heavy a load. Wash your feet and change your socks regularly. During lunch stops take off your boots and socks and let them dry in the sun. Attend to any blister as soon as you feel it developing.

Blisters There are a number of ways to treat blisters but prevention is far better than cure. Stop immediately you feel a 'hot spot' forming and cover it with a piece of moleskin or Second Skin. One trekker suggests using the membrane inside an egg-shell as an alternative form of Second Skin. If a blister does form you can either burst it with a needle (sterilized in a flame) then apply a dressing or build a moleskin dressing around the unburst blister to protect it.

Kilimanjaro seen from Lake Jipé
(from *The Kilima-njaro Expedition – A Record of Scientific Exploration in Eastern Equatorial Africa* HH Johnston, 1886)

Sprains You can lessen the risk of a sprained ankle by wearing boots which offer good support. Watch where you walk, too. If you do sprain an ankle, cool it in a stream and keep it bandaged. If it's very painful you'll probably have to abandon your trek and return to your hotel. Aspirin is helpful for reducing pain and swelling.

Knee problems These are most common after long stretches of walking downhill. It's important not to take long strides as you descend; small steps will lessen the jarring on the knee. It may be helpful to wear knee supports and use walking poles for long descents, especially if you've had problems with your knees before.

PART 7: TRAIL GUIDE AND MAPS

Using this guide

ABOUT THE MAPS IN THIS GUIDE

Scale
Most of the **trekking maps** in this guide are drawn to the same scale, namely 19mm to 1km (1¼ inches to the mile). The exceptions are those maps depicting the routes up to the Kibo summit – ie, those maps that depict the final ascent to the top, which is usually made at night. In these maps the scale has been doubled (ie 38mm to 1km or 2½ inches to the mile) to allow for more detail to be drawn on them.

Walking times
The times indicated on the maps should be used as an approximate guide. They refer to **walking times only**, and do not include any time for breaks and food: don't forget to add on a few minutes for breaks when estimating the total time for a particular stage. Overall you may find you need to **add between 10% and 30%** depending on your walking speed and the average lengths of the breaks you take.

Gradient arrows
You will also notice that we have drawn '**gradient arrows**' on the trekking maps in this book. The arrows point uphill: two arrows mean that the hill is steep, one that the gradient is reasonably gradual.

The Marangu Route

Because this trail is popularly called the 'Tourist Route' or '**Coca Cola Trail**', some trekkers are misled into thinking this five- or six-day climb to the summit is simply a walk in the (national) park. But remember that a greater proportion of people fail on this route than on any other. True, this may have something to do with the fact that Marangu's reputation for being 'easy' attracts the more

---

❏ In the following descriptions, the treks have been divided into stages, with each stage roughly corresponding to a day's trekking. For this reason, throughout the text the words 'stage' and 'day' have been used interchangeably.

WHAT'S IT LIKE ON THE TRAIL?

Fun. It really is. Sure, the last push to the summit is hard, as some of the quotes used later in this book clearly indicate, but don't let it put you off. Kilimanjaro is a delightful mountain to climb:

But we had much to compensate us for all we had to give up. The charm of the mountain scenery, the clear, crisp atmosphere, the tonic of 'a labour we delight in' and the consciousness now and again of success achieved, all went far to make our fortnight's arduous toil a happy sequence of red-letter days. **Hans Meyer** *Across East African Glaciers*

The days are spent walking through spectacular landscapes which change every day as you pass through different vegetation zones; the pace is never exhausting, as you have to walk slowly in order to give yourself a chance to acclimatize. And as for the end of the day, while the guides are cooking your dinner, you are free to wander around the campsite; and, as you bump into the same people time and again over the course of the trek, a sense of community soon develops. Then as night falls, and you tuck into the huge plates of food cooked by your crew, the stars come out, stunning everyone into silence. This is the favourite time of day for most people: rested, replete with food, and with a day of satisfactory walking behind and a good night's sleep ahead, it's natural to feel a sense of comfort and contentment, with the thought of wild animals possibly lying nearby serving to add a pleasing hint of excitement.

Bed? It's too early. I feel too good. Aaah I wonder if there'll ever be another time as good as this. **Gregory Peck**, in the film version of *The Snows of Kilimanjaro*.

Of course, walking up from around 1800m to 5892.55m or thereabouts does, as you can probably imagine, take a lot of effort, and the night walk to the summit is unarguably tough. But short of actually carrying you up, your crew will do everything possible to make your entire experience as comfortable as possible. In fact, they'll spoil you: not only do they carry your bag, but at the end of the day's walk you'll turn up at camp to find your tent has already been erected, with a bowl of hot water lying nearby for you to wash away the grime of the day. A few minutes late and a large plate of popcorn and biscuits will be served with a mug of steaming hot tea or coffee.

What to put in your daypack

Normally you will not see your backpack from the moment you hand it to the porter to carry in the morning to at least lunchtime, and maybe not until the end of the day. It's therefore necessary to pack everything that you may need during the day in your bag that you carry with you. Some suggestions, in no particular order:

- sweets
- water and water purifiers
- camera and spare film/batteries
- this book/maps
- sunhat/sunglasses and suncream
- compass
- toilet paper and trowel
- rainwear
- walking sticks and knee supports
- medical kit, including chapstick
- watch
- whistle

Accommodation on the trail

I got back in time to see P.D. lying on sloping ground, slipping off the stretcher, and in great pain. Small fire had been made under the root of a great tree. Rain soon came on and wiped out the fire ... tent was not put up and we were all in great misery. Men with tent lost in the darkness. Thought if the rain stopped we could go on in the moonlight. Rain did not stop. **Peter MacQueen** *In Wildest Africa*

Unless you are on the Marangu Route (or the latter part of the Rongai Route where it coincides with Marangu), accommodation on the mountain will be in tents brought up by your porters. (Do not be tempted to sleep in any of the caves, which is against the park regulations.) On the Marangu Route, camping is forbidden and instead people have to sleep in huts along the route. The sleeping arrangements in these huts are usually dormitory-style, with anything from four to twenty beds per room.

Confusingly, away from the Marangu Route, many of the campsites on Kilimanjaro are actually called huts, but don't be fooled: they are called huts merely because of the green shacks that you'll find at these campsites, and which are usually inhabited by the park rangers. Trekkers used to be allowed to sleep in these huts too, but no longer, although porters and guides still sometimes sleep in them depending on the mood of the ranger and the space available

The only other buildings you will possibly see along some trails are the toilets. Most are of the same design, namely a little wooden hut with a hole in the floor. Some are in better condition than others; all I will say is that some people are terrible shots, while other latrines are in desperate need of emptying before they become Kilimanjaro's fourth peak.

Food on the trail

Remember to tell your agency if you have any special dietary requirements – because both meat and nuts form a substantial part of the menu on Kilimanjaro.

A typical **breakfast** will involve eggs (boiled or fried), porridge, a saveloy (possibly with some tomatoes too), a piece of fruit such as a banana or orange, some bread with jam, honey or peanut butter, and a mug or two of tea or coffee.

Lunch is usually prepared at breakfast and carried by the trekker in his or her daypack. This packed lunch often consists of a boiled egg, some sandwiches, a banana or orange, and some tea kept warm in a flask and carried by your guide.

At the end of the day's walking, **afternoon tea** is served with biscuits, peanuts and, best of all, salted popcorn. The final and biggest meal of the day, **dinner** usually begins with soup, followed by a main course including chicken or meat, a vegetable sauce, some cabbage, and rice or pasta; if your porters have brought up some potatoes, these will usually be eaten on the first night as they are so heavy.

Drink on the trail

Porters will collect water from the rivers and streams along the trail. Some of this they will boil for you at the start of the day to carry in your water bottles. On the lower slopes you can collect water yourself from the many streams and purify it using a filter or tablets. Note, however, that as you climb ever higher the water becomes more scarce. On the Machame trail, for example, the last water point is at the Karanga Valley, the lunch-stop before Barafu; on Marangu, it's just before the Saddle. For this reason it is essential that you carry enough bottles or containers for *at least* two litres.

In camp, coffee and tea is served, and maybe hot chocolate too – all usually made with powdered milk. Remember that all of these are dehydrating, which can be bad for acclimatization, and are diuretics too (ie you will want to urinate frequently – something you will already be doing a lot as you adapt to the higher conditions).

inexperienced, out-of-condition trekkers who don't realize that they are embarking on a **forty-kilometre uphill walk**, followed immediately by a forty-kilometre knee-jarring descent. But it shouldn't take much to realize that this is not much easier than any other trail: with the Machame Route, for example, you start at 1800m and aim for the summit at 5895m. On Marangu, you start just a little higher at 1828m and have the same goal, so simple logic should tell you that it can't be that much easier.

The main reason why people say that Marangu is easier is because it is the only route where you **sleep in huts**, rather than under canvas. The accommodation in these huts should be booked in advance by your tour company, who have to pay a US$30 deposit per person per night to KINAPA in order to secure it. To cover this, the tour agencies will probably ask you to pay them some money in advance too. This deposit for the huts is refundable or can be moved to secure huts on other dates, providing you give KINAPA (and your agency) at least seven days' notice.

Unfortunately, some of the cheaper agencies prefer to trust to luck when it comes to accommodation on the Marangu Route, deciding that it is too much bother to travel all the way to Marangu Gate to pay a deposit. Instead they prefer to assume/pray that there will be room in the huts for their clients when they get there. In days gone by this resulted in some trekkers sleeping on dining tables or hall floors in situations where the huts were overbooked. More and more frequently, however, KINAPA are refusing to allow trekkers without a reservation even to start their walk if the huts are fully booked. For your own peace of mind, therefore, you should ask your agency to show you a receipt confirming that they have paid a deposit for your accommodation on the trek. Furthermore, **be suspicious of any agency that *doesn't* ask for at least some of your trekking fee upfront to cover these deposits**, or who agrees to accept a last-minute booking for the Marangu Route – they should have at least a day's notice in order to book the huts and pay the deposits. Of course, in most cases these agencies get away with their lackadaisical approach to hut booking, simply because the huts aren't always fully booked and there are usually enough spaces for you, especially if your party is a small one of only two or three trekkers. But don't be surprised if, having booked with one of the cheaper and less reputable agencies, it transpires that there is no room for you at the huts and you get turned away at Marangu Gate. Incidentally, there are 70 spaces at Mandara Huts, 148 at Horombo – the extra beds are necessary because this hut is also used by those descending from Kibo, as well as those coming from the Rongai Route – and just 58 at Kibo. If any one of those are already booked to capacity on the night you wish to stay there, you will not be allowed to start your trek and will have to change your dates.

The fact that you do sleep in huts makes little difference to what you need to pack for the trek, for sleeping bags are still required (the huts have pillows and mattresses but that's all) though you can dispense with a ground mat for this route. You may also need some small change should you give in to temptation and decide that the exorbitant price of sweets and drinks that are available at the huts is still a price worth paying. The fact that there's no tent to carry, however, means you can probably get away with just two porters per person, or even one if you carry your own bag – something of a false economy I've found, as explained on p151. Regarding the sleeping situation, it does help if you can get to the huts early each day to grab the better beds. This doesn't mean you should deliberately hurry to the huts, which will reduce your enjoyment of the trek and increase the possibility of AMS. But do try to **start early each morning**: that way you can avoid the crowds, beat them to the better beds, and possibly improve your chances of seeing some of Kili's wildlife too.

In terms of **duration**, the Marangu Route is one of the shorter trails, taking just five days (or 24 hours if you happen to be as nutty as the Brazilian mentioned in the introduction to this book). Many people, however, opt to take an extra day to acclimatize at Horombo Huts, using that day to visit the Mawenzi Huts Campsite at 4538m. In theory this is entirely sensible, though in my experience just as many 'six-day' people fail as those who take five days. Aesthetically such a plan cannot be argued with, however, for the views from Mawenzi across the Saddle to Kibo truly take the breath away (assuming, that is, that you have some left to be taken away after all that climbing).

One aspect of the Marangu Route that could be seen by some as a drawback is that it is the only one where you **ascend and descend via the same path**. However, there are a couple of arguments to counter this perception: firstly, between Horombo and Kibo Huts there are two paths, and it shouldn't take too much to persuade your guide to use one trail on the ascent and a different one on the way down; and secondly, we think that the walk back down the Marangu Route is one of the most pleasurable parts of the entire trek, with splendid views over the shoulder. Furthermore, it offers the chance to greet the crowds of sweating, red-faced unfortunates heading the other way with the smug expression of one for whom physical pain is now a thing of the past, and whose immediate future is filled with warm showers and cold beers.

STAGE 1: MARANGU GATE TO MANDARA HUTS   [MAP 1, p174]

The woods are lovely, dark and deep, but I have promises to keep, and miles to go before I sleep.   **Robert Frost** as seen on a signwriter's wall in Moshi

As the headquarters of KINAPA (Kilimanjaro National Park), you might expect Marangu Gate (altitude 1800m) to have the best facilities of all the gates, and it doesn't disappoint. Not only does the gate have the usual **registration office**, but there's also a picnic area, a payphone and some latrines, and a **shop-cum-tour-agency** that sells stamps, has a good collection of books and souvenirs and allows you to make international phone calls (at premium rates, of course). There's also a small booth run by the Kilimanjaro Guides Cooperative where you can **hire any equipment** you may have forgotten to bring along, from essentials such as hats and fleeces, sleeping bags and water bottles, to camping stuff that you almost certainly won't need on the trail such as stoves and so forth, which should be provided by your agency. Sample prices: ski poles Ts3000 per trip, sleeping bags Ts6000.

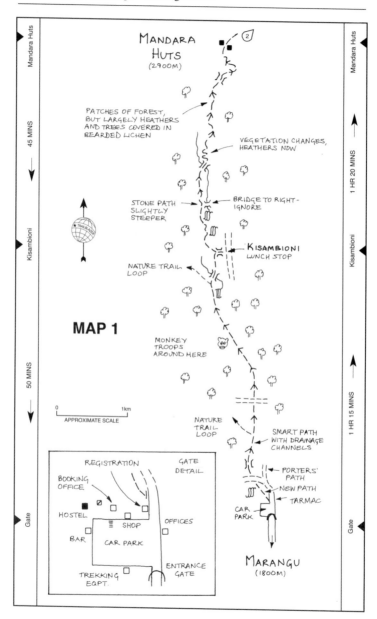

MANDARA HUTS
(2900M)

PATCHES OF FOREST, BUT LARGELY HEATHERS AND TREES COVERED IN BEARDED LICHEN

VEGETATION CHANGES, HEATHERS NOW

STONE PATH SLIGHTLY STEEPER

BRIDGE TO RIGHT – IGNORE

KISAMBIONI
LUNCH STOP

NATURE TRAIL LOOP

MAP 1

MONKEY TROOPS AROUND HERE

0   1km
APPROXIMATE SCALE

NATURE TRAIL LOOP

SMART PATH WITH DRAINAGE CHANNELS

PORTERS' PATH

NEW PATH

TARMAC

CAR PARK

REGISTRATION

GATE DETAIL

BOOKING OFFICE

HOSTEL

SHOP

OFFICES

BAR

CAR PARK

ENTRANCE GATE

TREKKING EQPT.

MARANGU
(1800M)

Side margins (left): Mandara Huts · 45 MINS · Kisambioni · 50 MINS · Gate

Side margins (right): Mandara Huts · 1 HR 20 MINS · Kisambioni · 1 HR 15 MINS · Gate

Having gone through the laborious business of **registering** (a process that usually takes at least an hour, though it can be quicker if you manage to get here before the large tour groups arrive), you begin your trek by following the wide, sealed road leading off to the north-west behind reception. After a few minutes the path divides. Take the left-hand trail; the right-hand path is a 4WD track used by the porters. Unfortunately, it is customary for some guides to send their trekkers on ahead with a porter on the first morning while they sort out the paperwork back at Marangu Gate, and as a result some trekkers unwittingly take the wider, uglier porters' trail. Avoid this by insisting to whoever accompanies you that you take the trekkers' trail, which is signposted (albeit not clearly) at the junction. **NB** During the research for this book, construction of a new trekkers-only path that begins right at Marangu Gate – thereby avoiding the 4WD road altogether – was already well under way, and by the time you read this should have been completed. This new path is marked on the map opposite.

This first day's walk is a very pleasant one of about 6km or so, and though the route is uphill for virtually the entire time, there are enough distractions in the forest to take your mind off the exertion, from the tall and solid *Macaranga kilimandscharica* trees with their smooth grey bark by the entrance gate to troops of **vervet monkeys** further along. In the early stages the path is so neat and well maintained, lined with stones and with drainage channels on either side, that it feels at first as if you are walking in the grounds of an English country house rather than on the wild slopes of Africa's highest mountain. Gradually, however, the forest closes in on all sides and the mountain's endemic flora – the vivid red *Impatiens kilimanjari* and its violet cousin *Impatiens pseudoviola* – make their first appearance by the wayside, thereby confirming that you are on Kili and not at Chatsworth. The path soon veers towards and then follows the course of a mountain stream; sometimes through the increasingly impenetrable vegetation to your right you may be able to glimpse the occasional small **waterfall**.

After about an hour and a quarter a wooden bridge leads off the trail over this stream to the picnic tables at **Kisambioni** and a reunion with the 4WD porters' trail. This is the half-way point of the first stage, and in all probability it is here that you will be served lunch.

At a height of 6,300 feet, however, all these were merged in the primaeval forest, in which old patriarchs with knotted stunted forms stood closely together, many of them worsted in the perpetual struggle with the encroachments of the parasitical growths of almost fabulous strength and size, which enfolded trunks and branches alike in their fatal embrace, crippling the giants themselves and squeezing to death the mosses, lichens, and ferns which had clothed their nakedness. Everything living seemed doomed to fall prey to them, but they in their turn bore their own heavy burden of parasites; creepers, from a yard to two yards long, hanging down in garlands and festoons, or forming one thick veil shrouding whole clumps of trees. Wherever a little space had been left amongst the many fallen and decaying trunks, the ground was covered with a luxurious vegetation, including many varieties of herbaceous plants with bright coloured flowers, orchids, and the modest violet peeping out amongst them, whilst more numerous than all were different lycopods and sword-shaped ferns.
Lieutenant Ludwig von Höhnel *Discovery by Count Teleki of Lakes Rudolf and Stefanie,* 1894.

Returning to the trail and turning right, you continue climbing north for thirty minutes to another bridge, this time leading off to the right of the trail; your path, however, heads off to the left, due west directly away from the bridge. The trail is a little steeper now as you wind your way through the forest; this is a very pretty part of the walk, with varieties of *Impatiens* and begonias edging the path; though by now you may be feeling a little too tired to enjoy it to its fullest.

Press on, and fifteen minutes later a second bridge appears which you *do* take. Like some sort of botanical border post, the bridge heralds the first appearance of the **giant heathers** (*Erica excelsa*) on the trail, intermingling with the camphorwood tree, with masses of **bearded lichen** liberally draped over both; and though the forest reappears intermittently right up to the Maundi Crater, it's the spindly heathers and stumpy shrubs of the second vegetation zone, the alpine heath, that now dominate.

From this second bridge, the first night's accommodation, the **Mandara Huts (2700m)**, lies just thirty-five minutes away. There are some smaller private rooms here, though most trekkers sleep in the large dormitory in the roof above the dining hall. If you have the energy, a quick fifteen-minute saunter to the parasitic cone known as the **Maundi Crater** (see Map 2) is worthwhile both for its views east over Taveta and north-west to Mawenzi and for the wild flowers and grasses growing on its slopes. On the way to the crater, look in the trees for the bands of semi-tame vervet monkeys that live here and are particularly active at dusk.

Incidentally, the Mandara Huts are the only huts on the mountain to be named after a person rather than a place. Mandara was the fearsome chief of Moshi, a warrior whose skill on the battlefield was matched only by his stunning greed and cupidity off it. Mandara once boasted that he had met every white man to visit Kilimanjaro, from Johannes Rebmann to Hans Meyer, and it's a fair bet that all of them would have been required to present the chief with a huge array of presents brought from their own country. Failure to do so was not an option, for those who, in Mandara's eye (he had only one, having lost the other in battle), were insufficiently generous in their gift-giving, put their lives in peril. The attack that led to the death of Charles New (see p84), for example, was said to have been orchestrated by Mandara after the latter had 'insulted' him by refusing to give the chief the watch from his wrist. Read any of the nineteenth-century accounts of Kilimanjaro and you'll usually find plenty of pages devoted to this fascinating character – with few casting him in a favourable light.

STAGE 2: MANDARA HUTS TO HOROMBO HUTS
[MAP 2 OPPOSITE; MAP 3, p179]

On this eleven-kilometre stage, in which you gain almost a kilometre in altitude, you say a final goodbye to the forest and spend the greater part of the day walking through the bleaker landscape of Kilimanjaro's moorland. If the weather's clear you will get your first really good look at the twin peaks of Kili, namely spiky Mawenzi and snow-capped Kibo; they will continue to loom large, and will doubtless appear in just about every photo you take, from now to the summit. The giant groundsels (*Senecio kilimanjari*) and phallic lobelias *Lobelia*

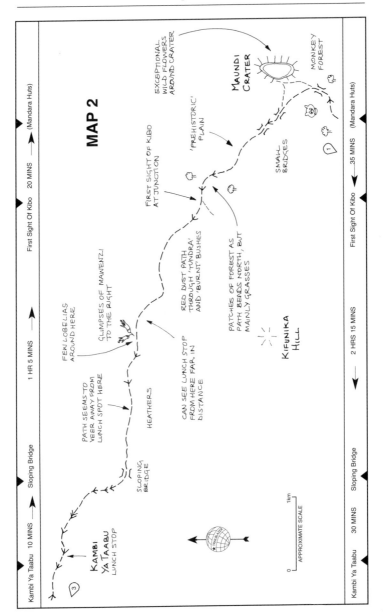

MAP 2

Kambi Ya Taabu 10 MINS — Sloping Bridge — 1 HR 5 MINS — First Sight Of Kibo — 20 MINS — (Mandara Huts)

KAMBI YA TAABU
LUNCH STOP

SLOPING BRIDGE

PATH SEEMS TO VEER AWAY FROM LUNCH SPOT HERE

HEATHERS

CAN SEE LUNCH STOP FROM HERE FAR IN DISTANCE

FEW LOBELIAS AROUND HERE

GLIMPSES OF MAWENZI TO THE RIGHT

RED DUST PATH THROUGH 'TUNDRA' AND 'BURNT' BUSHES

FIRST SIGHT OF KIBO AT JUNCTION

'PREHISTORIC' PLAIN

EXCEPTIONAL WILD FLOWERS AROUND CRATER

MAUNDI CRATER

MONKEY FOREST

PATCHES OF FOREST AS PATH BENDS NORTH, BUT MAINLY GRASSES

KIFUNIKA HILL

SMALL BRIDGES

TRAILBLAZER

APPROXIMATE SCALE

0 — 1km

Kambi Ya Taabu — 30 MINS — Sloping Bridge — 2 HRS 15 MINS — First Sight Of Kibo — 35 MINS — (Mandara Huts) *deckenii* also make their first appearance in this stage, with the former growing in some abundance towards the latter part of the walk.

The whole landscape as far as the eye could reach was a medley of dull grey lava slabs, dotted with the red-leafed protea shrub (Protea Kilimandscharica) and stunted heaths, which became smaller and smaller as we rose higher. Not a sound disturbed the silence of this uninhabited mountain mystery; not a sign of life broke the stillness save a little ashy-brown bird that hopped about the boulders, flipping its tail up and down. And to add to the impression created by the eerie scene, huge senecios lifted to a height of 20ft their black stems and greyish-yellow crowns and stood spreading out their arms in the deep moist gullies, like ghostly sentinels of the untrodden wilds.

Eva Stuart Watt *Africa's Dome of Mystery, 1930*

The day begins with a stroll through the monkey forest towards the Maundi Crater. After fifteen minutes you cross the small bridge and, leaving the last significant expanse of forest behind, enter a land of tall grasses and giant heathers. **Wild flowers** rarely seen elsewhere in the park, such as the pinkish *Dierama cupiflorum*, abound in this little bumpy corner of the mountain. Crossing bridges over (often dry) water courses, you eventually come to gently undulating fields that feel somehow vaguely prehistoric. Passing through these, the path continues north-west through slopes of heather directly towards Kibo, with Mawenzi peering over the horizon to your right and **Kifunika Hill** – the main water source for many of the villages – on your left.

The vegetation here has clearly suffered from the fires of the past few years, the green heathers emerging between the blackened sticks of burnt bushes. If it's a clear day, you may be able to make out, atop one of the many undulations, a small green hut; this will be your lunch stop, called **Kambi Ya Taabu** after a nearby stream and reached after a fairly trying thirty-minute climb. The guides typically call this the halfway point in the day, but they're being unnecessarily pessimistic: the Horombo Huts lie just 90 minutes away, the path tracing a generally westward course across a number of (dry) stream beds.

The **Horombo Huts** (3657m) are generally regarded as the most pleasant of those on the route: small A-frame shelters partitioned down the middle, with each side holding beds for four people. They cater for a transient population of about 100 trekkers plus porters and guides, as well as a more permanent population of four-striped grass mice whose numbers are now almost at plague proportions; indeed, some of them have now forsaken their grassy homeland to scavenge in the main dining hall. The huts are also the busiest on the mountain, catering not just for those ascending the mountain, but those coming back down from Kibo too, as well as those who spend the day here acclimatizing. As such the whole place tends to get rather busy, which can be a problem when it comes to feeding-time, there being only one dining hut at Horombo and a rather officious caretaker who refuses to allow eating in the dorms. Try to arrange with your guide to have dinner slightly earlier than normal to avoid the main dinner-time rush, or you could be waiting for hours.

If you have opted for the acclimatization day, the chances are you'll be led by your guide on the northern route (aka Mawenzi Route, see p213) past the

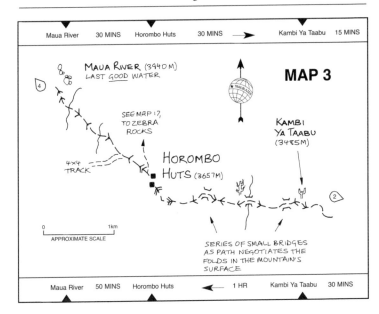

| Maua River | 30 MINS | Horombo Huts | 30 MINS → | Kambi Ya Taabu | 15 MINS |

MAUA RIVER (3940M)
LAST GOOD WATER

4

SEE MAP 17,
TO ZEBRA
ROCKS

MAP 3

KAMBI
YA TAABU
(3485M)

HOROMBO
HUTS (3657M)

4×4
TRACK

0   1km
APPROXIMATE SCALE

2

SERIES OF SMALL BRIDGES
AS PATH NEGOTIATES THE
FOLDS IN THE MOUNTAIN'S
SURFACE

| Maua River | 50 MINS | Horombo Huts | ← 1 HR | Kambi Ya Taabu | 30 MINS |

Zebra Rocks and up to the **Mawenzi Huts** at 4600m (see Map 17). Not only will this exercise allow you to cope with the thin air of Kibo later on, but it also affords magnificent views of your ultimate destination across the Saddle, and yet is near enough to allow you to return to Horombo for a late lunch.

STAGE 3: HOROMBO HUTS TO KIBO HUTS
[MAP 3 ABOVE; MAP 4, p181; MAP 5, p183]

The path to Kibo from the Horombo Huts now divides into two; almost invariably you will be led along the southern (left-hand) route, which we describe now. If your guide is amenable, however, you may like to ask him on the return from Kibo to use the more northerly route, particularly if you did not take a day to acclimatize at Horombo (those who did will already be familiar with much of this northerly path, which we have called the Mawenzi Route and have described, in reverse, on p213).

The eleven-kilometre **southern path** seems rather steep at first as it bends left (north-west) and up through the thinning vegetation of the moors. Looping north, just under an hour after leaving Horombo you come to the tiny mountain stream known as the **Maua River** (3940m). You should fill up your water bottles here, for the water from this point on is rather brackish. The terrain gradually levels out after Maua, passing the junction with the **Southern Circuit** as it does so, and some of Kibo's many parasitic cones move into view for the first time. Still bending north, the path leaves the scant vegetation behind for even more barren terrain. The **Last Water Point**, well signposted and rather incongruously furnished with picnic tables, marks the beginning of the approach to the Saddle, the dry, barren terrain separating Kilimanjaro's two major peaks which lies on the other side of **Middle Red Hill**, the small parasitic cone you see ahead of you to the right of the path. You are now in a rather flat, extremely windswept and dramatic landscape, the only decoration provided by a few tufts of grass, some hardier floral species such as the aptly named everlastings, and a number of boulders and smaller stones, some of which have been arranged into messages by previous trekkers. The path begins to loop north between the Kibo summit on your left and the Middle Red, whose western slopes shelter trekkers from the often howling wind and usually provide the venue for **lunch**.

Your path for the afternoon continues northwards across the Saddle; it's a bit of a weary trudge on a steadily inclining path to **Jiwe Lainkoyo**, a former campsite with some toilet huts and a huge boulder. (Jiwe means 'Rock' in Swahili.) It is also the meeting point between the two main paths from Horombo. Thereafter the path turns sharply westwards towards the **Kibo Huts**, which nestle snugly at the foot of the summit after which they were named. Though the huts look close, you still have more than an hour of walking from Jiwe Lainkoyo, and it's a tough walk too, a gradual but relentless uphill slog to

Mawenzi

Though less than 6km of nothingness (namely the Saddle) separates the foot of one from the foot of the other, the twin peaks of Kibo and Mawenzi could not be more different. Where Kibo is all gentle slopes and perfectly circular craters, Mawenzi is spiky, steep, and rises to a series of peaks like the back of a stegosaurus; where the former is at least partially covered in glaciers, the other stands naked, or at least wears no permanent raiment of ice, its sides too steep to allow the glaciers a secure enough footing; and while Kibo is easily accessible to walkers, any assault on Mawenzi involves some serious preparation, specialist equipment, and no small amount of technical skill.

Indeed, the only similarity between the two peaks is their enormity: after Kibo, Mawenzi's **Hans Meyer Peak**, at 5149m, is, (after Mount Kenya, 50m taller) the third highest in Africa. Its smaller size when compared to Kibo can be ascribed to the fact that the Mawenzi volcano died out first, while the forces that formed Kibo continued to rage for a further few thousand years after Mawenzi had become extinct, pushing Kibo above the height of its older brother. Erosion then caused the collapse of Mawenzi's entire north-east wall, releasing the waters of a lake that had formed in its crater down into the valley below. The jagged appearance of its summit is due to the formation of **dykes**. This is where lava, pushed into gaps in the crater rim, solidified over time and, being harder than the original rock, remained while the softer rock eroded. Today, this hardened lava is also rather shattered, which, combined with its steep gradients, makes Mawenzi extremely dangerous to climb. John Reader tells of two Austrian climbers who perished on their descent from the summit of Mawenzi, with the body of one of them found dangling by a rope snagged to the rocks. Such is the difficulty associated with any climb of Mawenzi that, rather than risk climbing up the peak to recover the corpse, the park authorities decided instead to hire a marksman to shoot at the rope with a rifle.

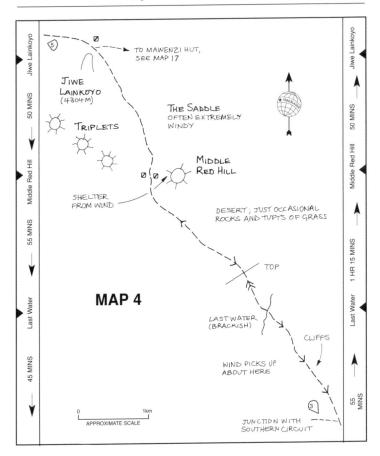

round off what has already been a fairly wearying day. The huts themselves are basic, built of stone and rather chilly. A sign on the door of the main hut tells you that you are now at 4750m; a second sign warns you that Gillman's Point is still five hours away...

STAGE 4: KIBO HUTS TO GILLMAN'S AND UHURU PEAK [MAP 5, p183]

And so you come to the testing part of the walk. No matter how tough you have found the trekking so far, it has been but a leisurely stroll compared to what lies ahead of you tonight. The path to Gillman's Point on the crater rim has been in your sights since the previous afternoon when you crossed the Saddle and saw it rearing up at an angle of 16° (John Reader's estimate) on your left behind the

Kibo Huts. By common consent, it is the easiest of the three leading up to the crater rim. But don't be fooled by this, for it is still an extremely demanding hike: the chances of failure are high – and those of making it, but throwing up or passing out along the way, are even higher. Just remember the golden rule: when it comes to climbing Kibo, there is no such thing as too slow.

I find a rhythm and try to lose my thoughts to it but feel the first pain of a stomach cramp and then another, and I feel the nausea starting and the headache that I recognise all too well ... The pain is sharp in my head and my cramping is still with me; if I feel this way how is Danny doing with no sleep and nothing in his stomach from the vomiting after dinner?
Rick Ridgeway, *The Shadow of Kilimanjaro – On Foot Across East Africa*

What you can't see from Kibo Huts, and yet what is rather good about this path, is that there are a number of landmarks on the way – the main ones being William's Point at 5000m and Hans Meyer Cave at 5151m – that act as milestones, helping both to break up the journey and to provide you with some measure of your progress. **William's Point** – or rather, the large east-facing rock immediately beneath it – lies 1hr 45min from Kibo Huts, and is usually the first major resting point. **Hans Meyer Cave**, a small and undistinguished hollow adorned with a plaque commemorating the Hungarian hunter, count and *bon viveur* Samuel Teleki who rested here in 1887, is another 30min further on. Reach here and you can take some pride from the fact that you have already passed the highest altitude achieved by Jon Amos in 1998. Mind you, Mr Amos did have something of a disadvantage when he made his attempt: he was in a wheelchair raising money for the British Wheelchair Sports Foundation. Though he failed to go any further, he still set a new world record for the highest altitude – 4812m – reached by somebody in a wheelchair.

From Hans Meyer Cave, it's a case of following the scree **switchbacks**; if you've mastered the art of walking in a zombie-like trance, now is the time to put that particular technique into action. This part, as you pinball back and forth on a stretch of fine scree bounded by two boulder-strewn slopes, is extremely exposed, and if there's any wind about, you will almost certainly feel it here. If you bought one in Moshi, now is the time to put on your balaclava: your friends will be too concerned with their own situation to laugh at you now anyway.

Gradually the switchbacks begin to reduce in size like the audiograph of an echo, and 2hr 30min after leaving Hans Meyer Cave you begin to clamber between and then over rocks. This is the final phase of the climb to Gillman's, though it takes over an hour to complete and you'll probably be breathless the whole way. There doesn't seem to be a set course to take through these rocks, so don't be too surprised if you see other trekkers to the left and right of you on a different path. If your guide is at least halfway competent, however, you should find yourself at the crater's edge at **Gillman's Point**. (If, upon arrival at the crater rim, you find no signpost welcoming you to Gillman's, then the chances are the guide has got his bearings slightly wrong and has led you to the slightly lower point of **Johannes Notch**. No matter: Gillman's is just a three-minute scramble up to your left.)

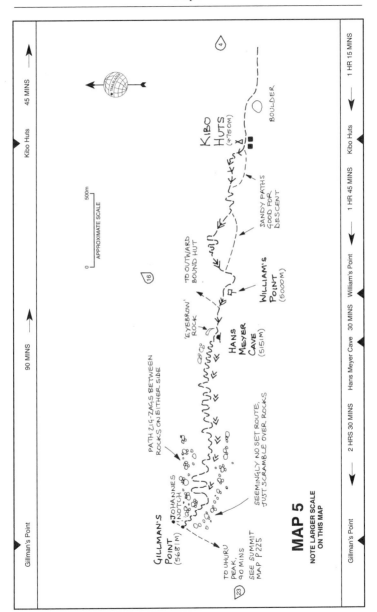

MAP 5

NOTE LARGER SCALE
ON THIS MAP

GILLMAN'S
Point
(5681M)

TO UHURU PEAK,
90 MINS
SEE SUMMIT
MAP P 225

JOHANNES'
NOTCH

PATH ZIG-ZAGS BETWEEN
ROCKS ON EITHER SIDE

SEEMINGLY NO SET ROUTE,
JUST SCRAMBLE OVER ROCKS

HANS
MEYER
CAVE
(5151M)

'EYEBROW'
ROCK

TO OUTWARD
BOUND HUT

WILLIAM'S
POINT
(5000M)

SANDY PATHS
GOOD FOR
DESCENT

KIBO
HUTS
(4750M)

BOULDER

APPROXIMATE SCALE

0   500m

TRAIL & ROCKS

Gillman's Point   90 MINS   Kibo Huts   45 MINS

2 HRS 30 MINS   Hans Meyer Cave   30 MINS   William's Point   1 HR 45 MINS   Kibo Huts   1 HR 15 MINS

Gillman's Point is 960m above Kibo hut, that is almost the equivalent of three Empire State Buildings standing one on top of another. The horizontal distance between Kibo Hut and Gillman's Point is roughly 3000 metres, so the gradient averages about 1:3.3 and the distance covered on the way up is about 3300m – the equivalent of nine Empire State Buildings laid end to end up the incline. **John Reader** *Kilimanjaro*

If the wind is not too high, Gillman's is a good spot to sit for a few minutes, get your head together, contemplate the star-spangled night with the silhouette of Mawenzi to the east, and congratulate yourself on having completed the hardest part of the trek. At least, it's the hardest part physically; the hardest part from a psychological point of view now awaits you, as you try to muster up the energy and enthusiasm to tackle the walk to **Uhuru**. Though the time varies throughout the year, as a rough guide you need to be at Gillman's at around 4.30am, in order to have a chance of seeing the sunrise at Uhuru at 6.10am or so. If you've no chance of making it by then, consider seeing the sunrise from somewhere along the way: from Stella Point, for example, or overlooking the Rebmann Glacier, or from one of the lesser peaks before Uhuru.

See Map 23 on p225 for details of the summit. The first part of this walk to Uhuru is easy enough, being either flat or, in some places, even slightly downhill. You will, however, need your head torch, because you will be walking in the moon-shadow of the crater rim for at least the first few minutes. The difficult part starts after **Stella Point**, forty-five minutes to the south of Gillman's, when the path begins to climb steadily again. Though nothing like as steep as that which has gone before, at this stage any incline is a major challenge. Don't be too disheartened by the many false summits you will encounter along the last part; instead, distract your mind from the pain you are feeling by looking at the huge and beautiful icefields to your left. A golden dawn at the summit, and a golden certificate back at Marangu Gate, are the prizes that await...

For details of what you can actually see at the summit, turn to p224, while for a description of the designated descent route, turn to the Marangu Route descent on p213.

The Machame Route

Then they began to climb and they were going to the East it seemed, and then it darkened and they were in a storm, the rain so thick it seemed like flying through a waterfall, and they were out and Compie turned his head and grinned and pointed and there, ahead, all he could see, as wide as all the world, great, high, and unbelievably white in the sun, was the top of Kilimanjaro. And then he knew that there was where he was going. **Ernest Hemingway**, *The Snows of Kilimanjaro*

Ask any guide or tour agent which is the best walk to do on Kilimanjaro, and nine times out of ten they will choose this, the Machame-Mweka Route (usually just shortened to the Machame Route, a convention we have adopted here). Though some of them doubtless say this because it's easier to organize – requiring no hut-booking or long-haul driving – it is not difficult to see why the route is so popular with everyone: beginning on the south-western side of the mountain and ascending to the summit from Kibo's south-eastern side, the trail passes through some of the mountain's finest features, including the **cloud forest** of Kili's southern slopes, the dry and dusty **Shira Plateau**, the delightful senecio-clad **Barranco Campsite** and finally the daunting **Barafu trail** to the summit, with the Rebmann Glacier edging into your field of vision on your left as dawn breaks behind Mawenzi on your right; unlike the Marangu Route, the Machame Route does not double back on itself either, but comes down via the Mweka Route, a quick but very pretty descent encompassing inhospitably dry mountain desert and lush lowland forest in a matter of a few hours. (For details of the New Alternative Mweka trail that you may well be obliged to use, see p218.)

Curiously, though the Machame Route is widely reckoned to be that much harder than the Marangu Route (and is thus nicknamed the Whiskey Route, in opposition to Marangu's softer soubriquet of the Coca Cola Trail), the proportion of trekkers who reach the top using this route is marginally but significantly higher. Whether this is evidence that the Machame Route allows people to acclimatize better – at one point on the third day the trail climbs to 4530m, before descending again to finish the day at 3950m – or whether this higher success rate is merely an indication that more experienced, hardened trekkers – ie the very people who are most likely to reach the summit – are more inclined to choose this route, is anyone's guess.

The walk traditionally lasts for six days and five nights, though it is becoming more common for trekkers to opt for an extra night during the ascent, usually in the Karanga Valley. Not only does the extra day aid acclimatization, but this also reduces from around six to just over three the number of hours walked on the day that precedes the exhausting midnight ascent to the summit, thereby allowing trekkers more time to recover their faculties, relax and prepare themselves for the final push to the top.

STAGE 1: MACHAME GATE TO MACHAME HUTS
[MAP 6, p186; MAP 7, p188]

Coming from Moshi, the drive to the Machame Gate, at an altitude of 1800m, takes just under an hour; the tarmac doesn't last that long, petering out after about 40 minutes. On the way to the gate ask the driver to point out the house of the local chief, a simple yet large bungalow on the left-hand side of the road. Passing through Machame village you'll soon arrive at the gate itself, a small collection of buildings huddled around a 4WD car park. Register in the office, set a few metres back down the hill, and use the toilet facilities behind them – you may not think much of them now, but believe me, compared to some of the latrines on the trail these are heavenly.

Back at the car park, porters are busy haggling over who is going to take what, water-sellers and walking-pole vendors are accosting new arrivals, while the trekkers themselves are quietly steeling themselves for the rigours ahead. To one side of this chaos is the beginning of the trail...

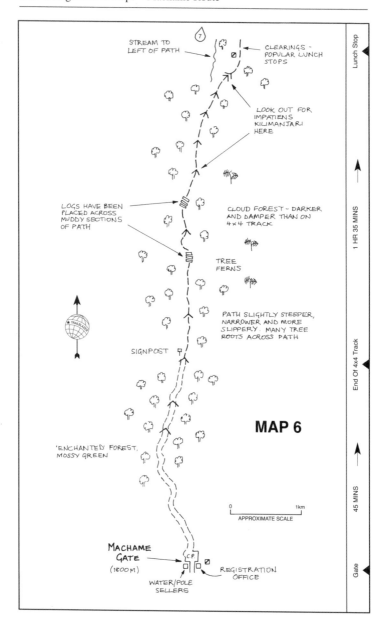

STREAM TO LEFT OF PATH

⑦

CLEARINGS - POPULAR LUNCH STOPS

LOOK OUT FOR IMPATIENS KILIMANJARI HERE

LOGS HAVE BEEN PLACED ACROSS MUDDY SECTIONS OF PATH

CLOUD FOREST - DARKER AND DAMPER THAN ON 4×4 TRACK

TREE FERNS

PATH SLIGHTLY STEEPER, NARROWER AND MORE SLIPPERY. MANY TREE ROOTS ACROSS PATH

SIGNPOST

MAP 6

'ENCHANTED' FOREST, MOSSY GREEN

0   1km
APPROXIMATE SCALE

MACHAME GATE
(1800 M)

WATER/POLE SELLERS

REGISTRATION OFFICE

Lunch Stop

1 HR 35 MINS

End Of 4x4 Track

45 MINS

Gate

The ten-kilometre, first-day **walk** itself starts with a three-kilometre amble up a 4WD track, a wide snaking trail that cuts through the kind of deep dark enchanted forest that Hansel and Gretel would be familiar with. Green moss hangs thickly from the branches that creak and groan in the wind. It's a magical start to a wonderful adventure. After 45 minutes, the track arrives at a sign advising hikers that Machame is for those ascending the mountain only. The sign also marks the end of the 4WD road, the gentle curves and steady incline giving way to a narrower, steeper, more slippery, pedestrians-only path. The forest closes in on all sides now, with tree roots encroaching onto the trail itself, forcing trekkers to watch their step and alter their stride to ensure they don't stumble. It is this breaking of the walker's rhythm – as much as the humidity and the gradient of the slope – that makes this first day such a tiring one. To aid walkers, logs have been placed across the muddier sections of the trail. If you do manage to look up from the path you'll notice that the vegetation is already changing as you progress deeper into the **cloud forest**; the scarlet and yellow *Impatiens kilimanjari* and the violet *Viola eminii* and *Impatiens pseudoviola* now flourishing between the roots of the huge 30-metre tall trees; tree ferns also proliferate here.

Ninety minutes or so from the end of the 4WD track, the path widens momentarily to form two small **clearings** (the first with en-suite toilet facilities) that make for popular lunch stops. Those who've already drunk their water bottles dry can replenish their supplies from the stream down in the valley to the west. Listen out for the primate-like call of the black and red turacao which nests around here, and watch your lunch too: it's not uncommon for the forest rodents to sneak into lunchboxes and drag off a samosa or two.

The post-prandial hike varies little from that which has gone before, though the gradient of the path increases slightly the higher you climb. As the forest gradually begins to thin out you'll notice that you are actually walking on a narrow forested spine between two shallow valleys. A stream – more audible than visible – runs briefly to the right of the trail.

Forty minutes later a second signpost of the day appears, this time warning against the careless discarding of cigarette butts; as well as dispensing some sound advice, this signpost also demarcates the border between the cloud forest and the heath, where the long grasses dominate, and the robust trees of the forest give way to the spindly, tree-like giant heathers. *Kniphofia thomsonii* (known to you and me as red hot pokers) make their first appearance at this altitude, as do a number of other wild flowers and shrubs such as the bushy *Phillipa excelsa*. With the forest thinning, the **Kibo peak** hoves into view for the first time to the east.

It is only fifteen minutes from the signpost to **Machame Huts** (3000m), a series of level pitches cut into the grass, each with its own toilet. Make sure you sign your name in the **registration book**, and aim to pitch your tent as high as possible for the best views: by the green hut is a good spot, affording views to the east up to Kibo, and south-west towards Mount Meru.

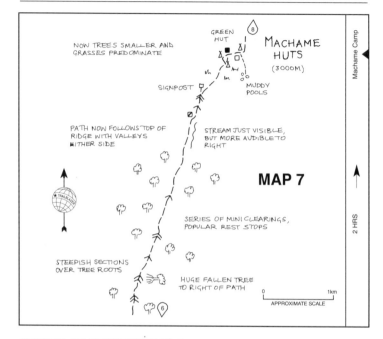

STAGE 2: MACHAME HUTS TO THE NEW SHIRA CAMP [MAP 8, OPP]

This leg of the trek is short (7km) but a little strenuous as you ascend from 3000m up to the Shira Plateau, finally coming to a halt at the New Shira Camp at just over 3800m. Parts of this walk are a bit steep, and the skinny, naked trees at this altitude provide little shade from the heat; what's more, the path is extremely dusty, so if you have gaiters you'll probably be thankful of the protection they provide (and remember to keep your camera bag tightly closed too). In spite of all this, by taking it slowly, resting frequently and enjoying the en-route views that encompass Kibo, Meru and all points in between, this day needn't be too taxing – indeed, it's probably the easiest day of the whole ascent.

The walk starts as it goes on for much of the day, with a steepish climb north up through forests of stunted, twisted, trees that are bare of vegetation and blackened by fire; ahead of you in the distance is the lip of the **Shira Plateau**. The path winds its way up to the top of a ridge formed by a petrified lava flow, occasionally allowing trekkers some splendid views over last night's campsite, Machame village and the flat Tanzanian plains beyond. **Senecia**, the squat, dry-looking trees with a leafy crown growing from the top, begin to dot the path, and Kilimanjaro's dessicated **helichrysums**, ubiquitous above 3000m, appear here for the first time too. Note, too, how most of the trees not only diminish in size as you climb higher but seem to bend as one towards the plateau, as if

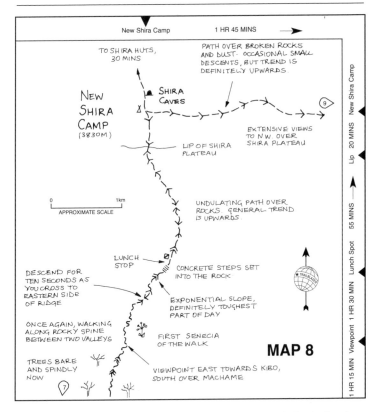

New Shira Camp — 1 HR 45 MINS →

PATH OVER BROKEN ROCKS AND DUST. OCCASIONAL SMALL DESCENTS, BUT TREND IS DEFINITELY UPWARDS.

TO SHIRA HUTS, 30 MINS

NEW SHIRA CAMP (3830M)

SHIRA CAVES

9

EXTENSIVE VIEWS TO N.W. OVER SHIRA PLATEAU

LIP OF SHIRA PLATEAU

0 — 1km
APPROXIMATE SCALE

UNDULATING PATH OVER ROCKS. GENERAL TREND IS UPWARDS.

LUNCH STOP

DESCEND FOR TEN SECONDS AS YOU CROSS TO EASTERN SIDE OF RIDGE

CONCRETE STEPS SET INTO THE ROCK

TRAIL BLAZE

EXPONENTIAL SLOPE, DEFINITELY TOUGHEST PART OF DAY

ONCE AGAIN, WALKING ALONG ROCKY SPINE BETWEEN TWO VALLEYS

FIRST SENECIA OF THE WALK

MAP 8

TREES BARE AND SPINDLY NOW

7

VIEWPOINT EAST TOWARDS KIBO, SOUTH OVER MACHAME

New Shira Camp | Lip 20 MINS | 55 MINS | Lunch Spot | 1 HR 30 MIN | Viewpoint 1 HR 15 MIN

pointing the way. After passing a number of viewpoints and clambering from one side of the ridge to the other, the gradient of the trail increases exponentially towards the **lunch stop**, hidden from view behind a rocky outcrop. The effort expended in reaching there is worth it, for while munching your sandwiches you can savour yet more views of Kibo and all points south.

By following the line of porters and trekkers on the path ahead, you can also pick out the afternoon's trail, which initially continues north and up, before bending fairly sharply to the north-west, cutting a near horizontal line beneath the rim of the plateau. But though the worst of the day's climbing is now behind you, don't be fooled into thinking this is an easy section, for the path on this north-westerly trail undulates considerably as it climbs over rocks and boulders, and it can be fairly tiring in the searing afternoon heat. As a distraction, the first of Kilimanjaro's celebrated **lobelias** (*Lobelia deckenii*), both phallic and cabbage-shaped, of which the former can grow to a height of three metres or more, appear by the trail.

Just an hour after lunch the plateau is gained and the path continues northwards. Note how much more barren the landscape is up here, with trees now all but extinct and only the dry white helichrysums and yellow everlastings thriving. Look out, too, for the Shira Plateau's distinctive, shiny black **obsidian** rock.

Your camp for the night, which we have called the **New Shira Camp** to distinguish it from the other sites around here, lies just 20 minutes into the plateau. On most maps this new, sprawling campsite is not marked, leading many trekkers to think mistakenly that they are actually camping at Shira Huts. In fact, this New Shira Camp lies just a few minutes' walk to the south of the **Shira Caves** – which *are* marked on most maps – which in turn are located a good 30 minutes to the south of the Shira Huts. Looking west from the New Shira Camp, ask your guide to point out the **Shira Cathedral**, the **Needle** and the **East Shira Hill** which line the southern boundary of the Shira Plateau, and, behind them to the far west, **Johnsell Point** and **Klute Peak**, the highest points of the Shira Ridge, the western rim of the oldest of Kili's three craters. Mount Meru, too, is still visible to the west on the horizon.

STAGE 3: NEW SHIRA CAMP TO BARRANCO HUTS
[MAP 8, p189; MAP 9, OPP; MAP 10, p194]

Camp-life on Kilimanjaro is a capital school for the practice of self-denial.
Hans Meyer *Across East African Glaciers*

During this section of the trek you cover a total of just over 10km as you move from the western to the southern slopes of Kilimanjaro; by the end of it you may feel slightly disappointed to learn that, for all your efforts, you will have gained just 150m in height, from the New Shira Camp at 3830m to Barranco, situated at an altitude of 3950m. Nevertheless, this leg of the trek is vital for acclimatization purposes, for during the day you will climb to a respectable **4530m**.

'...an extraordinary arborescent plant, since named *Senecio Johnstonii*... Its trunk was so superficially rooted and so rotten that, in spite of its height and girth, I could pull it down with one hand.
(from *The Kilima-njaro Expedition*, HH Johnston, 1886)

Don't be surprised, therefore, if by the end of it you have a crashing headache: this is normal, and is only cause for concern if it is accompanied by other symptoms of mountain sickness, or if the pain hasn't diminished by the morning.

The day begins with a steady, gentle ascent towards the western slopes of Kibo through the dry, boulder-strewn terrain of the Shira Plateau. At first the path meanders somewhat and rises and falls regularly as it negotiates the gentle folds of the plateau, before finally settling on a roughly easterly direction, with a steady, shallow incline, for most of the next 6km. Notice how the vegetation has deteriorated to such an extent that only a few everlastings and lichen successfully cling to life up here. Soon after the **junction** with the

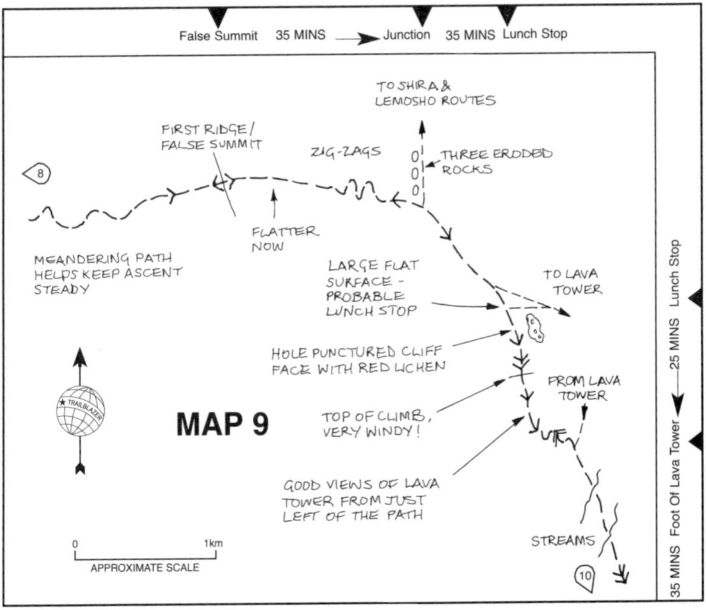

False Summit 35 MINS → Junction 35 MINS Lunch Stop

TO SHIRA &
LEMOSHO ROUTES

FIRST RIDGE/
FALSE SUMMIT   ZIG-ZAGS   THREE ERODED
                                 ROCKS

8

MEANDERING PATH
HELPS KEEP ASCENT
STEADY

FLATTER
NOW

LARGE FLAT
SURFACE -
PROBABLE
LUNCH STOP

TO LAVA
TOWER

HOLE PUNCTURED CLIFF
FACE WITH RED LICHEN

FROM LAVA
TOWER

TRAILBLAZER

MAP 9

TOP OF CLIMB,
VERY WINDY!

GOOD VIEWS OF LAVA
TOWER FROM JUST
LEFT OF THE PATH

STREAMS

10

0   1km
APPROXIMATE SCALE

25 MINS Lunch Stop

35 MINS Foot Of Lava Tower

Lemosho Route (see p209) the path loops to the south-east and divides into two. It is here that those people who have opted to tackle the summit from the more difficult Western Breach branch off and head east towards the **Lava Tower** (see p192), while the rest (the majority) follow the more southerly, gentler trail as it bends round to the right. Just two minutes after the fork the latter route comes upon a large flat, rocky surface – the **lunch** stop on this third leg.

The highest point of the day's walk, 4530m, lies just 15 minutes further on. At the top, by walking just off the path to the left, you can enjoy unrivalled views of the strange and isolated Lava Tower, with Lava Tower Camp sitting in its shadow to the north, and the path to the Arrow Glacier Hut leading off behind it. (For details of this ascent, see p192.)

The Lava Tower continues to loom to your left for the next 10min as you descend quickly via a series of zigzags into the gully separating you from Kibo's southern slopes. Crossing the tiny stream at the bottom, the path bends south-east once more, following the contours of Kibo's lower reaches as it crosses two more streams. Less than an hour later the trail meets with the **Umbwe Route** (see p210), a junction that is marked by a proliferation of signposts. From here it's downhill all the way as the route descends once more, this time into the delightful **Barranco Valley**, rich in senecio and lobelia. A huge gouge in the southern face of Kibo to the south-west of Uhuru Peak, the valley is in places 300m deep and was formed when a huge landslide swept south-

Ascent of Kibo via the Arrow Glacier (Western Breach)

Without doubt Kibo is most imposing as seen from the west. Here it rises in solemn majesty, and the eye is not distracted by the sister peak of Mawenzi, of which nothing is to be seen but a single jutting pinnacle. The effect is enhanced by the magnificent flowing sweep of the outline, the dazzling extent of the ice-cap, the vast stretch of the forest, the massive breadth of the base, and the jagged crest of the Shira spur as it branches away towards the west. **Hans Meyer** *Across East African Glaciers*

This route is less popular than the alternative, Southern Circuit route around the southern side of Kibo to Barafu Huts. It is much harder, steeper, and gives trekkers less time to acclimatize. The path can also be a little treacherous – rocks occasionally tumble down the steep side, particularly on the way up to the crater rim from the Arrow Glacier Campsite. What's more, when you reach the campsite you'll have a lot of hanging around to do, for the walk to it from the previous night's camp, at Lava Tower, takes only an hour or two.

The advantage with the walk is that, on reaching the crater, you are close to the path that leads to the inner Reusch Crater, thereby allowing you to explore the summit in far greater detail than the average 'summiteer'. (Indeed, if you want to reach Uhuru Peak you have to cross the crater in order to gain the rim at Stella Point.) As the night-time walk from Arrow Glacier Campsite to the crater rim takes four hours, it also allows you more time than the other paths to explore the summit.

The starting point for this ascent of Kibo is from **Lava Tower Camp** (4600m) on the lower western slopes of Kibo. This a good campsite, with pleasing views down the massive expanse of the Shira Plateau. No matter what time of day you reach this campsite, **don't** be tempted to press on to Arrow Glacier Camp. Not only is this latter camp markedly inferior – positioned in a rather inhospitable spot higher up the slope – but you need to rest at Lava Tower for acclimatization purposes.

Instead, spend the next morning marching up to **Arrow Glacier Camp** (4800m), stop there, and conserve your energy for the night time scramble. The huts have long since been ruined here, and the glacier itself has receded greatly and is no longer the feature it once was. The night-time walk to the summit is a direct but painful and sometimes precarious hike of four hours or so on scree and rocky outcrops. After snowfall the route can be icy and an ice axe may be required, though for most of the year it should be OK. At the top you enter into the crater; there is a path directly up to Uhuru from here, but usually you have to cross the crater from west to east to reach **Stella Point**, at the top of the trail up from Barafu Huts. From here you double back on yourself, heading west along the rim to Uhuru Peak (see Map 23).

wards down from the summit about 100,000 years ago. From the **campsite** (3950m) and its environs you'll have spectacular views of Kibo's southern face, the Western Breach and the mighty Heim Glacier, with glacial moraine tumbling southwards towards the camp. Few are the trekkers who do not rank this campsite as their favourite on this trail – hope the toilets have been cleaned up now, though.

Opposite: Buffeted by strong winds, the walk across the Saddle is not as easy as it would seem.

STAGE 4: BARRANCO HUTS TO BARAFU HUTS
[MAP 10, p194; MAP 11, p195]

This is a long stage, so long that many trekkers now prefer to tackle it over two separate days, camping for the night in the Karanga Valley. Make sure you fill your containers in this valley as this is the last place to get water on the Machame Route and, if the cold wind's rushing through, it's possibly the last place you'd want to be stopping at too, though its beauty cannot be denied. As you walk along the path today the great glaciers of Kili's **Southern Icefields** – the Heim, Kersten and Decken glaciers – will appear on your left one after the other. Curiously, although this stage sets you up nicely for the final push to the summit, by the end of the day you will actually be further away from Uhuru Peak (as the buzzard flies) than you were at the start of the day at Barranco.

The hardest part of the day occurs right at the beginning, with a near-vertical scramble up the **Great Barranco Wall** (or **Breach Wall**) to the east of the campsite. You'll have to stash your walking poles away for this first section, for at times you'll need to use both hands to haul yourself up the senecio-dressed slopes. False summits along the way further sap the strength and spirit, but after about an hour and a quarter you'll reach the true summit of the wall; here you can sit on the bare rock and enjoy the views south and east, with the great **Heim Glacier** over your shoulder to the north, and relish the prospect of the relatively gentle descent into the next gully below.

At the bottom of this pretty little gully, and having crossed the small stream that flows through it, you come to a **flat gravel area**, a possible camping spot and, by the amount of loo roll hanging from the bushes, a popular pit stop too. To the east a path snakes towards a high pass, but in all probability your guide will instead lead you away from this larger, quicker route to Barafu, and bring you instead along an easier trail cutting south-east into a series of mini-valleys. Climbing out of these valleys, the path then cuts across a barren, desert slope where the silence and stillness are positively deafening, before finally descending down the western, lusher slopes of the **Karanga Valley**. Ferns, heather and other greenery reappear for a while as you descend along the rock-and-mud path, a path that you share in places with a mountain stream.

The Karanga Valley is, in the words of John Reader, 'narrow, steep and exquisite'. It is also your last place to collect water before the summit, so it is vital you fill all your water bottles here. Try to collect your water from as high a point in the stream as possible and purify it: there are plenty of toilets within 20m of the stream around here, and giardia could be present. The valley itself is like a small oasis of green, albeit a cold and windswept one; the beautiful shimmering green **malachite sunbirds** nest around here; you may spot them feeding on the lobelias.

Opposite Top: The desolate 'moonscape' of the trail to Barafu Huts; Machame Route.
Bottom: Porters on the steep second day of the Machame Route.

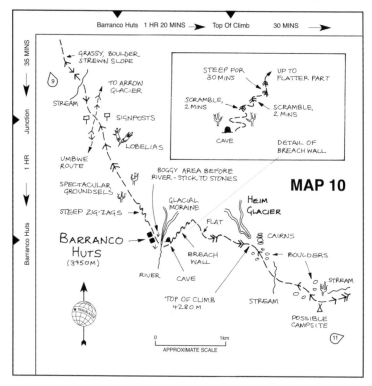

Those who plan to split this leg into two days will either camp by the stream itself, or above the valley at the top of the next climb, a very steep twenty-minute ascent on a switchback path. At the top the trail takes a sharp leftward turn, heading in an easterly/north-easterly direction on a relatively gentle incline, with the Decken Glacier a permanent presence to your left.

The scenery now becomes even more barren, as you make your way between the boulders and over the shattered rocks and stones of this misty mountain ridge. Even the trail is faint. Only the occasional cairn marking out the way gives an indication that man has passed this way before (unless, of course, some bastard has dropped some litter). If George Lucas is looking for somewhere wild, inhospitable and unearthly as a location for his next Star Wars instalment, he could do a lot worse...

At the top the path bends more to the east and descends into a shallow valley that, if anything, is even drier and more blighted than the previous section. Once again, the Southern Icefields loom ominously to your left, with the **Rebmann Glacier** appearing for the first time.

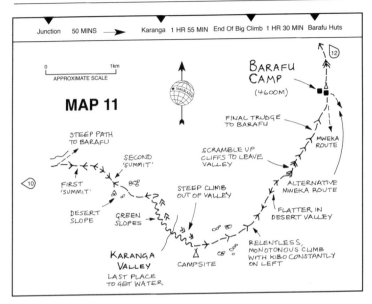

Junction 50 MINS → Karanga 1 HR 55 MIN End Of Big Climb 1 HR 30 MIN Barafu Huts

MAP 11

0 ___ 1km
APPROXIMATE SCALE

BARAFU CAMP
(4600M)

FINAL TRUDGE TO BARAFU

STEEP PATH TO BARAFU

SECOND 'SUMMIT'

SCRAMBLE UP CLIFFS TO LEAVE VALLEY

MWEKA ROUTE

FIRST 'SUMMIT'

STEEP CLIMB OUT OF VALLEY

ALTERNATIVE MWEKA ROUTE

DESERT SLOPE GREEN SLOPES

FLATTER IN DESERT VALLEY

KARANGA VALLEY

CAMPSITE

RELENTLESS, MONOTONOUS CLIMB WITH KIBO CONSTANTLY ON LEFT

LAST PLACE TO GET WATER

Barafu Camp (4600m), your destination for this leg, lies at the end of this valley, reached after a short scramble up the cliff-face and a 25-minute walk almost due north. Barafu means 'Ice' in Swahili, and the camp is probably called this because of its proximity to the Rebmann Glacier, away to the north-west. Hopefully, your tent should have been set up for you by the time you arrive. Try to get some food and rest as soon as possible, and sort out your equipment for the next stage before it gets dark: you've got a long night ahead.

STAGE 5: BARAFU TO STELLA POINT AND UHURU PEAK
[MAP 12, p197]

But now, apparently, the mountain was inhabited by fiery beings who baffled man's adventurous foot: the mountain receded as the traveller advanced, the summit rose as he ascended; blood burst from the nostrils, fingers bent backwards .. even the most adventurous were forced back. **Richard Burton** in *Progress of Expedition to East Africa*, reporting the rumours he had heard about Kilimanjaro while residing in Tanga.

And so you come to the final ascent, a rigorous, vigorous push to Stella Point and the crater rim, followed by a 45-minute trudge up to Uhuru Peak, the highest point in Africa. It's tough, no doubt about it, but if you manage to avoid sickness or injury there's no reason why you, too, shouldn't be clutching a golden certificate come tomorrow evening. This final stage usually begins at around midnight; this not only allows trekkers the chance to see sunrise from the summit but also leaves enough daylight to allow for the long descent to the next night's campsite, with an hour's recuperation back at Barafu on the way. As such, you can leave most of your **luggage** at Barafu while you tackle the ascent, though you should take any valuables with you (there have been a few robberies from tents left unguarded), as well as your **camera**, spare film and batteries and all your **water** (which should be kept in **insulated bottles** or it'll freeze up and be useless on the ascent). Cameras, particularly the modern auto-focus varieties, have been known to freeze in these conditions as well, so keep them insulated. Wear all your **clothes** too – you can always take a layer or two off in the unlikely situation that you find yourself getting too hot – and have your **head-torch** readily to hand when you wake up, so you don't have to spend time and energy looking around for it before you go.

Good luck!

At 4am by the light of a hurricane lamp, and wrapped in everything that could give warmth, I started with Mawala, the headman, and Jonathan, our guide, on the long uphill pull of 4000ft over loose scree and fissured rocks. The cold was intense, and Mawala got two of his toes frost-bitten ... our breathing had become so difficult that we could barely drag ourselves along and had to sit down every few yards to recover breath, now and again sucking icicles and nibbling Cadbury's Milk Chocolate. Yet the steep ascent was mostly over projecting ridges of lava slabs and presented no real obstacle beyond the extreme altitude. Here and there, however, we struck a bed of loose shingle, which mockingly carried us backwards at every footstep almost the whole distance of our tread.
Eva Stuart Watt *Africa's Dome of Mystery*, 1930

The way to the summit starts, as you've probably already observed from Barafu, by scrambling over the **small cliffs** at the northern end of camp; after fifteen minutes or so the path flattens a little as you walk in the moon-shadow of a second set of cliffs rising up to your left. Twenty-five minutes on from there the path descends minimally; I mention this not because the descent is in any way remarkable or extensive – it lasts for maybe ten seconds in total – but merely because it is the only descent I can recall for the whole of the next six hours.

Immediately after this the path takes a fairly sharpish turn to the left (northwest). You are now heading directly for the summit and Stella Point, a direction you will maintain for nearly the entire night. After another fifteen minutes or so you begin to walk on the distinctive **shale and gravel slopes** of Kibo, which cause you to slip back with every step. Everybody has their own way of tackling this, with some trekkers stabbing their poles hard into the ground to aid their balance, while others walk with a Chaplin-esque gait, their feet splayed outwards to stem the slide back. Whatever way you choose, you'll find it hard work.

The situation was appalling, there was a grandeur and a magnificence about the surroundings which were almost too much for me; instead of exhilarating, they were oppressive.
Charles New *Life, Wanderings, and Labours in Eastern Africa*, 1873

An hour or so after turning west you take another left turn and cross to the top of the ridge that has been a constant companion on your left-hand side for the past hour or so. The **switchback path** begins in earnest now and continues for the next three hours. It is pointless describing the scenery on this section, for the chances are you won't be able to see much beyond the radius of your torch-beam, and won't be keen on surveying the landscape now anyway; if it's a clear

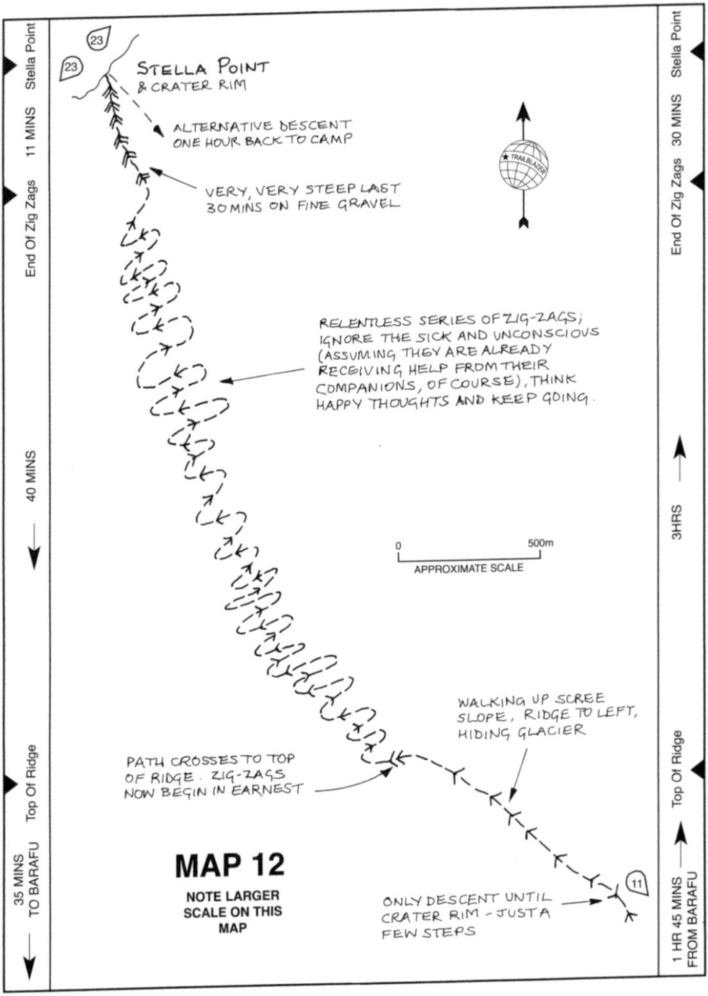

Stella Point

11 MINS

End Of Zig Zags

40 MINS

Top Of Ridge

35 MINS
TO BARAFU

(23) STELLA POINT
& CRATER RIM

ALTERNATIVE DESCENT
ONE HOUR BACK TO CAMP

VERY, VERY STEEP LAST
30 MINS ON FINE GRAVEL

RELENTLESS SERIES OF ZIG-ZAGS;
IGNORE THE SICK AND UNCONSCIOUS
(ASSUMING THEY ARE ALREADY
RECEIVING HELP FROM THEIR
COMPANIONS, OF COURSE), THINK
HAPPY THOUGHTS AND KEEP GOING.

0   500m
APPROXIMATE SCALE

WALKING UP SCREE
SLOPE, RIDGE TO LEFT,
HIDING GLACIER

PATH CROSSES TO TOP
OF RIDGE. ZIG-ZAGS
NOW BEGIN IN EARNEST

MAP 12
NOTE LARGER
SCALE ON THIS
MAP

ONLY DESCENT UNTIL
CRATER RIM - JUST A
FEW STEPS

Stella Point

30 MINS

End Of Zig Zags

3HRS

Top Of Ridge

1 HR 45 MINS
FROM BARAFU

night, however, you may be able to see the **Rebmann Glacier** ahead of you to your left, with the snow-less Stella Point a little to your right in the distance. Picking your way through the trail of vomiting trekkers and exhausted assistant guides, ignore the sound of people retching and sobbing and remember to keep your pace constant and very slow, even if you feel fine: you've come this far, and now is not a good time to get altitude sickness.

Though you probably won't notice it, the path actually drifts slightly to the north over these three hours, before crossing a frozen stream which marks the end of the zigzags. You are now just thirty minutes from Stella Point (5795m), a painful, tear-inducing half-hour on sheer scree. The gradient up to now has been steep, but this last scree slope takes the biscuit; in fact, it takes the entire tin.

Lift one foot and then the other, just enough to place it higher; don't use any more energy than you need to and to breathe deeply between each move. Rhythm is everything, rhythm and pacing, and when you are in it your thoughts go and it is dreamlike, but you are still here in the moment, the cone beam of light coming from your forehead tying you through the blackness to the lava slope of this mountain that in your mind you see rising to a rare glacial height above the acacia-studded plain of Africa.
Rick Ridgeway *The Shadow of Kilimanjaro – on Foot across East Africa*

Make it to the top and you can afford to relax a little. If you really, absolutely, positively, definitely can't do anymore, take comfort from the fact that you have already matched the feat of respected climber HW Tilman, for whom Stella Point was the highest point reached on his first attempt on the summit; and you can always use his excuse – that he thought that this *was* the highest point – too. (Mind you, as if to prove that it was ignorance and not a lack of fortitude that prevented him from reaching Uhuru, he then went on to conquer Mawenzi Peak a few days later). Take comfort, too, from the fact that you have also earned yourself an impressive green certificate. Those who want an even more impressive gold one, however, must push on for another 45 minutes around the crater rim, turning left (south) and then right (west), passing minor pinnacles such as **Hans Meyer** and **Elveda** points before finally arriving, just as Hans Meyer himself did over a century ago, at Uhuru Peak: the true summit of the mountain and the highest point in the whole continent (see Map 23, p225). You are now enjoying an unrivalled view of Africa – nobody on this great, dark continent is currently gazing down from as lofty a vantage-point as you.

From the summit, it's usual for trekkers who took the Machame Route up to take the Mweka or the new Alternative Mweka Route back down, and it is these two routes we describe beginning on p214.

The Rongai Route

Please convey to the seven blind climbers who reached the summit of Kilimanjaro my warm congratulations on their splendid achievement. **Queen Elizabeth II** in a telegram to Geoffrey Salisbury who, with his team of young, blind African trekkers, used the Rongai Route for their attempt on the mountain.

The name **Rongai Route** is actually something of a misnomer. Sure, it's the name that everybody uses but, strictly speaking, it's not the correct one. The real, original Rongai Route used to start at the border village of the same name but was closed a couple of years ago by the authorities who decided that two trails on a side of the mountain that few trekkers visit was unnecessary. You will still see this route marked on many maps, but today all trekkers who wish to climb Kili from the north now follow a different trail, commonly called the **Loitokitok Route** after the village that lies near to the start. (Just to confuse the issue still further, this isn't officially the correct name either, for along the trail you'll see various signs calling this trail the **Nalemuru Route** – or, occasionally, Nalemoru – though this name is rarely used by anybody.)

At first glance, this trail seems decidedly unattractive. The lower slopes at the very start of the trail have been denuded by farmers and present a bleak landscape, while the forest that follows is little more than a narrow band of woodland which soon gives way to some rather hot and shadeless heathland. Indeed, the parched character of Kili's northern slopes often means trekking parties have to carry water a long way (often all the way from the Third Cave Campsite to the Outward Bound Hut), so make sure you have enough porters to cover this eventuality. Furthermore, because of its proximity to Kenya this route is also prone to the occasional foray by opportunist bandits from the Kenyan side who indulge in a little light larceny, before escaping Tanzanian jurisdiction by hot-footing it back to their homeland again. For this reason, groups trekking on the Rongai Route are accompanied by an armed guard (though to be honest, I didn't realize our party had one until he appeared out of the heather on the second day to bid his farewells). And then there's the expense: if you are booking your trek in Moshi, Arusha or Marangu, the cost of transporting you to the start of the trail can be quite exorbitant, pushing the price up above most other trails.

So why, if this route is more expensive, dangerous and barren than all the others, should anybody do it at all? Well for one thing, there's the **wildlife**. Because this side of the mountain sees fewer tourists, and because animals tend to gather where humans don't, your chances of seeing the local wildlife here are greater than on any other route bar, perhaps, those starting in the far west on the Shira Plateau. During the research for this book we encountered a troop of colobus monkeys, while later that same day we came across an elephant skull, with elephant droppings and footprints nearby; and at night our little party was kept awake by something snuffling around the tents (a civet cat, according to our guide, though presumably one wearing heavy hobnail boots to judge by the amount of noise it was making). Buffaloes also frequent the few mountain streams on these northern slopes (though, as previously mentioned, these streams, never very deep, are almost always dry except in the rainy season, and consequently the buffaloes choose to bathe elsewhere for most of the year). The **flora** is different here too, with its juniper and olive trees. And if at the end of the ascent you do feel you've somehow missed out on some of the classic features of Kili – lobelias, for example, or the giant groundsels, which don't appear often on the northern side – then fear not, as both can be found in abundance on the Marangu Route, the designated descent for those coming from Rongai. Furthermore, opt for the extra day (see p202) – which I strongly advise, for reasons not only of acclimatization – and you will spend that extra night at the **Mawenzi Tarn Hut**, which not only allows you to savour some gobsmacking views across to Kibo – and a grove of splendid senecia – but also gives you the chance the following day to walk across the Saddle, many people's favourite part of the mountain. And finally, when it comes to the ascent, I found the walk from the Outward Bound Hut to Gillman's Point to be *marginally* easier than that from Kibo Hut, (though admittedly the two do share, for the last three hours or so to the summit, the same path).

Other advantages include the drive to the start: if you're coming from Kenya you'll drive through a landscape populated by giraffes and zebra, while from Moshi the road passes through rural Chagga heartlands, so giving you the chance to see village life Chagga-style (see p100). Furthermore, if you manage to find other trekkers to join you and split the cost, the transport should not be too expensive.

But perhaps the best thing about the Rongai Route is the fact that it is **so unpopular**. Choose to undertake this route and you'll often be the only party on the whole of this side of the mountain. According to the only statistics available, 130 people climbed it in 2000. That's 130 out of more than 20,000 who climbed the mountain that year. When compared with the human jungle of Kili's other side, the sense of isolation one feels when walking the Rongai Route is simply wonderful – and that is reason enough to recommend this trail.

PREPARATION

When booking your trek, it is important to get details right: are you staying at the campsite for the first night (in which case you won't need to pay any park or camping fees to the authorities for that first day, though you will have to pay something to Snow Cap – see p153 – for using their campsite). Check too that lunch on the first day is included, for this is usually taken at a café in Tarakea. Finally, as the gate at the start of the route is a one-man operation, permits have to be collected at Marangu Gate before you begin; make sure your guide has that permit before embarking on the long drive to the gate.

The journey to Loitokitok

From Marangu Gate, the car returns down the hill to the bus station before continuing round the dry, eastern side of the mountain, through the villages of Mwika and Mrere, host to a big market on Saturday, in the heart of the **Rombo District**. After them, in order, the villages of Shauritanga (site of a horrific tragedy in June 1994, when 42 schoolgirls were burnt to death in a dormitory fire started by a candle), Olele, Usseru, Mashima and Kibaoni emerge through the dust before, finally, around an hour and a quarter from the Marangu junction, you arrive at Tarakea, the largest settlement in the district and the usual venue for lunch. Don't let your guide drink too much here – we've heard some horror stories about this.

There is also a border post with Kenya in Tarakea; presumably your guide will know not to take the road leading to it but instead to keep on hugging the track which now heads north-west. The road continues to deteriorate until it is little more than pure sand and dust; keep your windows wound up.

Thirty minutes after leaving Tarakea, you reach the wooden settlement of Loitokitok, where a track on the left branches up to the park gate, situated at 2100m. From the gate you can see the smart **Snow Cap Campsite**.

STAGE 1: LOITOKITOK TO FIRST CAVE CAMPSITE [MAP 13, p203]

It is an inauspicious start to the trek. Having registered with the park official in his little wooden booth, your guide will then take you up the slopes through what, for many trekkers, is the ugliest part of Kilimanjaro, a hot and dusty blemish of corn and **cypress plantations** pockmarked here and there with the wooden shacks of those who eke out a living from the soil.

It is almost an hour before you escape this desolate scene for the lush green haven of the forest. When you do so, you'll be disappointed to find just how quickly the tall trees of the cloud forest give way to the smaller, less robust varieties. The forest does make a second, equally brief appearance later on in the day fifteen minutes after the first one, but even then the **heathland** is quick to assert itself and thereafter remains the dominant landscape for the rest of the day.

It's tempting to blame the untrammelled agriculture for the paltry amount of decent rainforest here. No doubt the farmers have played their part, but the truth of the matter is that this side of Kili has never had much in the way of rainforest – simply because it never gets much in the way of rain. Besides, this narrow band of forest is still teeming with wildlife, in particular **colobus monkeys**, with a troop of six often grazing in the first tree by the entrance to the forest.

Leaving the forest on a trail that slowly steepens, half an hour afterwards you cross a stream and a few minutes later reach the first campsite on this route, known as the **First Cave Campsite** (though there are no significant caves nearby), at an altitude of 2650m. You have already gained 550m in altitude in the 6km since you started walking. It's always good to get to a campsite, and this one in particular is pleasant:

Colobus monkey
(from *The Kilima-njaro Expedition,* HH Johnston, 1886)

with things snuffling about the tent at night, and birdsong from the Hunter's cisticolas in the morning, this spot has a pleasingly wild, isolated ambience.

STAGE 2: FIRST CAVE TO THIRD CAVE CAMPSITE [MAP 14, p204]

This stage perhaps lacks the variety of other stages. For most of the day you will be walking up slopes flanked with heather and erica, with the twin peaks of Kilimanjaro keeping a watchful eye as you progress. If you're on a five-day trek, during this stage you will bid farewell to those lucky trekkers who opted to take the extra day and visit the Mawenzi Tarn Hut; they will go their own way after lunch. (That route is described in the box below.) For the 'five-dayers', by the end of today you will have ascended more than 1100m, from 2650m at the First Cave Campsite to 3875m at your campsite at the end of this stage, the Third Cave. But there's no gain without pain, and today is long, involving four and a half hours or more of steady walking on a steep, dusty path. Take comfort from the fact that tomorrow is much easier, and that you have already ascended more than 1775m from the gate, and are now well over halfway to the summit.

The path at the start of this eight-kilometre stage is, perhaps surprisingly, a westward one, its goal seeming to be the northern slopes of Kibo rather than the eastern slopes that you will eventually climb. The heathers are gradually shrinking in size now too, and while there are still some trees clinging on to survive at this altitude, they are few in number and scattered. For these reasons, the first part of this stage is rather shadeless, and very hot. After 45 minutes a **river bed** (dry for the best part of the year) joins you from the left, and the path follows its course for most of the next hour. Look back occasionally and, weather permitting, you should be able to see a number of villages on the Kenyan side of the border, the sunlight glinting off the tin roofs. Continuing upwards, the path steepens slightly and begins to turn more to the south, passing the **junction** with the old Rongai Route, where an armed guard you never knew you had may suddenly appear and bid you farewell. Most strange.

The terrain up here is rather rocky and bumpy. The path continues south-south-west, rounding a few minor cliffs and hills, crossing a number of false

The Mawenzi Tarn Hut Route

From the Second Cave the path takes an abrupt south-easterly turn directly towards the jagged peak of Mawenzi. Traversing open moorland, the path is straightforward if occasionally a little indistinct through lack of use. Your camp on this second day is near a small set of caves known as **Kikelewa Caves**. These lie just below the Saddle, set in a valley of the same name that is rich in senecia. The caves lie at an altitude of around 3600m; since the Second Cave you have walked about 3km, but have gained just 150m in altitude.

The next two days are short (about two to three hours of walking each day). Initially, the path continues its idle south-easterly course, before rising steeply to your destination, the **Mawenzi Tarn Hut**, shedding the moorland vegetation as it does so. One of the most spectacular settings of any campsite, the Mawenzi Tarn Hut lies in a cirque right beneath the jagged teeth of Mawenzi. You are now at an altitude of 4330m, and assuming the walk here was trouble-free, you should have most of the afternoon to explore the barrancos and towers of this secondary peak. Make the most of it: very few people get here, and there's plenty to see and discover, including, of course, the Mawenzi Tarn. Wherever you go, take a guide.

On the third day you strike a direct westerly course, tiptoeing along the northern edge of the beautifully barren Saddle. You have two destinations, the School Hut (the more usual destination on this route) or the Kibo Hut. Both lie on the lower slopes of Kibo, and both are just a few hours' walk away along the largely flat Saddle. Depending on which hut you end up at, please see either p206 or p181 for the continuation of your walk up to Gillman's and Uhuru.

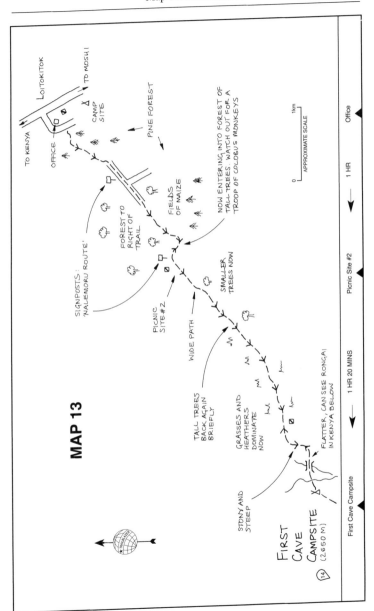

MAP 13

LOITOKITOK

TO MOSHI

TO KENYA

OFFICE

CAMP SITE

PINE FOREST

NOW ENTERING INTO FOREST OF TALL TREES. WATCH OUT FOR A TROOP OF COLOBUS MONKEYS

FIELDS OF MAIZE

SIGNPOSTS: 'NALEMORU ROUTE'

FOREST TO RIGHT OF TRAIL

PICNIC SITE #2

WIDE PATH

SMALLER TREES NOW

TALL TREES BACK AGAIN BRIEFLY

GRASSES AND HEATHERS DOMINATE NOW

FLATTER, CAN SEE RONGAI IN KENYA BELOW

STONY AND STEEP

FIRST CAVE CAMPSITE (2650 M)

14

0   1km

APPROXIMATE SCALE

	Office
1 HR	
	Picnic Site #2
1 HR 20 MINS	
First Cave Campsite	

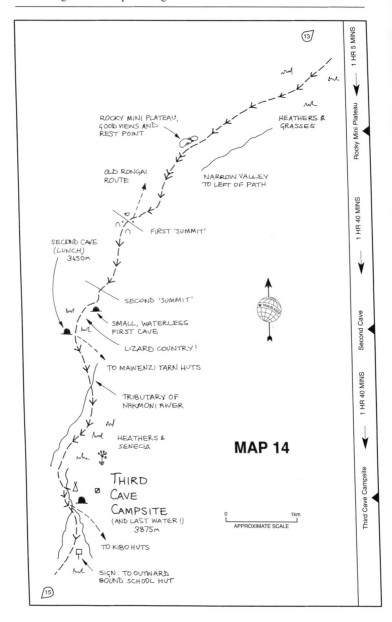

ROCKY MINI PLATEAU, GOOD VIEWS AND REST POINT

HEATHERS & GRASSES

OLD RONGAI ROUTE

NARROW VALLEY TO LEFT OF PATH

FIRST 'SUMMIT'

SECOND CAVE (LUNCH) 3450m

SECOND 'SUMMIT'

SMALL, WATERLESS FIRST CAVE

LIZARD COUNTRY!

TO MAWENZI TARN HUTS

TRIBUTARY OF NAKMONI RIVER

HEATHERS & SENECIA

THIRD CAVE CAMPSITE (AND LAST WATER!) 3875m

TO KIBO HUTS

SIGN: TO OUTWARD BOUND SCHOOL HUT

MAP 14

0   1km
APPROXIMATE SCALE

1 HR 5 MINS → Rocky Mini Plateau ◄

1 HR 40 MINS → Second Cave ◄

1 HR 40 MINS → Third Cave Campsite ◄

summits, before eventually flattening out and arriving at a small, waterless cave. As inviting as the cave and the shade it offers now appear, this is not your lunch stop known as the **Second Cave** (3450m) which lies twenty minutes further on through lizard country of bare rocks and long grasses.

Before setting off, make sure you are on the right trail, for the path to the Mawenzi Tarn Hut branches off at this point (see p202), so if your destination is the Third Cave Campsite but you find yourself heading south-east, reconsider. The path to the Third Cave begins behind and above the caves, from where it now bears off in a more southerly direction than heretofore. Crossing a wide and usually dry riverbed, which in the rainy season is a popular playground for buffaloes, the path continues drifting southwards across increasingly arid terrain, the 'dry flower' *helichrysum* now interspersed amongst the heathers. As huge rocks begin to appear to left and right, temporarily obscuring Mawenzi and Kibo, the unmistakable outline of toilet huts appear ahead on the trail, a sure sign that the campsite is nearing, this time to your left across another broad riverbed. This is the Third Cave Campsite and the **last water point** before the summit.

STAGE 3: THIRD CAVE CAMPSITE TO SCHOOL HUT [MAP 15, p206]

This stage is little more than an hors d'oeuvre for the main course, which will be served at around midnight tonight. Yet it may surprise you to find out that over the course of this stage you climb 925m – just 250m less than the previous stage, even though today's walk takes less than half the time. By the end of it you will be on the eastern slopes of Kibo, with splendid views galore across the Saddle to Mawenzi just a few minutes' walk away.

If you haven't already been doing so, this is also the time to take things deliberately *pole pole* ('slowly slowly' in Swahili) – you're reaching some serious altitudes now, and mountain sickness stalks the unwary. Looking southwest from the Third Cave Campsite, you should be able to see today's path snaking over the undulations of Kibo. The path begins by retracing the last few steps of yesterday back to the river bed, which forks just a few minutes after the campsite into two distinct tributaries. The path, too, divides at this junction and is signposted, with your trail heading off to the right (west), crossing the western tributary and continuing on towards the foot of Kibo. It's a slow slog southwards up the hill. Even the heathers struggle to survive up here, disappearing for the last time less than an hour outside camp; only the *helichrysum*, including the occasional yellow everlasting, continue to thrive, providing a welcome relief to the relentless greys and browns of the rocky soil.

After about 75 minutes a summit of sorts is reached, whereafter the path now heads more to the west, directly towards Kibo. The Northern Circuit bisects our trail around here, though this path is so seldom used that the junction is easily missed. No matter, for your path is clear as it bends more to the south, traversing Kibo's eastern slopes with the western face of Mawenzi now in full view to your left. This last bit of the walk is steep, and with the drop in oxygen at this altitude, quite exhausting. But after little more than an hour from the western bend in the path, you finally reach the **School Hut** (marked as the

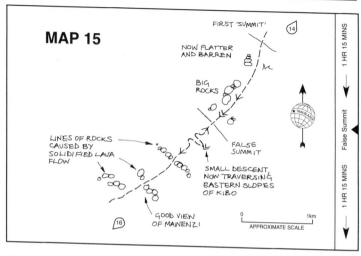

MAP 15

FIRST 'SUMMIT'

14

NOW FLATTER
AND BARREN

BIG
ROCKS

LINES OF ROCKS
CAUSED BY
SOLIDIFIED LAVA
FLOW

FALSE
SUMMIT

SMALL DESCENT,
NOW TRAVERSING
EASTERN SLOPES
OF KIBO

16

GOOD VIEW
OF MAWENZI

0   1km
APPROXIMATE SCALE

1 HR 15 MINS   False Summit   1 HR 15 MINS

Outward Bound Hut on some maps, though this is its former name, and one that KINAPA would prefer you didn't use), sitting in the shadow of some rather daunting cliffs. The huts sit at an altitude of about 4750m. If there are no tour groups that day, the chances are you'll have the place to yourself, save perhaps for an impressive mountain buzzard that likes to scavenge here from time to time when the place is deserted. Officially you should still use your tent rather than the hut to sleep in; for a small consideration, however, (namely a beer or two) the caretaker might consider letting you use the hut if that is what you prefer. Incidentally, if you need to fetch help for any reason, the Kibo Huts, larger and permanently manned by park staff, lie just 25 minutes to the south, the path beginning by the southernmost toilet hut.

STAGE 4: SCHOOL HUT TO KIBO TRAIL AND GILLMAN'S [MAP 16, OPP]

The higher we climbed the rarer grew the atmosphere and the more brilliant the light of the stars. Never in my life have I seen anything to equal the steady lustre of this tropical starlight. The planets seemed to grow with a still splendour which was more than earthly, ... Assuredly, the nights of lower earth know nothing of this silver radiance.
Hans Meyer *Across East African Glaciers*

There is no direct trekking route from the School Hut to the crater rim. Instead, the path heads south from the huts to join up with the 'Tourist Trail' running from Kibo Huts towards Gillman's Point. The junction between these two routes occurs between William's Point (5000m) and Hans Meyer Cave (5151m). In my experience, it takes slightly less time from School Huts to this junction than it does from Kibo Huts, so you may wish to start this section of the walk a little later – say at 12.15–12.30am rather than midnight.

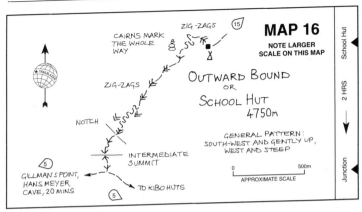

Finding the start of the path from the School Hut can be a little tricky in the dark, so we recommend that you or your guide conduct a little reconnaissance while it's still light to ensure one of you knows where you're supposed to be going. (Your guide should have been this way before, but if he has, it was probably a while ago.) Once you're on the path, which starts with a scramble up the rocks behind (ie to the west of) the School Hut, the trail becomes fairly clear, being marked with cairns the whole way. A repetitive pattern emerges during the walk to the junction: generally you are walking in a south-westerly direction over scree, but every so often the path turns more westerly and climbs more steeply over solid rock – these being petrified lava flows. At the end, a short descent brings you into the Kibo Hut 'valley' and a union with the path up to Gillman's. After the isolation of the last three days, the number of trekkers on this path comes as something of a shock. Hans Meyer Cave lies just twenty minutes above you along a series of switchbacks. For details of the path up to Gillman's Point from Hans Meyer Cave, turn to p182. For the descent you'll be using the Marangu Route, details of which can be found on p213.

The Shira Plateau and Lemosho routes

These two treks have been put together simply because they have a lot of features in common, the main one being that both involve a crossing of the expansive Shira Plateau which stretches out for some 15km to the west of Kibo. This plateau is actually a **caldera**, a collapsed volcanic crater: when you are walking on the plateau, you are walking on the remains of the first of Kilimanjaro's three volcanoes to expire, around 450,000 years ago; it was then filled by the lava and debris from the Kibo eruption.

As with the Rongai Route, the main advantage of these two trails is their isolation. Few trekkers make it this way, and as a result it's perfect for those who are hoping for a more solitary experience on Kili, and a chance to appreciate the sheer beauty of the mountain without the distraction of other people. The plateau also has a reputation for its **fauna**, largely thanks to its proximity to Amboseli National Park in Kenya, from where herds of elephant, eland, buffalo, and big cats such as the lion, have been known to wander. Indeed, it is not unusual for trekkers on these routes to be accompanied by a ranger, armed in case of encounters with predators. That said, you will be very, *very* lucky to see anything of the animals on the plateau, save for the occasional sun-dried lumps of scat and spoor. So while the proximity of Africa's finest wild beasts adds a certain frisson of excitement to the walk, don't choose either of these trails purely on the strength of their reputation for spotting game: it's a long way to come just to see dessicated elephant shit.

There are **many paths** on the plateau, a number of possible campsites too, and each year the guides alter slightly the routes taken by their trekkers. What's more, it is common for the new Lemosho Route to be referred to as the Shira Plateau Route. For these reasons, the following descriptions of the Lemosho and Shira Plateau trails may not tally exactly with your own experience on the plateau, though the difference should be negligible. However, you should ask your agency to indicate *exactly* which path you will be taking before you set off, to ensure there are no problems or disagreements on the trail itself.

The starting point for both of these trails is the **Londorossi Gate**, reachable via a long drive from Moshi or Arusha. As such, for much of the first day you won't be walking anywhere, but will be strapped into the back of a jeep as it glides along the Arusha–Moshi highway, before turning off at **Bomaya Ya Ng'ombe** (26km from Moshi). From there it bounces along for another two hours past **Sanya Juu** (22km from the turn-off and virtually the last place to get supplies) and **Simba Farm** (a huge estate to the left of the road) before finally pulling up at the village and gate of Londorossi. It's a weird place, a Spaghetti Western outpost stuck in the middle of Africa, made entirely of wood, divided up and shut off from the outside world by high wooden fences designed to keep the local fauna at bay. At Londorossi you can register and pick up a **permit** (the only other place outside of Marangu and Machame gates where this is possible). From here, the two trails divide, and are described separately below.

THE SHIRA PLATEAU ROUTE

This is the older of the two trails, and perhaps the inferior. From Londorossi Gate the four-wheel-drive track continues through some gorgeous forest scenery for another hour before climbing up and onto the plateau. This is the trail's main failing: by driving up to the plateau and a height of around 3500m, trekkers are not given enough time to acclimatize and may suffer later on as a result. Although this can be remedied by taking it easy for the next day or two – and your agency should have built into the itinerary some easy days – this is still not exactly ideal. Furthermore, by the time you are on the plateau you are already in Kilimanjaro's moorland zone and thus have missed out on the mountain's fascinating forest, which you will have only glimpsed through the car window. True, you will be walking back through the forest on the way down, but by then you may well be too tired, following your ascent of Kibo, to fully appreciate it.

Having finally reached the end of the road at the **Morum Barrier** (the track actually continues for a little way beyond this but is usually open only to rescue vehicles), it is probably already getting late and only an hour or two's walking can be completed before camp needs to be made; indeed, of the people I have met who have done this trail, many actually camp at the Morum Barrier and thus do no walking whatsoever on the first day. If you do manage to squeeze in some trekking on this first day, it is highly likely that your guide will lead you to **Simba Cave** (3454m), two hours away to the south-south-east.

The second day on the Shira Plateau Route is traditionally very short, involving just a couple of hours' hiking south-east along the plateau, thereby giving you some time to acclimatize. Your destination on this second day will depend on which route you have opted to take up Kibo: if you plan on taking the easier **Barafu Route** around the southern slopes of Kibo, the chances are you will be marched by your guide to the **New Shira Camp** – along a path that veers off south before the Shira 2 Camp – and a union with the Machame trail. From now on you will be walking with the many trekkers taking this trail; it can be quite a strange and unnerving experience for a party that started on the Shira Plateau Route, and who have in all probability spent at least one night in complete isolation on the mountain (the Shira Plateau Route being perhaps the least popular route of them all), suddenly to meet so many fellow walkers. For a description of the walk from the New Shira Camp to the summit, see p190.

The alternative route is for those hoping to ascend Kibo via the **Arrow Glacier Route**. The traditional destination for the second day in this case is the **Shira 2 Camp** (3850m) – again, just a couple of hours from the Simba Cave. From here, on the third day the path heads almost due east across the undulations of the plateau, picking its way between the boulders, joining with the Machame Route and heading on to the prominent Lava Tower, the huge and isolated lump of rock guarding the way up to the Western Breach. For details of this ascent up Kibo, turn to p192.

THE LEMOSHO ROUTE

The Lemosho Route is a relatively new variation on the traditional Shira Plateau Route. It is also a better one: by starting the trek lower down you get to walk through some fine forest, and although the walk up to the plateau is an exhausting one, the benefits of trekking rather than driving up will manifest themselves later on, as you saunter up Kibo with scarcely a headache, while littering the trail around you are the weeping, retching bodies of the AMS-sufferers who took the car up to the Shira Plateau.

Getting to the start of the Lemosho Route is a bit of a bind. Having registered at Londorossi, you must then return through wheat fields and cypress forests back south to **Lemosho Glades** (2100m), taking a left turn at the junction with the sawmill (where you have to pay a toll). It will already be late in the day by the time you start walking, although the first night's camp lies just two hours from the end of the road. The campsite is known officially (ie by nobody) as the **Forest Camp**, and unofficially (ie by everybody) as Mti Mkubwa, or the **Big Tree Camp** (2650m), for obvious reasons.

A whole day spent travelling, registering and walking, and you are still some way short of the plateau, which you will finally reach towards the end of day two, leaving the forest for the moorland as you do so. Having gained the Shira Ridge (3690m), most parties descend to make camp on the second night by the stream at **Shira 1** (3610m). The trail to get there is a long one, involving about six hours of walking all told and a gain of almost 1000m in altitude; some parties, particularly those planning to take the Barafu/Barranco route up to Kibo, press on even further to the old **Shira Huts**, safe in the knowledge that this longer route should provide time enough to acclimatize later on. If you can afford to spend the extra night on the plateau, however, it is by far the better option.

Assuming that you did stop overnight at Shira 1, day three offers alternative paths, the one you take depending largely on which of the two main trails you wish to follow to the summit. With either route, look to your right during the morning's trek and ask your guide to point out some of the more recognizable features of the Shira Plateau, namely the **Cathedral** and the **Needle** on the plateau's southern lip, the **Shira Cone**, rising 200m from the plateau slightly to the west, and further west over your right shoulder, on the Shira Rim, the high points of **Klute Peak** and **Johnsell Point** (3962m). For those aiming for the Barranco/Barafu trail, on the third day it is usual to walk via the Shira Huts, taking a path that veers south before Shira 2, and from there join up with the Machame Route and head on for a further six hours to the **Barranco Campsite**, in the valley of the same name. For details of the walk from Barranco to the summit via Barafu, see p193. If taking the Arrow Glacier Route, however, it is more usual to move on from Shira 1 just a little distance to **Shira 2** (3850m), a short day involving just 2hr 30min of walking, but a very necessary one in helping acclimatization. From here, trekkers typically spend the fourth day joining the Machame Route to the Lava Tower and the ruined **Arrow Glacier Hut**. For details of the trail from the Arrow Glacier Hut to the summit, see p192.

The Umbwe Route

This is the hardest trek up Kili, a thoroughly tough uphill struggle for a day and a half until the trail reaches Barranco Huts and a union with the Southern Circuit. As a reward for your endeavours, however, a clear day will provide you with views that many guides and porters insist are the best there are on Kilimanjaro. It's a little-used route, too, giving you time to appreciate the mountain without the chatter and clutter of other trekkers.

From Barranco you have two choices: the first is to continue your northerly course directly up to the Arrow Glacier and through the Western Breach to the summit. Alternatively, you can opt to take the Southern Circuit to Barafu Huts, and a scramble to the summit via Stella Point. Be warned that the first strategy is extremely risky without taking at least one acclimatization day en route to Arrow Glacier Hut. Otherwise, the trip from Moshi up to Arrow Glacier Hut, an increase in altitude of almost 4000m, will take just three days, which is far too rapid.

STAGE 1: UMBWE GATE TO UMBWE CAVE CAMPSITE

The drive to Umbwe Gate takes around an hour and a half, the 4WD track continuing up the hill for a long way. Permits should already have been secured from Marangu Gate. The start of the trail is at 1800m, the route initially following a 4WD forestry track before it narrows and steepens to climb a ridge between the Lonzo and Umbwe rivers.

This is the steepest part of the entire trek, and in places you'll be hauling yourself up by tree roots. Luckily, there are plenty of tree roots around. The forest around here is rich and dark, the forest canopy minimizing the amount of light that filters through to the path. In between breaths, look out for the beautiful red *Impatiens kilimanjari* growing in between the roots.

Eventually, after five hours of this exhausting exercise, and a gain in altitude of 1050m, you reach a rocky overhang. This is the Umbwe Cave (2940m), a popular first-night campsite with plenty of water sources available.

STAGE 2: UMBWE CAVE CAMPSITE TO BARRANCO HUTS

Roughly forty-five minutes after breaking camp you emerge from the forest gloom onto the heath, to be presented with two awesome sights: the breathtaking Breach Wall – all 1000m of it – and the glory of the Kibo summit. The path continues getting relentlessly steeper as you come to a short stretch of scrambling on rocks through the heath. Finally the gradient eases and the rest of the day is spent ambling through moorland vegetation to the Barranco Hut Campsite, nestling on your right – around five and a half hours from Umbwe Cave Campsite.

The next day another choice faces you. If you plan to follow the Southern Circuit Route, turn to p193 and follow the description from there. Those hoping to reach the summit via the Western Breach should head west up the senecio-clad valley to the ridge and continue north and west to Lava Tower Camp, about two hours away. See the box on p192 for details of this ascent.

The designated descent route for Umbwe is the Mweka (or Alternative Mweka) Route. Please see p214 (p218 for Alternative Mweka) for details of this descent.

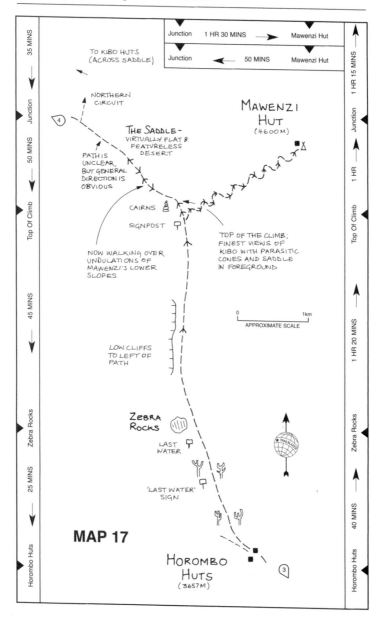

| Junction | 1 HR 30 MINS | → | Mawenzi Hut |
| Junction | ← | 50 MINS | Mawenzi Hut |

TO KIBO HUTS
(ACROSS SADDLE)

NORTHERN
CIRCUIT

④

THE SADDLE –
VIRTUALLY FLAT &
FEATURELESS
DESERT

PATH IS
UNCLEAR,
BUT GENERAL
DIRECTION IS
OBVIOUS

MAWENZI
HUT
(4600M)

CAIRNS

SIGNPOST

NOW WALKING OVER
UNDULATIONS OF
MAWENZI'S LOWER
SLOPES

TOP OF THE CLIMB;
FINEST VIEWS OF
KIBO WITH PARASITIC
CONES AND SADDLE
IN FOREGROUND

LOW CLIFFS
TO LEFT OF
PATH

0   1km
APPROXIMATE SCALE

ZEBRA
ROCKS

LAST
WATER

'LAST WATER'
SIGN

MAP 17

HOROMBO
HUTS
(3657M)

③

35 MINS · Junction · 50 MINS · Top Of Climb · 45 MINS · Zebra Rocks · 25 MINS · Horombo Huts

1 HR 15 MINS · Junction · 1 HR · Top Of Climb · 1 HR 20 MINS · Zebra Rocks · 40 MINS · Horombo Huts

The descent routes

MARANGU ROUTE

Stage 1: Gillman's Point to the Horombo Huts
[Map 5, p183; Map 4, p181; Map 3, p179]

Few people remain at the summit for long: weariness, risk of hypothermia and the thought of a steaming mug of *Milo* at the Kibo Huts are enough to send most people scurrying back down. There are two main ways of doing this: the first is to follow exactly the course you took getting up here, carefully retracing every zig and zag like somebody who has dropped a contact lens on the way up but can't quite remember when or where. Curiously, it is precisely those people who are in greatest need of getting down fast who are the ones who usually use this method to descend.

The second way is to cut straight through the switchbacks and simply head vertically downwards in a sort of ski-style, using the now defrosted scree to act as a brake on your momentum. After the tedium of the previous night's heel-to-toe exercise, the sheer abandon of this method, and the rapid progress made – it takes just over 90min to travel from Gillman's to the huts this way – comes as something of a relief. Take care, however: far more people are injured com-

---

Returning via the Mawenzi Route　　　　　　　**[Map 17, opposite]**

This is the more interesting path between Kibo and Horombo, encompassing not only entire groves of giant groundsels (*Senecio kilimanjari*) and the Zebra Rocks, but also the best panorama of them all on Kilimanjaro. It is, however, one that is seldom used, mainly because the majority of trekkers will already have done a lot of it during their acclimatization day up to Mawenzi Hut.

From Kibo Huts the path descends once more to **Jiwe Lainkoyo**. Though there appears to be but one path from Jiwe, there is in fact another, much fainter path heading almost due east across the Saddle towards Mawenzi. If you cannot make it out at first don't worry, just aim for Mawenzi and you will soon notice a faint but distinct path etched into the earth bisecting the Saddle. Ten minutes after Jiwe a junction with the even fainter **Northern Kibo Circuit** is reached (a signpost is the only evidence that there is a junction here at all), and twenty-five minutes after that the path begins to rise and fall as it follows the contours of Mawenzi's lower reaches. After half an hour of following this undulating terrain you come to a summit of sorts, from where you can rest and gaze back over the finest **panorama** this mountain has to offer: the alpine desert of the Saddle, with a string of parasitic cones leading from the foreground to the foot of Kibo and with Mawenzi just over your shoulder. Spectacular.

From here, the path runs due south through heather past the path leading to Mawenzi Hut to the **Zebra Rocks** (a collection of rockfaces coloured by water that resemble the flanks of a zebra), then down between the groundsel gullies until, one hour from the unforgettable panorama and two hours 35 minutes since leaving Jiwe Lainkoyo, the roofs of the **Horombo Huts** appear beneath you once more.

ing down than going up. Furthermore, do remember that every year at least ten thousand other pairs of feet tread on this part of the mountain and, at the risk of sounding like a killjoy, pushing down all that scree cannot be doing the mountain any good. If KINAPA are looking for a new problem to address now that they have finished constructing the Alternative Mweka Route, they should start by looking here.

Upon returning to camp, your guide should allow you to rest for an hour before moving on again to the Horombo Huts. Remember the advice given at the beginning of Stage 3 (see p179) and ask your guide to take you back via a different route to the one on which you ascended. This usually means returning via the Saddle on the Mawenzi Route, a route we have described in the box on p213. If you do return via the southerly route, expect it to take about three hours.

Stage Two: Horombo Huts to Marangu Gate
[Map 3, p179; Map 2, p177; Map 1, p174]

Don't be in too much of a hurry to finish your trekking, for today holds lots of treats for those who take the time to enjoy them. If you have come from the Rongai Route this is the first time you will have seen forest so thick and vast on Kilimanjaro, and it's worth taking the time to appreciate the different flora on this side of the mountain. But even if you ascended by the Marangu Route, it still warrants a second look on the way down. Much of the scenery may be old hat to you by now, but remember that you've still paid US$30 for the privilege of walking in the forest today, so you may as well get the most out of it. And just as Lee Marvin in *Paint Your Wagon* sang that he'd never seen a town 'that didn't look better looking back', so most people will agree that the forest seems so much more welcoming when you're walking *downhill* through it; and the views of Kibo are that much more appealing from over the shoulder, knowing that you'll never have to climb it again.

It takes about 2hr 20min to return from Horombo to the **Mandara Huts** which are, typically, the final lunch-stop of the trail. This is also your last chance to buy beer while it's still cheaper than water. From there, it's back into the forest and down to the **gate**, a journey of some 95 minutes. Name registered, tips dispersed and with certificate clutched close to your bosom, it's time to return to the land of hot showers and flush toilets. Your adventure is at an end, and civilization has rarely seemed so good.

THE MWEKA ROUTE

Stage 1: Uhuru Peak to Barafu and Mweka Camp
[Map 12, p197; Map 18, opp]

What goes up must come down, and that includes you. The path back to Barafu is little more than a retracing of your steps of the previous night (assuming you climbed this way), though there is a slightly quicker, if more hair-raising approach: walking past Stella Point, slightly to the north is the start of a straight ski-run down through the gravel that bypasses the zigzags of the regular route. Some people prefer to make it down as quickly as possible and so choose this

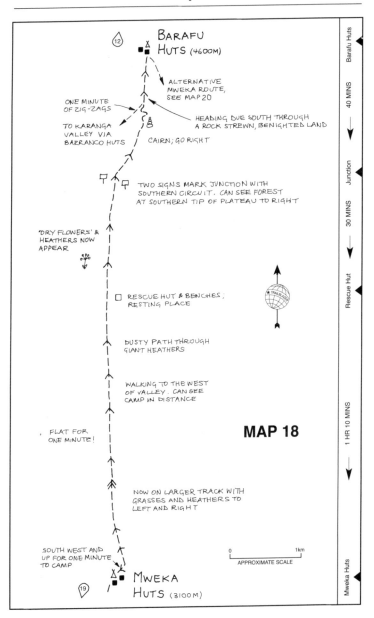

⑫

BARAFU
HUTS (4600M)

ALTERNATIVE
MWEKA ROUTE,
SEE MAP 20

ONE MINUTE
OF ZIG-ZAGS

HEADING DUE SOUTH THROUGH
A ROCK STREWN, BENIGHTED LAND

TO KARANGA
VALLEY VIA
BARRANCO HUTS

CAIRN; GO RIGHT

TWO SIGNS MARK JUNCTION WITH
SOUTHERN CIRCUIT. CAN SEE FOREST
AT SOUTHERN TIP OF PLATEAU TO RIGHT

'DRY FLOWERS' &
HEATHERS NOW
APPEAR

RESCUE HUT & BENCHES;
RESTING PLACE

DUSTY PATH THROUGH
GIANT HEATHERS

WALKING TO THE WEST
OF VALLEY. CAN SEE
CAMP IN DISTANCE

FLAT FOR
ONE MINUTE!

MAP 18

NOW ON LARGER TRACK WITH
GRASSES AND HEATHERS TO
LEFT AND RIGHT

SOUTH WEST AND
UP FOR ONE MINUTE
TO CAMP

⑲

MWEKA
HUTS (3100M)

0   1km
APPROXIMATE SCALE

Barafu Huts

40 MINS

Junction

30 MINS

Rescue Hut

1 HR 10 MINS

Mweka Huts

> **Mweka and Alternative Mweka**
> Note that there are now two Mweka routes: the standard, original Mweka Trail as described below, and a new trail described on p218. There's little variation in the scenery: you are, after all, still passing through the same vegetation zones on both routes, from desert to heathland to forest before finishing on the edge of the cultivated zone. Be sure about which route you should be following before setting off from Barafu.

trail; others find it too taxing on both nerves and knees, and opt for the gentler descent. Before deciding which is for you, read the advice about erosion on p160 – and then take the gentler descent! Either way, the two paths reunite back near the foot of the cliffs above Barafu. The entire descent takes about an hour and twenty minutes (plus breaks) from Stella Point, less if you take the 'fast' route.

You probably feel, on returning to camp, that you have earned the luxury of a brief rest at Barafu, and indeed you have. But make sure it *is* brief, for you still have another two and a half hours of knee-knackering downhill before you reach Mweka Camp, your home for the night. A pretty monotonous two and a half hours it is, too, as you head off due south and down for the entire 8km. In its defence, the descent is both large (dropping from 4600m to 3100m) and fairly gradual, which can only be good news for both AMS sufferers and those with aching knees. There is also some interest to be had in seeing how the vegetation changes along the way: at first, only the incredibly hardy yellow everlastings are able to survive at the high altitude, but they are soon joined by their dry-looking cousins in the *helichrysum* family, and soon after that the heathers appear.

After forty minutes or so you come to a huddle of **signposts** collected around the path; to your left on the slopes you can see paths from the Horombo Huts on the Marangu Route, while to your right are those coming from the Karanga Valley. Your path continues straight on, however, towards the green-roofed **rescue hut** – a popular rest stop. Coke and other soft drinks are available here. Immediately to the south, giant heathers grow for the first time by the dusty path; further down keep your eyes peeled for the heavy yellow-white flowers of the **protea**. You first glimpse **Mweka Camp** (3100m) about 40 minutes before you actually get there as you descend on a ridge between two valleys towards a small heather-clad hill. Rounding this, the path widens and flattens before turning south-west and climbing for one minute to the camp – the only ascent of the entire walk from Barafu. By the way, you may wish to share out your tips at Mweka Camp before you depart on this last leg: as porters all walk at different speeds, this may be the last time the whole group is together.

Stage 2: Mweka Camp to Mweka Gate   [Map 19, opp]

By now you'll probably just want to get off the mountain as quickly as possible – which would actually be rather a shame, for this last section follows a very pretty forest trail alive with birdsong and flowers.

This ten-kilometre stage begins in similar fashion to much of the previous one, by heading south and down. Less than five minutes after you start walking,

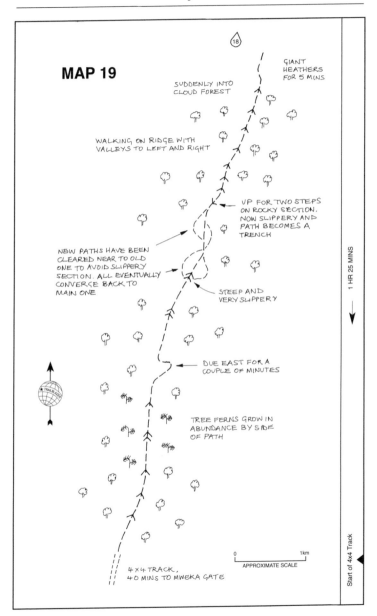

MAP 19

SUDDENLY INTO
CLOUD FOREST

GIANT
HEATHERS
FOR 5 MINS

WALKING ON RIDGE WITH
VALLEYS TO LEFT AND RIGHT

UP FOR TWO STEPS
ON ROCKY SECTION,
NOW SLIPPERY AND
PATH BECOMES A
TRENCH

NEW PATHS HAVE BEEN
CLEARED NEAR TO OLD
ONE TO AVOID SLIPPERY
SECTION. ALL EVENTUALLY
CONVERGE BACK TO
MAIN ONE

STEEP AND
VERY SLIPPERY

DUE EAST FOR A
COUPLE OF MINUTES

TREE FERNS GROW IN
ABUNDANCE BY SIDE
OF PATH

1 HR 25 MINS

Start of 4x4 Track

0   1km
APPROXIMATE SCALE

4 X 4 TRACK,
40 MINS TO MWEKA GATE

you find yourself in cloud forest, the border between this and the giant heather forest so definite and distinct that you could almost draw a line in the ground between the two. Once again walking on a narrow ridge between two valleys, look around and notice how the trees now grow in height and girth, how the moss that grows upon them is thick, green and hearty where before it was stringy and limp, and how flowers such as the *Impatiens kilimanjari* once again make an appearance on the trail. It's a lovely walk, marred only by the fact that the path is in patches *extremely* slippery and, if it has been raining heavily, very muddy too. In places the trail is so worn through overuse that it has become a two-foot deep trench. New paths that avoid the worst of the mud have been created along the way though all of these detours converge on the main trail eventually and it is hard to get lost on this section. Tree roots encroach to try to reclaim the path once more, and tree ferns appear in abundance; look out for armies of ants crossing the trail too.

Less than ninety minutes after breaking camp, you'll find yourself walking on the start of the 4WD track down to **Mweka Gate** (1500m), a further 40 minutes away. At the gate you can buy a souvenir T-shirt to advertise the fact you reached the summit (curiously, there are no T-shirts suitable for those that did not). You must also sign the last **registration book** at the nearby park office, from where those who were successful can collect the appropriate certificate. If you're with a company that has four-wheel drive vehicles you might be met at the gate (Roy's, I notice, is one such company); the rest have to walk ten minutes further down the hill to the lower station, where there are a couple of shops and a bar, the *Tobit Kilimanjaro View Centre*. Those who succeeded in reaching Uhuru Peak can usually be seen standing around, their golden certificates held casually yet deliberately so that they catch and glint in the sun, in much the same way that Ferrari owners are wont to display their car keys. Your mountain odyssey is almost at an end: from here, it's a 30-minute drive back to the land of power showers and flush loos.

ALTERNATIVE MWEKA (KIDIA) ROUTE

In September 2001 the park authorities closed the Mweka Route. As anyone who has walked down this trail in the last few years can testify, this was no bad thing. Simply put, it was in a terrible condition, with the passage of thousands of trekkers over time creating a foot-deep trench where once a path existed.

It is not surprising that the track fell into such a parlous state: originally the numbers on the Shira, Umbwe and Machame routes (Lemosho had yet to be created) were limited to just 16 trekkers on each trail per day, thereby limiting to no more than 48 the total number of trekkers on Mweka in any one day. With the abolition of those limits, however, and the soaring popularity of Machame, that figure has been nearer 200 trekkers per day for the last couple of years; that's an extra 304 feet treading on poor Mweka every day – not to mention the feet of all the attendant porters and guides – and the path was simply unable to cope with this increased volume.

In its place KINAPA have created – and are to be applauded for doing so – an alternative Mweka Route, which they have called, rather imaginatively, the **Alternative Mweka Route**. At least that is the name KINAPA, as the proud parents, have christened it: among the porters, guides and trekking agencies who actually use the path it has already become known as the **Kidia Route** after the village that lies at the end of it.

KINAPA are at pains to point out that they still regard Mweka as the main descent trail for those coming from the Machame, Shira, Umbwe and Lemosho routes, and its closure is but temporary, with estimates as to when it will reopen varying, depending on to whom you speak, from six months to five years. But there is strong speculation among many that this new trail is here to stay and that, if and when the original path does begin receiving trekkers again, the Alternative Mweka will remain open to ease the burden upon it. I note, too, that the Keys Hotel already has a campsite complete with bar and restaurant at the end of the path and appears to be testing the water with regards to establishing a hotel there – which they would surely do only if they felt that the new path was going to be permanent.

As to the relative merits of the two, while both have their attractions I have to say I still prefer the former, if only because the new trail is so exasperatingly long. Where the original sets off due south like a bullet from a gun towards civilization, and continues unwaveringly in that direction nearly all the way to Mweka Gate, the new path tends to dawdle somewhat; and after spending the entire night walking to the top of a very big mountain, dawdling will probably not be on your list of preferred activities at that moment. This criticism is particularly applicable both to the first day, which goes on for at least one eternity across valley after valley of heather and *helichrysum*, a repetitive and unvarying landscape that offers little to distract you from the screaming pain in your calf muscles; and of the latter part of the second day, where the path joins a 4WD track that twists, curls, loops and snakes all over the slopes like a python on its stag night.

In compensation, there is a brief section on the morning of the second day which is just divine: on the one side, meadows dotted with lobelias between which **malachite sunbirds** flit in search of nectar and insects; on the other, a slender grove of bearded forest following the course of a bubbling mountain stream, while looking over your shoulder all the while are Kibo and Mawenzi, posing for one last photo before ducking for good behind their lower slopes. If I should ever die on this mountain, I can think of no finer send-off than to have my ashes scattered here. (Although I hope whoever's responsible for the scattering will let them cool first: as many of the notices en route point out, wildfires can be a problem here.)

Stage 1: Barafu to Rau Campsite   [Map 20, p220; Map 21, p221]

To begin: from behind the twin green huts of Barafu the trail plummets down the western wall of the neighbouring **South East Valley**, crosses it in a southeasterly direction, then climbs up and out and into the next valley to the east. It

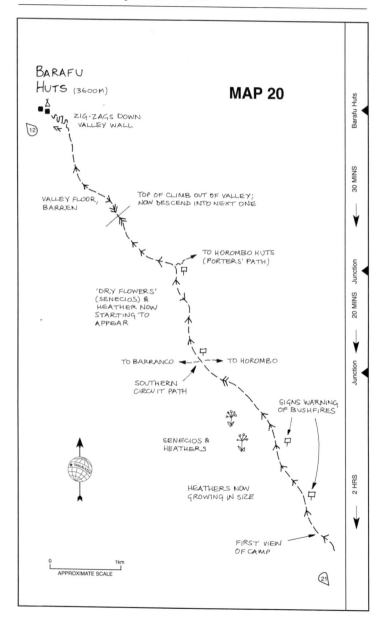

BARAFU
HUTS (3600M)

MAP 20

12

ZIG-ZAGS DOWN
VALLEY WALL

Barafu Huts

30 MINS

VALLEY FLOOR,
BARREN

TOP OF CLIMB OUT OF VALLEY;
NOW DESCEND INTO NEXT ONE

TO HOROMBO HUTS
(PORTERS' PATH)

Junction

'DRY FLOWERS'
(SENECIOS) &
HEATHER NOW
STARTING TO
APPEAR

20 MINS

TO BARRANCO ◄———————► TO HOROMBO

Junction

SOUTHERN
CIRCUIT PATH

SIGNS WARNING
OF BUSHFIRES

SENECIOS &
HEATHERS

HEATHERS NOW
GROWING IN SIZE

2 HRS

FIRST VIEW
OF CAMP

21

TRAILBLAZER

0   1km
APPROXIMATE SCALE

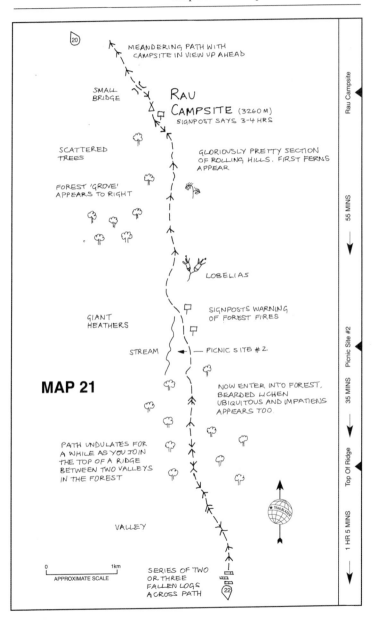

MEANDERING PATH WITH
CAMPSITE IN VIEW UP AHEAD

SMALL
BRIDGE

RAU
CAMPSITE (3260 M)
SIGNPOST SAYS 3-4 HRS

SCATTERED
TREES

GLORIOUSLY PRETTY SECTION
OF ROLLING HILLS. FIRST FERNS
APPEAR

FOREST 'GROVE'
APPEARS TO RIGHT

LOBELIAS

GIANT
HEATHERS

SIGNPOSTS WARNING
OF FOREST FIRES

STREAM — PICNIC SITE #2

MAP 21

NOW ENTER INTO FOREST.
BEARDED LICHEN
UBIQUITOUS AND IMPATIENS
APPEARS TOO.

PATH UNDULATES FOR
A WHILE AS YOU JOIN
THE TOP OF A RIDGE
BETWEEN TWO VALLEYS
IN THE FOREST

VALLEY

0   1km
APPROXIMATE SCALE

SERIES OF TWO
OR THREE
FALLEN LOGS
ACROSS PATH

Rau Campsite

55 MINS

Picnic Site #2

35 MINS

Top Of Ridge

1 HR 5 MINS

is a pattern that is repeated for much of the rest of the day. After a while the heathland become a little monotonous, with dullish greens growing out of soil a dullish grey-brown colour. At first this landscape is merely boring; but as impatience and tiredness set in, the unchanging scenery becomes downright aggravatingly, aggressively tedious. Cairns pick out the way, and signposts have been placed by the junctions with other paths (namely the **porters' path** to Horombo about thirty minutes after leaving Barafu, and a junction with the **Kibo Southern Circuit** twenty minutes further on).

Eventually the **Rau Campsite** (3260m), your home for the night, moves into view, though even this provides little cheer, being both far away (about 35 minutes from the point where you first see it) and clearly located upon a hill, thus requiring yet more work for those screaming calf muscles. But reach it you eventually will, there to sit and soak your feet in the bucket of water provided by your kindly porter, followed possibly by a trip to the tourists-only toilet, noteworthy insofar that they are of the sit-down variety; this is probably the first welcome piece of news your tired legs have received on this very, very long day.

Stage 2: Rau Campsite to Kidia Gate   [Map 21, p221; Map 22, opp]

The sign at Rau Campsite says that the end of the trek is but a three to four hour walk away. This is pushing the truth a bit. It probably did take the park warden (or whoever was responsible for arriving at this estimate) three or four hours to walk from the campsite down to the gate, but then you have to ask if he had spent the previous four or five days walking up to the summit of Kibo and back? I think not. Still, as mentioned in the introduction to this route, this final day has some glorious sections to it, the first of which, and the most spectacular, lies just fifteen minutes south of the Rau Campsite. It's not just I who thinks this section is worthy of greater attention: the authorities have decided to locate the first of two **picnic spots,** here on the route in the forest on the edge of the fields, and a more perfect spot to munch on a chicken drumstick it is hard to imagine. Be careful of the path along this first section, however: many small trees and bushes were uprooted or chopped down to make way for the trail, and their stumps and roots continue to protrude along the path, causing many a trip and stumble. Take care in the **forest** too, which you will enter an hour after Rau, for creepers and vines also pose potential hazards.

Having entered the forest, the path undulates as it first climbs to and then follows the top of a narrow ridge between two deep valleys. The **second picnic site** (called, confusingly, Picnic Site Number 1) is about 90 minutes or more into the forest, and cannot compete with the first; indeed, the forest at this second site looks rather bare and sparse, and the deep, steep drops on either side give this spot a rather isolated, lonely feel.

After this the path crosses and re-crosses a number of mountain streams and, later on, a couple of man-made water channels. It then descends along a pretty path lined with tree ferns, before climbing up a short hill to a large **aerial tower**. The 4WD track begins about now, and meanders on for the next few

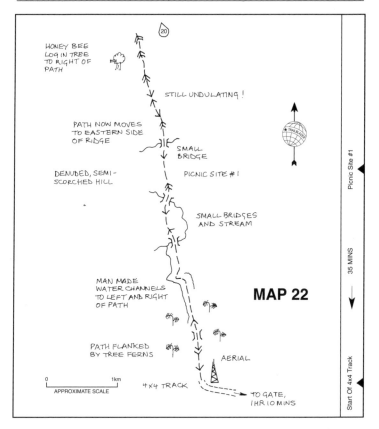

HONEY BEE
LOG IN TREE
TO RIGHT OF
PATH

STILL UNDULATING !

PATH NOW MOVES
TO EASTERN SIDE
OF RIDGE

SMALL
BRIDGE

DENUDED, SEMI-
SCORCHED HILL

PICNIC SITE # I

SMALL BRIDGES
AND STREAM

MAN MADE
WATER CHANNELS
TO LEFT AND RIGHT
OF PATH

MAP 22

PATH FLANKED
BY TREE FERNS

AERIAL

0   1km

APPROXIMATE SCALE

4 X 4 TRACK

TO GATE,
I HR I0 MINS

Picnic Site #1

35 MINS

Start Of 4x4 Track

kilometres. Every time you come to a bend in the path you think the gate is just around the corner; time and again, however, you will be disappointed. Eventually, after well over an hour from the aerial, the path descends for the final time and you reach **Kidia Gate** (1500m), where a nice man sits in a little cabin to the right of the gate and doles out certificates to those who deserve them. The trek is at an end, and all that remains to do is sign your name in the registration book, dish out the tips (if you haven't done so already) and catch your lift back past waving kids to your hotel, a warm shower and a cold Kilimanjaro beer. You've earned it – though if you do plan to celebrate in Moshi, please take more care than Meyer did upon his return to town:

In the evening, to show there was no ill-feeling, I treated the natives to a display of fire-works, in the course of which a spark from a rocket set fire to one of the men's huts.

PART 8: THE SUMMIT

What's at the top?

The crater of Kilimanjaro is a primeval place and decidedly uncomfortable, yet I was drawn to it. The idea of spending some days and nights awoke a compelling mixture of reverential fear and wonder; similar, I suspect, to the compulsion which draws some people unquestioningly to church. And like churches, the crater also invites contemplation of the eternal mysteries.   **John Reader** *Kilimanjaro*

It's only when you reach the top of Kibo that you realise that the mountain really is a volcano, and all you have done is climb to the crater rim.

The rim itself is largely featureless, though as the highest point on the mountain it has assumed a pre-eminent role and is the focus of all trekkers. The few bumps and tumescences on it have been dignified with the word 'Spitze' or 'Point' as if they were major summits in their own right. Heading clockwise around the rim from **Gillman's** – the lowest point on the crater rim, according to Tilman – these bumps in order are: **Stella** (the aim of those climbing from Barafu), **Elveda**, **Hans Meyer**, **Uhuru** and **Furtwangler** (named after the man who first used skis to descend); while just to the north of Gillman's is **Leopard Point**. The distance between Gillman's to Uhuru is about 1.5km, with the crater rim rising 207–210m between the two. The floor of the crater, covered in brown shale and rocks and boulders of all shapes and sizes, lies between 25m (at Gillman's or the Western Breach) and 200m (at Uhuru Peak) beneath this rim.

Trudging around the rim to Uhuru is achievement enough. There are, however, plenty of other diversions to keep you on the summit for longer ...

WALKING ON THE SUMMIT   [Map 23, opp]

For most people the conquest of Uhuru Peak, and a shiny gold certificate that says as much, is reason enough to climb Kilimanjaro. Some trekkers, however, always want to do just that little bit more, and if you still have some energy to burn once you've reached the summit you may care to take a quick tour around the crater itself. **Warn your guide in advance** of your intentions – preferably before you've even started your trek – for some react badly to the idea of spending any longer on the summit than is absolutely necessary; a little gentle cajoling, along with a few hints about the size of the tip that awaits them at the end of the trip, should do the trick. Make sure, too, that your guide knows his way

---

Opposite Top: The inevitable photo opportunity at Uhuru Peak.
          Bottom: The Southern Icefield on the summit of Kibo.
Overleaf: Trekkers on Kibo framed against the silhouette of Mawenzi.

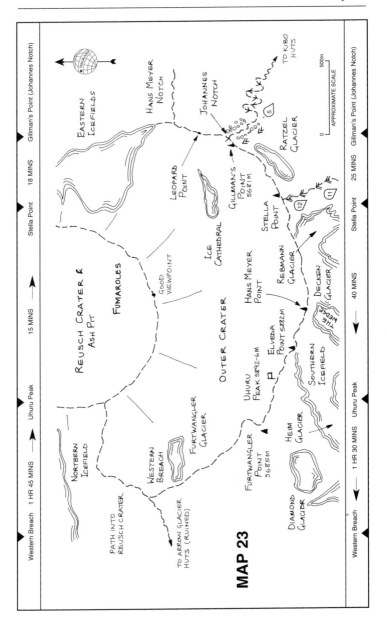

MAP 23

around up there: you'll probably be a little short of humour as well as breath on the crater rim, and following an ignorant guide while he tries in vain to locate the correct path to the Reusch Crater will do little to lighten your mood.

The standard way to reach the **Reusch Crater** is to ascend via the Western Breach, where a trail of sorts heads off to the north away from Uhuru Peak; for this reason, it is more common for those who have climbed via the difficult Arrow Glacier Route to visit Reusch than those who ascended by one of the other paths. But those who arrived at the crater rim at either Gillman's or Stella Point needn't despair, for there is also a possible trail, though unmarked and unclear, that crosses the crater floor to Reusch from somewhere between the two. The actual climb up to the rim of the Reusch Crater is surprisingly easy and can take as little as forty minutes, though this, of course, is assuming that you were in fairly good shape by the time you reached the summit in the first place; and this is a very big assumption. Having reached Reusch, check out the bright yellow sulphurous deposits, largely on its western side, and the fumaroles that occasionally puff smoke – proof not only that Kili is a volcano, but that it is also an active one. The smell of sulphur is all-pervasive in this crater, and the earth is hot to touch.

Within the Reusch Crater is the 120m-deep **Ash Pit** which, though it does not conspicuously contain ash, is said to be one of the most perfect examples of this sort of formation in the world. At 360m across, it's also one of the largest; and, we might suggest, one of the most inaccessible. If you reach the Ash Pit, you can truly say that you have conquered this mountain.

APPENDIX A: RECOMMENDED READING

Many of the following books, particularly those written during the great days of exploration in the 1800s, are now out of print and, short of a miraculous find in a secondhand bookstore, the only place you're going to find them is at the British Library in London or a similar institution abroad. For those books that *are* still in print, your best bet is in Tanzania itself, either in the small souvenir shop by Marangu Gate or, somewhat surprisingly, in the large bookshops in Stonetown, Zanzibar. Failing that, you could always try the Internet (Amazon etc) who will usually be able to track a copy down for you.

Fiction
The Snows of Kilimanjaro Ernest Hemingway (Arrow Books, 1994). Short story about a writer dying of a gangrenous leg and a rich wife, written by an honourary game warden based in Loitokitok in the early 1950s. Said to be his most autobiographical work.

Biography
Africa's Dome of Mystery Eva Stuart Watt FRGS (Marshall, Morgan and Scott Ltd, 1930). Brought up in East Africa, Ms Stuart-Watt describes her life among the Chagga people, including an account of her climb to Kibo's crater rim. Interesting if only for the fact that there are few accounts of Kibo from this period under British rule.

Chagga language, history and lifestyle
Chagga – A Course in the Vunjo Dialect of the Kichagga Language of Kilimanjaro, Tanzania Bernard Leeman and Trilas Lauwo (published in Europe by Languages Information Centre). The best Chagga language book I could find, this tome, written by an Australian who worked as a teacher in the region, deals with the basic structure and grammar and is an ideal introduction to the language.
Hunger and Shame – Child Malnutrition and Poverty on Mount Kilimanjaro Mary Howard and Ann Millard (Routledge). Comparatively rich by African standards it may be but, as this book proves, Kilimanjaro still suffers from more than its fair share of grinding poverty. With views from family members, health workers and government officials, this book discusses the moral and practical dilemmas of malnourishment.
Kilimanjaro and its People The Honourable Charles Dundas OBE (H, F and G Witherby, 1924; reprinted by Frank Cass & Co, 1968). Probably still the most authoritative account of the Chagga people, this tome is a little dry in places (particularly the rather involved history section), and outdated too (very few of the more extreme Chagga practices, described on p100 are still conducted today); nevertheless the sections on religion, witchcraft and ritual ceremonies are completely fascinating, and offer the most comprehensive insight into how the Chaggas used to be at least, if not how they are today.
History of the Chagga People of Kilimanjaro Kathleen M Stahl (Mouton & Co, 1964). Highly detailed account of the Chaggas, probably more for those with an academic interest in the subject.

Miscellaneous
Duel for Kilimanjaro Leonard Mosley (Weidenfeld and Nicolson, 1963). Account of the East African campaign during World War I.
Kilimanjaro – Animals in a Landscape Jonathan Kingdon (BBC Publications 1983). Born in Tanganyika, Kingdon is an artist specialising in the flora and fauna of his homeland. This book, based on a BBC series, contains examples of his work as well as an extended commentary on the creatures that live on the mountain.
Birds of Kenya and Northern Tanzania Popular guide by Dale A Zimmerman.
Field Guide to the Birds of East Africa Guide in the Poyser series.

Twentieth-century accounts

Bicycles up Kilimanjaro Richard and Nicholas Crane (Oxford Illustrated Press 1985). These two cycled up Kili with Mars Bars taped to their handlebars to finance the establishing of windmills for pumping water in East Africa. The only other person I met who had read this book said he enjoyed it, but I didn't.

Kilimanjaro John Reader (Elm Tree Books). Excellent, beautifully written coffee-table book with detailed accounts both of the history and geology of Kili, and the author's own experience of photographing it.

Kilimanjaro: to the Roof of Africa Audrey Salkeld, (National Geographic Books). The best-looking book on Kilimanjaro, this mighty coffee-table tome includes detailed sections on history and geology, as well as some excellent photographs of the mountain.

On Top of Africa – the Climbing of Kilimanjaro and Mount Kenya Neville Shulman (Element Books). Tale of the conquering of these two African giants by the author, along with the help of Zen philosophies and his own personal *shin* spirit.

The Road to Kilimanjaro Geoffrey Salisbury (Minerva Press, 1997). Though mainly auto-biographical, recounting Salisbury's busy life, this book includes a heart-warming, humbling account of an expedition in 1969 by the author to the summit of Kilimanjaro on the Loitokitok Route with a group of eight totally blind African youths, all but one of whom made it to the top.

Snow on the Equator HW Tilman (Bell and Son Books, 1937, republished as part of *The Eight Sailing/Mountain Exploration Books* by Baton Wicks, 1989). Inaccurate account (Kilimanjaro is not an extinct volcano, for example, but a dormant one) by coffee planter, explorer, mountaineer and all-round show-off Harold William Tilman. Nevertheless a very entertaining read, and for all his bluster Tilman comes across as an entirely likeable fellow.

In Wildest Africa Peter MacQueen, FRGS (George Bell and Sons, 1910). Account of one of the first tourists to Kilimanjaro, who visited the region during the German occupation. Includes a description of their ascent up Kili, during which some of their porters died, more were frightened by snow and fled (taking the food with them) and MacQueen himself only managed to find his way down by following the trail of porters' corpses left behind from an expedition five months previously. MacQueen went on to reach a highly credible 19,200 feet (the highest, at that time, by an English speaker).

The Shadow of Kilimanjaro – On Foot Across East Africa Rick Ridgeway (Bloomsbury 1999). Well-written account of a walk that begins on the summit of Kilimanjaro and ends at Malindi on the Kenyan coast. Though Kili is dealt with in a matter of pages at the front of the book, the narrative style is absorbing and this book is well worth reading.

Guidebooks

Kilimanjaro National Park (TANAPA, 1987). Available at Machame and Marangu gates, this is the official guide, and is very good with the descriptions of flora and fauna in the park, even though they do not use colour pictures. A little out of date now, but not bad.

Kilimanjaro and Mount Kenya – A Climbing and Trekking Guide Cameron M Burns (Cordee, 1998). If you want to do anything more technical than just walking up to Kibo on one of the accepted routes, this book is a must, detailing as it does a number of alternative routes up the glaciers, as well as ways of tackling Mawenzi.

Moshi Guide Karen Rooms (Coffee Shop, 2000). Locally produced guide to Moshi, very informative and perfect for anybody staying for more than a few days there.

The explorers

Across East African Glaciers – An Account of the First Ascent of Kilimanjaro Dr Hans Meyer, translated from the German by EHS Calder (George Philip and Son, 1891). Perhaps the most fascinating book ever written about the mountain, Meyer's beautiful work describes his unprecedented ascent of Kilimanjaro, all illustrated with some lovely little pictures by ET Compton. Splendid stuff.

An Essay on the Sources of the Nile in the Mountains of the Moon Charles T Beke (Neill and Company, 1848). This short work is of interest not only because it was written before Rebmann's visit of Kilimanjaro, but also, though written less than 200 years ago, the author still takes as his starting point the work of Ptolemy written 1800 years before, thus giving an indication of just how little was known about Africa at that time.

The Church Missionary Intelligencer (Seeleys, 1850). Definitely one you'll have to look for in the British Library, this august organ was the first to publish Rebmann's accounts of his three trips to Kilimanjaro, as well as Krapf's subsequent visit to the Usambara region. Volume 1, May 1849, contains most of the relevant texts.

Discovery by Count Teleki of Lakes Rudolf and Stefanie Lieutenant Ludwig von Höhnel, translated by Nancy Bell (Longmans, Green and Co, 1894). Lengthy, two-volume account of the Hungarian count as he shoots and slaughters his way through East Africa's fauna, written by his companion von Höhnel. Only about a sixth of the book deals specifically with Kili, though that sixth is interesting both for the account of their attempt to climb Kili, and in their dealing with Chagga chiefs Mandara (whom they try to avoid) and Mareale.

The Kilima-njaro Expedition – A Record of Scientific Exploration in Eastern Equatorial Africa HH Johnston (Kegan Paul, Trench and Co, 1886; republished by Gregg International Publishers Ltd, 1968). Widely dismissed as exaggeration going on fabrication, this is nevertheless a very entertaining read thanks to Johnston's sense of humour. Possible to pick up second-hand.

Life, Wanderings, and Labours in Eastern Africa Charles New (Cass Library of African Studies, 1971, originally 1873). Charles New set off in 1871 to spread the gospel to Africa's heathen population, but it was as an explorer that he is remembered, becoming the first white man to cross the African snow-line during a visit to the Chagga region. This book was written in the months spent in England between his first and second trips, on the latter of which he fell ill and died. Once again, though the account of his time on the slopes of Kili occupies only about a third of the book, it is for the most part fascinating, as much for his description of Mandara and the Chaggas as it is for his climb up the mountain.

Tracts Relating to Missions (Printed by A Lankester, 1878) Yet another work whose habitat is restricted almost entirely to the British Library these days, this collection of missionary accounts includes one by the Rev A Downes Shaw entitled *To Chagga and Back — An Account of a Journey to Moshi, the Capital of Chagga, Eastern Equatorial Africa*.

APPENDIX B: SWAHILI

Of the two main languages you will encounter, Swahili, the national tongue, is undoubtedly the more useful and the one you will see written on signs and notices. There are plenty of Swahili dictionaries around; street vendors sell little green Swahili dictionaries in Arusha for about Ts3000, or you can pick one up in souvenir stores for about a sixth of that. The other language, Chagga (along with all of its various dialects), is more common around Kili, but it is unlikely you will hear it outside the region. You will, however, curry favour with porters and guides on Kilimanjaro by learning a few words; see the box on p105 for a brief introduction to the language. Chagga dictionaries are rare, though you'll find one mentioned in Appendix A.

Basics

Yes	Ndiyo
No	Hapana
Good Morning	Jambo.
My name is. . .	Jina langu ni . . .
How are you?	Habari gani?
Please . .	Tafadhali. . .
Thanks (very much)	Asante (sana)
Do you speak English?	Unasema Kiingereza
Help!	Saidia!
How much is it?	Kiasi gani?
Slowly, slower	Pole, pole-pole
Let's go!	Twendai!

Numbers

1	moja
2	mbili
3	tatu
4	nne
5	tano
6	sita
7	saba
8	nane
9	tisa
10	kumi
11	kumi na moja
12	kumi na mbili
20	ishirini
21	ishirini na moja
30	thelathini
40	arobaini
50	hamsini
60	sitini
70	sabini
80	themanini
90	tisini
100	mia
200	mia mbili
1000	elfu
2000	elfu mbili

Places

Bank	Banki
Laundry	Kufulia
Post office	Posta

Days of the week

Monday	Jumatatu
Tuesday	Jumanne
Wednesday	Jumatano
Thursday	Alhamisi
Friday	Ijumaa
Saturday	Jumamosi
Sunday	Jumapili

Travel

Bus station	kituo cha mabasi
Airport	kiwanja cha ndege
Port	bandari
Train station	stesheni
Ticket office	wanapouza tikiti
When will we arrive at . . ?	tutafika . . jini?
Is this the direct way to . .?	hii ni njia fupi kwenda?

Food and drink

Beans	Maharagwe
Bread	Mkate
Chicken	Kuku
Coffee	Kahawa
Eggs	Mayai
Fish	Samaki
Meat	Nyama
Orange	Chungwa
Pork	Nyama ya nguruwe
Vegetables	Mboga
Venison	Nyama ya porini
Water	Maji

APPENDIX C: FLIGHTS TO KILIMANJARO

FLIGHTS TO KILIMANJARO INTERNATIONAL AIRPORT

Currently there are three main international carriers flying into Kilimanjaro: Air Tanzania, Air Ethiopia and the Dutch airline KLM.

KLM fly everyday in the high season to Dar, touching down first in Kilimanjaro. The flight currently leaves Schipol (Amsterdam) at 10.30 or 11am, arriving the same day at Kili at 8.20pm (total travel time 8hr 45min). This is certainly the most convenient way to get to Kili, particularly if you can get an early morning connecting flight to Amsterdam (there is a flight from London to Amsterdam at 6am, for example, making this the best connection from the UK). If you've bought a return ticket, you may find that on the return trip from Kilimanjaro (which usually leaves at 9.15pm) the plane flies first to Dar es Salaam, leaving there for the return (direct flight) to Amsterdam at 11.40pm, arriving at 8.15am the following morning.

Air Ethiopia operate a pretty comprehensive pan-African network and are renowned for being cheap. From London they have flights to Addis Ababa thrice weekly, usually leaving at night and arriving around 8.30am. At Addis Ababa you'll have to wait for a few hours before catching the 12.15pm flight to Kilimanjaro, a journey of 2hr 15min. This inter-African flight operates six times a week, though all but one of them fly via Nairobi first.

Air Tanzania operate a complicated schedule. However, it's worth remembering that there is a daily fifty-minute flight to Dar es Salaam (currently Ts85,000) usually leaving early in the morning. They also fly to Entebbe (1hr 10min) four-times weekly, Mwanza (55min) four-times weekly, Nairobi thrice weekly, Zanzibar thrice weekly, and one a week to Johannesburg. **Precision Air** also have flights to Kilimanjaro from various places in East Africa, including Mombasa (daily at 12.30pm), Nairobi (2 daily at 11.35am and 6.05pm) and one weekly from Shinyanga.

APPENDIX D: TANZANIAN EMBASSIES ABROAD

Belgium 363 Avenue Louise, 1050 Brussels (☎ 32-2 640- 6500, 🖹 646-8026; 🖳 tanzan ia@skynet.be)
Canada 50 Range Road, Ottawa, Ontario KIN 8J4 (☎ 613-232 1500 /232-1509, 🖹 232 5184; 🖳 tzottawa@synapse.net)
Egypt 9, Abdel Hamid Loutfy, Street, Dokki-Cairo (☎ 20-2 3374286, 704446, 346017, 🖹 704446; 🖳 tanrepcairo@infinity.com.eg)
Ethiopia PO Box 1077, Addis Ababa (☎ 251-1 511063, 612904, 518155, 🖹 517358; 🖳 tanzania@addisababa_serverl.telecom.net.et)
France 13 Avenue Raymond, Pointcare, 75116 Paris (☎ 01 47 55 05 46, 🖹 01 53 70 63 66; 🖳 tanzanie@infonie.fr)
Germany Theaterplatz 26, 5300 Bonn 2 (☎ 0228 353219, 340139, 58051/4, 🖹 358226; 🖳 balozi@tanzania-gov.de)
Italy 9,Via Giambattista Vico, 00196, Rome (☎ 06-3610901, 🖹 4549660; 🖳 tanzarep@ pcg.it)
Japan 21-9, Kamiyoga 4, Chome Setagaya-Ku, Tokyo 158 (☎ 03-425 4531/3, 🖹 03-425 7844; 🖳 tzrepjp@japan.co.jp)
Kenya Continental House, Harambee Avenue/Uhuru Highway, PO Box 47790, Nairobi (☎ 331056/7, 331104, 🖹 054-2721874; 🖳 tanzania@users.africaonline.co.ke; consulate: Mombasa (🖳 tancon@users.africaonline.co.ke)
South Africa PO Box 56572, Arcadia, 0007, Pretoria (☎ 3424371/93, 🖹 002712 434 383; 🖳 tanzania@cis.co.za)
Sweden Oxtorgsgatan 2-4, Box 7255, 103-89 Stockholm (☎ 08 244870, 🖹 00468 109815; 🖳 mailbox@tanemb.se)
Uganda 6 Kagera Road, PO Box 5750, Kampala (☎ 41 257357, 242815, 256272, 🖹 041 242890; 🖳 tzrepkla@imul.com)
UK 43 Hertford Street, London W1Y 8DB (☎ 020-7499 8951, 7491 3600, 🖹 020-7491 9321; 🖳 www.tanzania-online.gov.uk)
US 2139 R. Street, Washington D. C. 20008 (☎ 202-9939 6129, 🖹 202-797-7408; 🖳 www.tanzaniaembassy-us.org/)
consulate: 205 East 42nd St, New York, N.Y. 10017 (☎212-972 9160, 🖹 682 5232; 🖳 tzrepny@aol.com)
Zimbabwe Ujamaa House, 23 Baines Avenue Harare (☎ 263-4 721870, 722627, 882265, 🖹 724172; 🖳 tanrep@icon.co.zw)
Zambia Ujamaa House, 5200 United Nations Avenue, PO Box 31219, 10101 Lusaka (☎ 227698/227702, 🖹 254861; 🖳 tzreplsk@zamnet.zm).

APPENDIX E: KENYAN EMBASSIES ABROAD

Australia QBE Building, 33 Ainslie Ave, Canberra ACT 2601 ☎ (062)474788
Belgium 1-5 Ave de la Joyeuse, 1040 Brussels ☎ (02) 230-3065
Canada 415 Laurier Ave, Ottawa, Ontario KIN 6R4 ☎ (613) 563-1773
Egypt 20 Boulos Hanna St., PO Box 362, Dokki, Cairo ☎ 704455
Ethiopia Fikre Miriam Rd, Hiher 16 Kebelle, PO Box 3301, Addis Ababa ☎ 180 033
France 3 rue Cimaros, 75116 Paris ☎ 45-53-35-00
Germany Villichgasse 17, 5300 Bonn-Bad Godesburg 2 ☎ (0228) 356042
India E-66 Vasant Marg, 110057 New Delhi ☎ 672 280

Italy Icilio 14, 00153 Rome ☎ 578-1192
Japan 24-20 Nishi-Azobu 3-Chome, Minato-Ku, Tokyo ☎ (03) 3479-4006
Netherlands Koninginnegracht 102, 2514 A1, The Hague ☎ (070) 504 215
Nigeria 52 Queens Drive, Ikoyi, PO Box 6464, Lagos ☎ 682768
Pakistan Sector G-6/3, House 8, Street 88, PO Box 2097, Islamabad ☎ 811243
Rwanda UN Toit Toi Bldg, Rue Kadyiro, PO Box 1215, Kigali ☎ 72774
Somalia Km. 4 Via Mecca, PO Box 618, Modagishu ☎ 80857
Sudan Street 33 Amarat, PO Box 8242, Khartoum ☎ 43758
Sweden Birger Jarlsgatan 37, 2tr, 10395 Stockholm ☎ (08) 218 300
Tanzania NIC Investment House, Samora Ave, PO Box 5231, Dar es Salaam ☎ 46362/6
Uganda Plot 60, Kira Rd, PO Box 5220, Kampala ☎ 231861
United Kingdom 45 Portland Place, London W1N 4AS ☎ (071) 636-2371
USA 2249 R Street NW, Washington DC 20008 ☎ (202)387-6101
    Consulate: 424 Madison Ave, New York NY 10017 ☎ (212) 486-1300
Zaire 5002 Ave de l'Ouganda, BP 9667, Gombe, Kinshasa ☎ 30117
Zambia Harambee House, 5207 United Nations Ave, PO Box 50298, Lusaka ☎ 212531
Zimbabwe 95 Park Lane, PO Box 4069, Harare ☎ 792901

OTHER TREKKING GUIDES FROM TRAILBLAZER

Trekking in the Dolomites *Henry Stedman*
1st edn, 224pp, 52 trail maps, 13 town plans, 30 colour photos
ISBN 1 873756 34 8, £11.99, US$17.95
The Dolomites region of northern Italy encompasses some of the most beautiful mountain scenery in Europe. This new guide features selected routes including Alta Via II, a West-East traverse and other trails, plus detailed guides to Cortina, Bolzano, Bressanone and 10 other towns. Also includes full colour flora section and bird identification guide.

New Zealand – The Great Walks *Alexander Stewart*
1st edn, 272pp, 60 maps, 40 colour photos
ISBN 1 873756 78 X, £11.99, Can$28.95, US$19.95
New Zealand is a wilderness paradise of incredibly beautiful landscapes. There is no better way to experience it than on one of the nine designated Great Walks, the country's premier walking tracks which provide outstanding hiking opportunities for people at all levels of fitness and proficiency. Also includes detailed guides to Auckland, Wellington, National Park Village, Taumaranui, Nelson, Queenstown, Te Anau and Oban.

The Inca Trail, Cusco & Machu Picchu *Richard Danbury*
2nd edn, 288pp, 45 maps, 24 colour photos
ISBN 1 873756 64 X, £10.99, Can$24.95, US$18.95
The Inca Trail from Cusco to Machu Picchu is South America's most popular hike. This practical guide includes 20 detailed trail maps, plans of eight Inca sites, plus guides to Cusco and Machu Picchu.
'Danbury's research is thorough...you need this one'. **The Sunday Times**

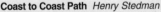

Coast to Coast Path *Henry Stedman*
1st edition, 224pp, 95 maps & town plans, 40 colour photos
ISBN 1 873756 58 5, £9.99, Can$22.95, US$16.95
A classic 191-mile (307km) walk across northern England from the Irish Sea to the North Sea. Crossing three fabulous national parks – the Lake District, the Yorkshire Dales and the North York Moors – it samples the very best of the English countryside.

For other trekking guides and the full Trailblazer list see p234

❏ TRAILBLAZER GUIDES

Adventure Cycling Handbook	1st edn mid 2005
Adventure Motorcycling Handbook	4th edn out now
Australia by Rail	4th edn out now
Azerbaijan	3rd edn out now
The Blues Highway – New Orleans to Chicago	2nd edn out now
China by Rail	2nd edn Sep 2004
Coast to Coast (British Walking Guide)	1st edn out now
Cornwall Coast Path (British Walking Guide)	1st edn out now
Good Honeymoon Guide	2nd edn out now
Inca Trail, Cusco & Machu Picchu	2nd edn out now
Japan by Rail	1st edn out now
Kilimanjaro – a trekking guide to Africa's highest mountain	1st edn out now
Land's End to John O'Groats	1st edn mid 2005
The Med Guide	1st edn mid 2004
Nepal Mountaineering Guide	1st edn Sep 2004
New Zealand – Great Walks	1st edn out now
Norway's Arctic Highway	1st edn out now
Offa's Dyke Path (British Walking Guide)	1st edn out now
Pembrokeshire Coast Path (British Walking Guide)	1st edn out now
Pennine Way (British Walking Guide)	1st edn out now
Siberian BAM Guide – rail, rivers & road	2nd edn out now
The Silk Roads – a route and planning guide	1st end out now
Sahara Overland – a route and planning guide	2nd edn Sep 2004
Sahara Abenteuerhandbuch (German edition)	1st edn out now
South Downs Way (British Walking Guide)	1st edn out now
South-East Asia – The Graphic Guide	1st edn out now
Tibet Overland – mountain biking & jeep touring	1st edn out now
Trans-Canada Rail Guide	3rd edn out now
Trans-Siberian Handbook	6th edn out now
Trekking in the Annapurna Region	4th edn Sep 2004
Trekking in the Everest Region	4th edn out now
Trekking in Corsica	1st edn out now
Trekking in the Dolomites	1st edn out now
Trekking in Ladakh	3rd edn July 2004
Trekking in Langtang, Gosainkund & Helambu	1st edn out now
Trekking in the Moroccan Atlas	1st edn out now
Trekking in the Pyrenees	2nd edn out now
Tuva and Southern Siberia	1st edn mid 2005
West Highland Way (British Walking Guide)	1st edn out now

For more information about Trailblazer and our expanding range of guides,
for where to find your nearest stockist, for guidebook updates
or for credit card mail order sales (post-free worldwide)
visit our web site:

www.trailblazer-guides.com

ROUTE GUIDES FOR THE ADVENTUROUS TRAVELLER

UPDATE – 2004

For this update I am indebted to the following who kindly wrote to me with their updates, corrections, thoughts and opinions: Maisy Luk; Stephen J Davies; Gard Karlsen; Ally Ibrahim Akaro, managing director of Akaro Tours Ltd; Ake Lindstrom of Hoopoe; and the stars of Montreal, namely Annaliese Di Betta, Valdina Di Betta, Maria Mangiocavallo and Isabelle Gryn.

PART 1: PLANNING YOUR TRIP

Page 19: Trekking agencies in the UK

In general, a credible local (ie Tanzanian) agency should not ask for the whole fee to be paid prior to your arrival in the country. If you are sceptical about the service of an agency, either visit the Tanzanian High Commission (☎ 020-7407 0566, 💻 www.tanzatrade.co.uk), 80 Borough High St, London SE1 1LL, for a list of recommended agencies, or you can visit the agency's office on arrival in Tanzania before making the final decision. A reliable agency should be able to allocate their manpower for a trekking holiday most days of the week, even in the high seasons.

Most agencies in the UK have policies on porters' rights and their working conditions. This means that the agencies are obliged to ensure there is no exploitation of porters and to observe working conditions (wages, loads, equipment, and what happens if porters have accidents or become ill during the trek). These companies include: Abercrombie and Kent; Dragoman; Explore Worldwide; Exodus Travels; Footprint; Gane and Marshall International; Guerba Expeditions; KE Adventure Travel; Tribes Travel; World Expeditions (the above information was cross-referenced with Tourism Concern, registered Charity No 1064020-0).

Adventure Alternative Expeditions (☎ 028-9070 1476, 💻 www.adventurealternative .com), 31 Myrtledene Rd, Belfast BT8 6GQ, Northern Ireland. Long serving and experienced tour leader/operator, recommended by a number of trekkers.

Africa Travel Resouces (ATR; 💻 www.africatravelresources.com) Excellent agency with a website filled with comprehensive, detailed information. Uses African Walking Company (see p237).

IntoAfrica (☎ 0114-255 5610, 💻 www.intoafrica.co.uk), 59 Langdon St, Sheffield, S11 8BH. A more expensive tour operator, directed by Chris Morris. They claim to operate to fair-trade standards where fully-qualified local staff are paid at above average rates without money being taken off to compensate vehicles, park fees, equipment and services. For Machame, they were charging US$1120 per person for two persons. A deposit is required in the UK prior to flying to Tanzania.

Page 22: Trekking agencies in Norway

Hvitserk (💻 www.hvitserk.no) has trips to lots of mountain ranges including Kilimanjaro.
EcoExpeditions (💻 www.ecoexpeditions.no/), PO Box 2028 Hillevåg, 4095 Stavanger.

Page 28: Park fees

As at July 2004, all the park fees (entry fee, camping/hut fee, rescue fee and entry fees for porters/guides) are unchanged.

Page 30: Porters

The issue of porters' welfare on Kilimanjaro continues to engender much debate and concern, particularly on the internet. Regarding tipping, sadly I have heard that some budget agencies are not paying porters now — in such an over-supplied labour market, they've no need to — and thus many locals on Kilimanjaro are working merely for tips. One website that discusses this, and which I urge you to look at, is the site of the International Porter Protection Group, 💻 www.ippg.net. They do not publish the names of companies but they do cite instances of porter abuse and exploitation, and, better still, they contact the company directly to encourage them to change their ways.

Another porter-friendly organization is International Mountain Explorers Connection (IMEC; International PO Box 3665, Boulder, CO 80307, USA; 💻 www.hec.org), which has opened a branch in Moshi and now runs the Kilimanjaro Porter Assistance Project, publishes the *Kilimanjaro Volunteer Handbook* and organizes cultural trips up the mountain.

Page 41: What to take
We have received the following suggestions for additional things to take:

Poncho A cheap one from a dollar store is fine, having the advantage of being small. Make sure it goes over your clothes at least; over the backpack is even better.

Plastic bags Two industrial-strength plastic bags, which can double as ponchoes, especially if you brought along Duct tape and two small grocery bags (to line boots in case they get wet). Also useful for segregating your wet gear from the rest of your stuff.

Water containers One reader suggested taking enough capacity to carry four litres of water on summit day.

Emergency aluminium sheet blanket Provides extra comfort if your sleeping bag is not as warm as you thought.

Bismuth subsalicylate (the active ingredient in Pepto-bismol); for soothing upset stomachs.

Binder clips (bulldog or office clip) Said to be superior to the clothes pegs we recommend because they take up less room, are stronger and are more functional.

PART 2: TANZANIA

Page 48: Internet sites
Some additional reliable and very useful internet sites are:

💻 **www.cdc.gov/travel/diseases** US Center of Disease control. Details on the illnesses you cannot pronounce. Thankfully, you will realize the likelihood of getting many or any in Tanzania is low.

💻 **www.travel.state.gov/travel_warnings** (US site) Or your country's equivalent site.

💻 **www.voyage.gc.ca** Consular affairs' website for Canadians abroad

💻 **www.atol.org.uk** To verify if your UK agency is financially sound, look at the Air Travel Organisers' Licensing website.

💻 **www.cia.gov/cia/publications/factbook/geos/tz** CIA website; good for Tanzania statistics

💻 **www.gardkarlsen.com** Includes a diary, talks about equipment, has a review of Marangu Hotel, and lots of pictures.

Page 59: Money
Latest exchange rates as at July 2004: UK£1 = Ts1907; €1 = Ts1287; US$1 = Ts1088; Can$1 = Ts782; A$1 = Ts748; NZ$1 = Ts855

Page 63: Tanzania – Email
The cost is now around TS600 for 30 minutes and some internet-café owners allow an additional two minutes to users.

Page 65: Tanzania – Things to buy
Afri-café was described by one (over-)enthusiastic reader to be the best instant coffee in the world and an affordable souvenir.

PART 4: FLYING TO EAST AFRICA – NAIROBI AND DAR ES SALAAM

Page 118: Nairobi – Arrival
Interestingly, two correspondents have written to tell us that it's possible to negotiate the excess-baggage charge downwards! Humour, politeness, respect and charm are, as always, important weapons.

PART 5: ARUSHA, MOSHI AND MARANGU

Page 133: Arusha – Communications
The internet service at Impala Hotel is reliable and reasonably priced but a bit more expensive than the usual rate.

Page 134: Arusha – Where to stay
Movairo Coffee Lodge (☎ 255 3243). Upscale accommodation, a bit outside town down a long dirt road. Its advantages include a garden, pool and lovely rooms in semi-attached one-level buildings. Disadvantages include its out-of-the-way location and expensive meals.
Meru House Inn The quality of the furnishings in the rooms varies greatly so check out a few before choosing one. Victoria Expedition, the hotel's resident agency, is known for its extreme persistence in making sales. However, the hotel does pick up their clients outside Novotel at the shuttle bus station twice daily.

Page 136: Arusha – Where to eat and drink
One reader wrote to say that they found the VIP Club to be too intimidatingly, well ... authentic! Instead, they recommended the *Barbeque Hut*, on the main road across from Novotel, which is spacious, clean and charges Ts5000 for three courses. I would appreciate any other reviews of this place. The Indian-owned restaurant below *Meru House Inn* serves good portions of Indian, Chinese and Italian dishes at reasonable tourist prices.

Page 140: Arusha – Trekking agencies
Supplementary information about touts Owing to mass unemployment (the average unemployment rate across Tanzania reached 13% in 2003) many local residents opt to work as self-employed touts. Few agencies officially hire them but they generally do appreciate touts bringing business to them. Whilst recognizing how wearying their attentions can be, please bear in mind the straitened circumstances they live in when dealing with them.

Roys Safari Further to my review, one reader wrote in to say that they were a well-respected Indian-owned safari company, having strong business links with luxury hotel establishments around nearby national parks.
Safari Makers They claim to limit the weight each porter carries to 15kg and unlike some other trekking companies, they give them full climbing salaries and ensure their guides choose to work only with porters who have proper gear/clothing for the weather on the trek.
Shidolya This agency remains popular but according to one reviewer, has no policy regarding porter welfare and, according to another source, asks them to carry up to 45kg!
African Walking Company (☎ 254 4461). Owned by Westerners, this is an agency that's been recommended more than once, and which, according to their clients, serves great food!

Page 154: Moshi – Trekking agencies
According to the National Geographic website, two years ago two porters working for Zara Tours (see p154) died due to fatigue/exposure (improper clothing) during a spell of unexpectedly poor weather. And according to one report, this popular and previously highly recommended agency continues to exploit the porters.

Page 158: Marangu – Where to stay
Marangu Hotel The phone number has changed to: ☎ 275 6594/6361

PART 7: TRAIL GUIDE AND MAPS

Page 185: Machame Trail, Stage 1: Machame Gate to Machame Huts
The trail from Machame gate to Machame camp was being 'upgraded' in late 2003 and work may still be in progress when you get there. After you leave the 4WD trail you get onto a new path which (I guess) is better than the old one (with slippery roots and mud).

INDEX

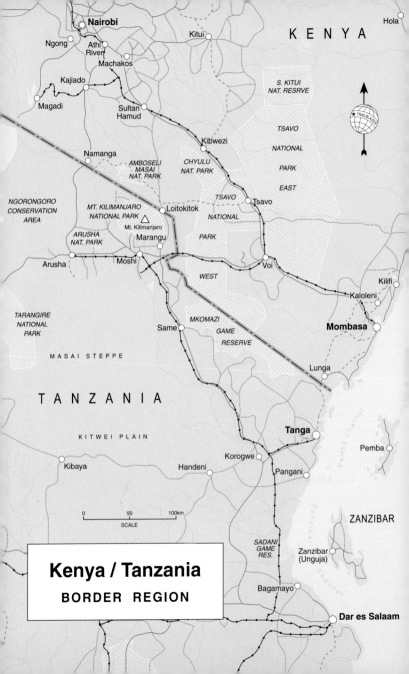

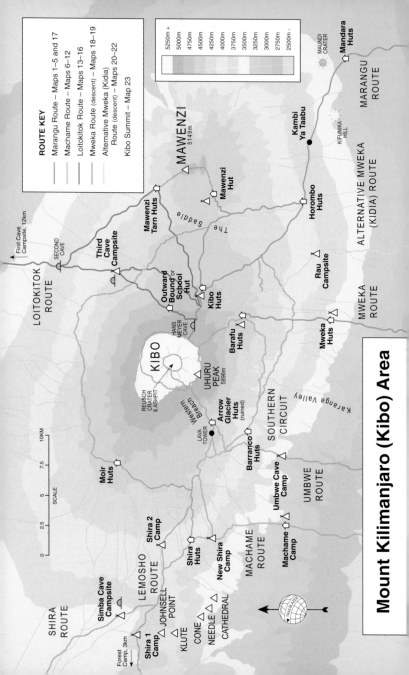

Mount Kilimanjaro (Kibo) Area